Lewis Bostock Radford

Thomas of London before his Consecration

Lewis Bostock Radford

Thomas of London before his Consecration

ISBN/EAN: 9783337397104

Printed in Europe, USA, Canada, Australia, Japan

Cover: Foto ©ninafisch / pixelio.de

More available books at **www.hansebooks.com**

Cambridge Historical Essays. No. VII.

THOMAS OF LONDON

BEFORE

HIS CONSECRATION.

BY

LEWIS B. RADFORD, M.A.

LATE SCHOLAR OF ST JOHN'S COLLEGE, CAMBRIDGE;
SECOND MASTER OF WARRINGTON GRAMMAR SCHOOL.

PRINCE CONSORT DISSERTATION, 1894.

Cambridge:
AT THE UNIVERSITY PRESS.
1894.

EXTRACT FROM THE REGULATIONS FOR THE PRINCE CONSORT PRIZE.

"There shall be established in the University a prize, called the 'Prince Consort Prize,' to be awarded for dissertations involving original historical research."

"The prize shall be open to members of the University who, at the time when their dissertations are sent in, have been admitted to a degree, and are of not more than four years' standing from admission to their first degree."

"Those dissertations which the adjudicators declare to be deserving of publication shall be published by the University, singly or in combination, in an uniform series, at the expense of the fund, under such conditions as the Syndics of the University Press shall from time to time determine."

INTRODUCTION.

An attempt has been made in this Essay to present in detail and in order all the valuable information extant as to the life and work of Thomas of London up to his consecration. It is a period of his career which has not received as thorough a treatment as it deserves at the hands of the modern historian. The archbishop has robbed the chancellor of his due. The interest taken in the life of Thomas has centred naturally in the conflict between the primate and the king, and the story of his earlier services in Church and state has been sketched in brief outline, except where the contemporary biographers expatiate on a signal instance of his grandeur, or else it has been viewed too exclusively in the light of a sympathy or antipathy arising from a prior estimate of his subsequent position. It is only sixteen years since the late Regius Professor of Modern History at Oxford in his controversy with Mr Froude appealed in the pages of the *Contemporary Review* for justice to the chancellor, and claimed a fuller investigation for his chancellorship. Much has been done since then in that direction, by Miss Norgate, for instance, in her *England under the*

Angevin Kings, in which the figure of Thomas the chancellor stands out boldly in the historical foreground of Henry II.'s reign. But no monograph has yet appeared in response to Prof. Freeman's appeal. A second call has now come from the sister University in the list of optional subjects for the Prince Consort Dissertation of 1894; and this Essay is an answer to the call. It is an attempt to rescue the earlier half of the career of Thomas of London from its position of secondary importance and give it a chance of speaking for itself.

It is difficult to be original in places where much of the ground has been covered so often already, but the attempt has been made, and, it is hoped, not without success. The subject-matter has been increased by the addition, from various sources, of fresh facts which are not found collected together in any existing account of Thomas' life. They will no doubt be recognised as they occur, e.g., in the details of Thomas' education, his ecclesiastical services as clerk to Theobald, and his judicial and financial work as chancellor. There was an obvious opening for originality in the method of arrangement, and it has been utilised, especially in the history of Thomas' chancellorship. This epoch in his life seemed to fall most conveniently under the different heads of military and diplomatic affairs abroad and judicial and financial administration at home, the question of his ecclesiastical policy coming last as an appropriate introduction to the climax,—his promotion to the primacy. This arrangement of course has its defects. The line cannot always be drawn sharply.

Facts which fall primarily under one head have to be reconsidered under another from a different standpoint. The case of Battle Abbey, for instance, serves to illustrate both the position of the chancellor in the Curia Regis and his views of ecclesiastical privilege. Similarly the scutage of 1159 finds an appropriate place in more than one section. Its constitutional importance has to be noticed incidentally under the reforms of Thomas' chancellorship; but it reappears for discussion along with the earlier scutage of 1156 under the head of ecclesiastical affairs, because its chief importance in his career is its bearing on his attitude towards the Church and her possessions. Still on the whole this arrangement seemed to give the clearest view of the chancellor's work.

It now remains to acknowledge with gratitude the help that I have received in writing this Essay. My thanks are due to Bishop Stubbs and Mrs J. R. Green, and above all to Miss Norgate, for assistance in following out the question of *perdona* granted at the Exchequer; and to the librarian of the Owens College, Manchester, for the generous permission to consult or borrow works of importance from the College library, which is especially valuable from the fact that it contains the historical collection of the late Professor Freeman.

WARRINGTON,
June, 1894.

WORKS CONSULTED.

I. ORIGINAL AUTHORITIES.

(a) Biographies.

William of Canterbury, vol. i.
John of Salisbury ⎫
Alan of Tewkesbury ⎬ , vol. ii.
Edward Grim ⎭
William Fitzstephen ⎫ , vol. iii.
Herbert of Bosham ⎭
Auctor Anonymus I. ⎫
Auctor Anonymus II. ⎬ , vol. iv.
Lansdowne MS. 2nd fragment ⎬
Quadrilogus ⎭

⎫
⎬ "Materials for history of Archbishop Thomas Becket," Rolls Series, No. 67, ed. Canon Robertson.
⎭

Thomas Saga Erkibyskups, vols. i, ii. Rolls Series, No. 65, ed. M. Eiríkr Magnússon.
Garnier de Pont S. Maxence, ed. Hippeau, Paris, 1859.

(b) Letters (Materials, vols. v, vi, vii).

Thomas, archbishop, Epp. 223, 224, 250.
Theobald, archbishop, Epp. 7, 8.
John of Salisbury, Epp. 3, 4, 5, 6, 9, 194, 252, 263.
Gilbert Foliot, Epp. 10, 15, 225.
Arnulf, bishop of Lisieux, Epp. 1, 12.
Anonymous friend of Thomas, Ep. 339.
Clergy of the Church of England, Ep. 205.
[Other letters of John of Salisbury are quoted from Dr Giles' edition of his works.]

(c) *Chronicles, records, and literary works.*

    Gervase : Acta Pontificum Cantuariensium.
              Chronicon.
    Ralph de Diceto : Abbreviationes Chronicorum.
                  Imagines Historiarum.
    William of Newburgh.
    Robert de Monte : Chronicon Normanniae.
    John of Hexham.
    William of Malmesbury : Historiae Novellae.
    Chronicle of Battle Abbey (Latin text, ed. Anglia Christiana Society, 1846; also Materials vol. iv, and Wilkins, Concilia, vol. i). Engl. translation by Mr Lower, 1851.
    Annals of Winchester.
    Historia Pontificalis (Pertz, Hist. German. Mon. vol. xx).
    Pipe Rolls : 2, 3, 4 Henry II. (ed. Hunter).
                 5, 6, 7, 8 Henry II. (ed. Pipe Rolls Society).
    Charters of Stephen, Henry II. (ed. Stubbs).
    Dialogus de Scaccario (ed. Stubbs, Select Charters, pp. 168–248).
    John of Salisbury : Polycraticus and Metalogicus (ed. Giles).

II. MODERN AUTHORITIES.

Lord Lyttelton, Henry II. vols. i, ii (ed. 1767).
Lord Campbell, Lives of the Chancellors.
Wilkins, Concilia.
Foss, Judges of England.
Madox, History of the Exchequer.
Ducange, Glossary of Mediaeval Latin.
Thierry, Norman Conquest, vol. ii (trans. by Hazlitt, Bohn's series, ed. 1885).
R. Hurrell Froude's Remains, vol. iv.
Canon Robertson, " Becket, a biography."
Dean Milman, Latin Christianity, vol. iii (ed. 1854).

Dean Hook, Archbishops of Canterbury, vol. ii (ed. 1862).
Hallam, History of the Middle Ages.
Stubbs : Lectures on Mediaeval and Modern History.
    Constitutional History, vol. i.
    Select Charters.
    Early Plantagenets.
J. A. Froude, "Life and Times of Thomas Becket" (Nineteenth Century, 1877; reprinted with modifications in his Short Studies on Great Subjects, vol. iv).
Freeman : Norman Conquest, vol. v.
    Historical Essays, 1st series.
    "Life and Times of Thomas Becket" (a reply to Froude, in Contemporary Review, 1878).
Lingard, History of England, vol. ii (6th ed. 1855).
J. R. Green, History of England, vol. i.
Mrs J. R. Green, Henry the Second.
Miss Norgate, England under the Angevin kings.
Introduction to the Pipe Rolls.
Father Morris, Life of S. Thomas Becket (2nd ed. 1885).
Lord Tennyson, "Becket."
Miss Lambert, "The real Thomas Becket" (Nineteenth Century, 1893).

CONTENTS.

CHAPTER I.
Thomas of London, 1118–1143 1–26

CHAPTER II.
The Servant of Theobald, 1143–1154 . . . 27–56

CHAPTER III.
Thomas the Chancellor 57–75

CHAPTER IV.
Foreign Affairs 76–95

CHAPTER V.
Judicial Administration and General Reform . 96–122

CHAPTER VI.
Financial Administration 123–152

CHAPTER VII.

	PAGE
The Chancellor and the Church	153–184
Note A. Meaning of the word *peremptorius*	184–187
Note B. The Chancellor and the Battle Abbey Case	187–190

CHAPTER VIII.

The Primacy	191–221
Note C. The election at London (Thomas Saga)	222–224

CHAPTER IX.

Character of Thomas of London	225–239
Note D. "The real Thomas Becket"	240–243

APPENDIX.

The Biographers of Thomas	244–259

CHAPTER I.

THOMAS OF LONDON.

THE uncertainty which attaches to so many incidents in the early life of "Thomas à Becket"— to give him for once his traditional name—has left room for conjecture at the very outset as to his birth and parentage. The place of his birth, it is true, is known for certain. He was a native of London[1], where his parents had been resident for some time. Our information goes still further. He was born in the parish of S. Mary Cole-church[2] in the northern part of Cheapside, in a house which has now given place to the Mercers' Chapel. In that same church he was baptized after evensong on the day of his birth, the 21st of December, the

His birth, 1118.

---

[1] Joh. S. ii. 302: Thomas Londoniensis urbis indigena. Will. C. i. 3: ex Londoniarum civibus oriundus. Grim, ii. 358, mentions a great fire on Thomas' birthday which began at his father's house and destroyed a large part of the city. Grim of course interprets it as symbolical of the influence of the archbishop in days to come.

[2] Dugdale, *Monasticon*, vi. 646 (ed. 1846).

festival of S. Thomas,—a coincidence which determined his baptismal name[1]. These minor details have every appearance of certainty, but there is some doubt about the year. According to Herbert of Bosham[2], Thomas was in his forty-fourth year at the time of his consecration in June 1162. This would give 1118 as the year of his birth. Gervase places his consecration in his fortieth year; but the evidence of Herbert, the confidential friend of the archbishop, is more likely to be correct[3].

His name. The first real difficulty is suggested by the surname which tradition has attached to the simple "Thomas" of his baptism. His father's name, it is true, is given by more than one authority as "Gilbert surnamed Becket[4]." But it is very doubtful

---

[1] Auct. Anon. I. iv. 4. Dean Hook (*Archbps. of Canterbury*, ii. 356) refers to a grant of Henry IV. licensing a brotherhood of S. Katharine in connexion with S. Mary Cole-church, "because Thomas Becket and S. Edmund the archbishop were baptized therein" (Newcourt, *Repertorium*, i. 448).

[2] Herb. iii. 189.

[3] Benedict of Peterborough supplies corroborative proof of the date 1118. He says (ii. 19) that Thomas was in his 53rd year at the time of his death in 1170. As his birthday fell on Dec. 21, and he died on Dec. 29, it was his 52nd year that was completed in 1170. He was therefore born in 1118.

[4] Grim, ii. 356. Auct. Anon. II. iv. 81: Gillebertus cognomine Beket. The name is also spelt Becchet, Beketh. Thierry (*Norm. Conqu.* ii. 53), who makes him a Saxon by birth but rich enough to associate with the Normans resident in London, thinks that his real name was perhaps Bek, and that Beket was a familiar diminutive by which he was known to his Norman friends and neighbours, just as Bekie was the Saxon diminutive current in ballad usage. But Robertson points out that Becket was itself a Norman surname occurring in the *Rotuli Scaccarii Normanniae* for

whether that surname was usually borne by the son. In the twelfth century, at any rate in the earlier half of that century, surnames appear to have been still personal, not hereditary; and the evidence is on the whole against the contemporary application of the surname Becket to the young Londoner. Roger Hoveden, it is true, in mentioning the appointment of Thomas to the archdeaconry of Canterbury, styles him "Thomas Beket." And Edward Grim[1], in describing the tragic scene within the cathedral, tells how the infuriated knights, clamouring for their victim, raised the cry, "Where is Thomas Beketh, traitor to his king and country?" But the archbishop was within hearing, and the surname may have been used contemptuously as a taunting reminder of his origin[2]. As a matter of fact he seems generally to have been known and described at the outset of his career as "Thomas of London[3]," and then, after the successive steps of his promotion, as "Thomas the archdeacon," "Thomas the chancellor," and finally "Thomas the archbishop." After his canonisation he naturally became "S. Thomas of

1180, e.g. Manzer de Becket. The original word *beck* was "a remnant of Teutonic vocabulary" surviving in Normandy, e.g. the famous abbey of Bec. And the diminutive *bequet* or *becket* occurs frequently in Norman charters with the meaning of a little brook. (Robertson, *Becket, a biography*, p. 13.)

[1] Grim, ii. 435.

[2] Hook, ii. 356, is of opinion that the designation "Thomas the archbishop," "if it superseded, did not suppress the other appellative Becket."

[3] e.g. Gervase (A.D. 1154): dedit archiepiscopus Cantuariensis archidiaconatum cuidam clerico suo *Thomae de Londonia*.

Canterbury," and such he remained for more than three centuries and a half. It was not until after the Reformation apparently that the name "Thomas à Becket[1]" forced its way into the prominence which it held, until a comparatively recent date, to the exclusion of all other designations.

His parents, (1) their nationality,

It is round the parentage of Thomas that controversy thickens. The two points at issue are (1) their nationality and (2) their social position. The former seems however by this time established beyond a doubt. The evidence at our disposal is quite sufficient to prove that the parents of Thomas, though Londoners by residence, were Normans by birth. It is true that M. Thierry in his history of the Norman Conquest, like Lord Lyttleton in his life of Henry II., has taken the opposite line. He has described Thomas as a Saxon of Saxons, and has allowed this assumption to colour his view of more than one phase in Thomas' career. Lyttleton dwells upon his promotion to the Chancellorship as the first instance since the Conquest of the elevation of an Englishman to high office, and has a warm word of praise for the generous and impartial policy which it betokened on the part of a semi-foreign king. Thierry, starting from the same standpoint, accounts for the opposition of the "Anglo-Norman" bishops and barons, both at the election of Thomas to the primacy and throughout the conflict between

---

[1] The original authorities know nothing of the prefix à or a', as it is variously spelt. Robertson considers it a remnant of "vulgar colloquial usage." Hook retains it "as a distinction conventionally conferred" upon a popular hero of English history.

the king and the archbishop, on the ground of Norman prejudice against a prelate of English origin,—and this in spite of a remark of John of Salisbury which might have been intended to anticipate and refute any such theory[1].

The Saxon descent of Thomas was never more than an assumption, and it has given way, on a more critical study of the evidence, to the certainty of his Norman origin. The very names of both parents point to that conclusion, and it is placed beyond doubt by two explicit statements in the original authorities. One of the anonymous biographers says that they were among the Normans who were attracted to London after the Conquest by the advantages which it offered as a commercial centre. Gilbert, he adds, was a native of Rouen, his wife Roesa (Rose) a native of Caen[2]. The other statement is an incidental allusion made by Fitzstephen in his account of Thomas' introduction to Theobald. He attributes the young man's promotion partly to

[1] Joh. S. Ep. 193 (ed. Giles), noted by Robertson in the introduction to his biography of Becket: qui persequuntur in hac causa Cantuariensem episcopum, non hoc persequuntur quod Thomas est, quod natione Londoniensis...sed quod annunciat populo Dei scelera eorum.

[2] Auct. Anon. II. iv. 81. Other authorities give her name as Matilda (Grim, ii. 356) or Mahalt (Fitzst. iii. 14) or Machilde (Auct. Anon. I. iv. 3), evidently different forms of the same word. Robertson, p. 15, by way of reconciling the discrepancy, ingeniously suggests that perhaps the grandparents of Thomas bore the names Gilbert and Roesa, and were the first of the family to settle in London, bringing with them a son Gilbert born in Normandy, whose wife was called Matilda. Thomas, it should be noted, had a sister named Roesa (Robertson, App. xxx. p. 253).

his father's previous acquaintance with the archbishop. In birth and rank, as Gilbert reminded Theobald, they had begun life upon the same footing, both of them Norman in descent, and both born in the same neighbourhood, near a place called Thierceville[1]. The mistaken idea that Thomas was of English extraction seems to have arisen from the fact that he was "the first Englishman, in the sense of a native of England of whichever race," who rose to the primacy after the Conquest[2]. It is true that "in all but actual descent he was a thorough Englishman," but it is precisely his Norman descent which points the moral of his career for the student of English national character. In fact the most important point to notice in this connexion is simply this—to quote once more Dr. Freeman's eloquent summing up of the whole question—that, "Norman by descent, English by birth and feeling, proud of England as his native land, of London as his native city,—trained by travel and study in other lands, but never losing his love for his native soil,—trusted by the Angevin king, beloved by the English people,—Thomas of London is the very embodiment of that blending together of Normans and English on English ground which was the great work of the twelfth century, and of which we feel the blessings in the nineteenth[3]."

[1] Fitzst. iii. 15. Gilebertus cum domino archipraesule de propinquitate et genere loquebatur; ut ille ortu Normannus, et circa Tierrici villam, de equestri ordine, natu vicinus.

[2] Freeman, *Contemporary Review*, 1878, vol. 31, p. 835.

[3] *Contemp. Rev.* vol. 32, p. 499.

Fitzstephen's allusion to the knightly rank of Gilbert and Theobald raises the question of Gilbert's social position. It is a remark not easily reconciled with the testimony of other authorities. The anonymous biographer quoted above says that Gilbert's antecedents, like those of his wife, were respectable but belonged to the bourgeoisie[1]. And this statement seems to tally better with Thomas' own admissions towards the close of his life. In his reply to the famous letter of remonstrance in 1166 from the bishops and clergy of his province, charging him amongst other things with ingratitude to the king who, as they declared, had been the maker of his fortunes[2], he admits that his origin was comparatively humble,—"non sum revera atavis editus regibus"—, but he reminds them that even before his introduction to the king he had held his own, and won an honourable name among all, of whatever rank, with whom he came into contact[3]. In his letter to Gilbert Foliot bishop of London—the prime mover of this remonstrance—he is more specific in his language. Far from evading the reference to his parents, he frankly describes their position. They were, he says, citizens of London living peaceably in the midst of their fellow-citizens,

(2) their social position.

---

[1] Auct. Anon. II. iv. 81: honestam sed ex burgensibus originem duxit. *ibid.*, uxorem...genere burgensium non disparem.

[2] Epist. 205 (v. 410).

[3] Epist. 223 (v. 499). The archbishop then proceeds to make capital out of the charge by drawing a bold parallel between his own rise and the elevation of the shepherd David to the throne of Israel, the fisherman Peter to the supremacy of the Church!

and "not exactly citizens of the lowest class either[1]."
This admission however need not be pressed to
mean simply a denial of poverty, as though Thomas
were unable to say anything further to their credit.
The words may also be translated "by no means of
the lowest class," but the shade of meaning makes
only a very slight difference. It is more important
to notice that the apologetic tone of the language is
probably due in part to the fact that Thomas here,
like his biographers[2] elsewhere, is contrasting his
parents' position in life with his own subsequent
eminence or comparing their status as members of
the citizen-class with the status of the classes above
them, the nobility. It is possible that Gilbert may
have belonged to a collateral branch of a knightly
family in Normandy; but it seems certain that he
was engaged in commerce[3] in London before the
birth of Thomas, and with more than ordinary
success, for there is every indication that he was a
man of means. Fitzstephen says that he was a
citizen of the middle class who had held the office

---

[1] Epist. 224 (v. 515): quod si ad generis mei radicem et progenitores meos intenderis, cives fuerunt Londonienses in medio concivium suorum habitantes sine querela, *nec omnino infimi*. The contrast suggested in the text above is Robertson's idea (*Becket, a biography*, p. 15).

[2] e.g. Joh. S. ii. 302: parentum mediocrium proles illustris. Will. C. i. 3: majores radice sua ramos expandit.

[3] Auct. Anon. ii. iv. 81: in commerciorum exercitio vir industrius, domum propriam pro vitae genere satis honorifice rexit. The same author describes him as one of the Normans who chose to settle in London, eo quod mercimoniis aptior et refertior erat quae frequentare consueverant.

of sheriff of London[1], not actually engaged in trade, but living in good style on an income of his own[2]. And this testimony to Gilbert's wealth is confirmed by incidental allusions to his hospitality, which barons and ecclesiastics did not disdain to accept.

It is scarcely necessary to justify the rejection of the story of Thomas' eastern origin,—the legend which makes Gilbert a crusader and his wife a Saracen princess. The very picturesqueness of its

The Saracen legend.

---

[1] Fitzst. iii. 14: natus ex legitimo matrimonio et honestis parentibus, patre Gileberto qui et vicecomes aliquando Londoniae fuit, matre Mahalt, civibus Londoniae mediastinis neque foenerantibus neque officiose negotiantibus, sed de reditibus suis honorifice viventibus. The charter of Henry I. placed London on a level with the shires, giving it a sheriff and justiciar of its own, with the privilege of electing them itself. But in the Pipe Roll of 31 Henry I. we find *four* sheriffs (vicecomites) accounting jointly for the ferm of London, and the citizens are mentioned as paying 100 marks for the privilege of electing *one* sheriff of their own. Apparently they had been deprived of the chartered right of election bestowed earlier in the reign (Stubbs, *Const. Hist.* i. 406; *Select Charters*, pp. 107, 108).

[2] Freeman (*Contemp. Rev.* vol. 31, p. 836, note) accepts Fitzstephen's statement that Gilbert was not engaged in trade, in preference to the evidence of Auct. Anon. II. But the facts of the case may perhaps be satisfied by supposing that Gilbert had retired from trade after making his fortune, and was living on the proceeds of property thus acquired. Froude (*Nineteenth Century*, 1877), following Auct. Anon. II., assumed that "few Normans were to be found as yet in the English towns condescending to trade," and used the assumption apparently as an argument in favour of Gilbert's Saxon origin. In the reprint of this series of articles in his *Short Studies on Great Subjects* (vol. iv. p. 21), he omits the sentence quoted above, follows Fitzstephen, and adds a note questioning the authority of Auct. Anon. II. and ending with the casual remark that the Saracen extraction of Thomas is "a legend doubtless, but the Norman origin is unproved also."

details has an air of suspicion,—the crusader's vow of penitence, his capture in the Holy Land, the conquest and conversion of the Emir's daughter, her resolution to follow the prisoner whose escape she had planned, her lonely voyage with the magic password "London," the strange recognition in a London street, the solemn conclave of six bishops bent on satisfying the conscience of the orthodox Gilbert, the solution of the difficulty by the baptism of the fair heathen, her marriage, her husband's speedy departure for conscience sake to the Holy Land, and, last scene of all, his happy return to find his infant son growing in beauty and wisdom. The story has had firm believers, it is true, among historians of note until far into the present century. Thierry has fitted it into his sketch of the origin of his Saxon hero, though he is not certain whether Gilbert assumed the cross to fulfil a vow of penance or to carve out a fortune in the Christian kingdom of Palestine[1]. In the latter case, Thierry remarks, the Saxon adventurer was "less fortunate in Palestine than the squires and serjeants of Normandy had been in England." The tradition furnished a fine

---

[1] Thierry, *Norman Conquest*, iv. 53. Sir James Mackintosh, admitting the possibility of the tale, though not quite convinced of its truth, makes Gilbert a pioneer of foreign trade; others describe him as a pilgrim, others a gentleman travelling for love of knowledge and adventure. One writer mentioned by Robertson—J. G. Nichols—goes so far as to place Thomas' birth at Acre, because the knights of Acre, the order of S. Thomas, took him for their patron saint. But Robertson points out that the order was founded in commemoration, not of Thomas' birth, but of the capture of Acre in 1190.

theme for the ballad poet[1], and evidently found appreciative listeners and readers. But there is one conclusive argument against its acceptance. It never appears in the contemporary authorities for the life of Thomas. It only occurs as an interpolation in a later copy of Grim's life of Thomas printed in the first composite life, the Quadrilogus bearing the date 1495, and as part of the chronicle assigned to John of Brompton[2]. There can be little doubt, if any, that the story is a later fiction, the outcome of popular imagination, which loved to cast a halo of Christian chivalry and Saracen splendour round the birth of its hero-saint. It is not the only legend that has to be rejected in connexion with Thomas. The process of legendary accretion began early in the cycle of contemporary biographers. His life had scarcely ended before its beginning had assumed a miraculous appearance. Stories are told of wonderful visions that immediately preceded or followed his birth,—strange omens of his future greatness, which must have sorely bewildered his simple-minded mother, if they ever happened at all. Their credibility is very slight, and their historical value as illustrations of mediaeval life still slighter. But they certainly reveal in those early biographers an appetite for the miraculous which would never have

[1] An interesting specimen is given in full from Jamieson's *Popular Ballads* in Appendix iv. to Thierry's *Norm. Conqu.* vol. ii. p. 398:
"In London was young Beichan born."

[2] Robertson, Introduction to Grim, vol. ii. p. xlvii. The story is printed in an appendix to Grim, ii. 451, and in Brompton (Twysden, col. 1052 foll.).

Education: (1) home training,

allowed the story of Matilda's eastern birth to pass unnoticed if it had been current in their day[1].

Thomas' education began with a careful training at home as he grew from infancy to boyhood. He had a devout and pious mother, as keenly alive to the responsibility of his nurture as she was to the call of charity[2]; and from her lips came his first lessons in godliness, as he often told his friend John of Salisbury in after days. She taught him diligently to fear God, and, next to his Saviour, to trust the blessed Virgin Mary[3]. His devotion was not unrewarded, if we may believe his biographers in the matter of dreams and visions. Herbert of Bosham describes a vision of the Virgin Mary vouchsafed to Thomas in his boyhood. The lad lay fever-ridden on his sick bed, when a woman's form, "divinely fair and most divinely tall," stood by his side, and handed to him two golden keys with a promise of his restoration to health. "These are the keys of paradise," so spake the heavenly visitant, "of which thou shalt have charge hereafter." Herbert says that he heard the story from the lips of Thomas himself[4]. The fault of retrospective fiction, conscious

---

[1] Milman has worked out this argument from the silence of the early biographers in a forcible passage in his *Latin Christianity*, iii. 444, 445.

[2] Auct. Anon. I. (iv. 7) tells how the mother weighed her infant son from time to time against bread, meat, clothes, and money, all of which she then distributed to the poor.

[3] Joh. S. ii. 302. Auct. Anon. I. *ibid.*

[4] Herb. iii. 162. Whatever credit this story deserves, the quaint audacity of the legend in Hermann Corner's *Chronicle* (a work dating early in the fifteenth century) out-miracles miracle.

or unconscious, which the incredulous reader will no doubt see here at work, is shifted therefore in this case from the adoring biographer to the archbishop in person.

It is said that the fond parents had destined their boy for the service of the Church[1]. At any rate his school life began under the shelter of a religious foundation. His father placed him at the age of ten under the care of the Augustinian canons of Merton in Surrey[2]. Their prior Robert appears more than once at a later stage in Thomas' career under circumstances which cast a pleasing light on these Merton schooldays. He was private confessor to Thomas, and bore testimony as such to the personal purity of the chancellor[3]. He attached himself to the archbishop from the day of his conse-

(2) *Merton*,

It is reprinted by Robertson (*Materials*, ii. 297), and is worth reproducing as a specimen of hagiography run riot. Thomas had chosen the better part, but at the new year when every one of his schoolfellows had received a gift from friend or lady-love, Thomas had none. He betook himself to prayer, and asked for a visible token of his lady's favour to display to his schoolmates. It was laid upon the shrine in answer to his prayer, with a prophetic command to use it when he became a priest. It was a casket containing a set of ecclesiastical ornaments! Herbert's story is sobriety itself in comparison with this later flight of imagination. The story is related in Thomas Saga (i. 23, 25), where the incident is placed at a *parlement d'amour* during his student days at Paris.

[1] Auct. Anon. II. iv. 82.

[2] Fitzst. iii. 14. This house was founded in 1115 by Gilbert Norman, sheriff of Surrey. In 1121 Henry I. gave it a charter and granted the manor of Merton towards the erection of a church in honour of the Virgin Mary. (Manning and Bray, *History of Surrey*.)

[3] Fitzst. iii. 21.

cration as his chaplain and inseparable companion[1]; and he was one of the two faithful friends who, when the monks of Canterbury fled on that cruel December day, stood along with Fitzstephen by the archbishop's side to the last and saw him die in his own cathedral[2]. On the other hand, Fitzstephen tells us, it was at the suggestion of Thomas the chancellor that King Henry II. visited and befriended the monks of Merton[3]. These allusions point irresistibly to a welcome trait in the character of Thomas; they seem to prove at least his grateful recognition of past kindness. His old master had evidently won a firm hold on his respect and gratitude; and on the other hand there must have been something attractive in the lad, which did not lose its charm amid all the perplexing changes of his career, to keep the old prior close by his side to the very end. There is an interesting story attaching to this episode in the life of Thomas. It is recorded by one of the soberest of his biographers[4], and may

---

[1] Fitzst. iii. 147: capellanus et comes inseparabilis. It was Robert who disclosed to the wondering monks the fresh proof of the murdered archbishop's hidden sanctity—the haircloth worn next to his skin under the monastic garb.

[2] Fitzst. iii. 139. Edward Grim was the other.

[3] Fitzst. iii. 23: cancellarii consilio dominus rex canonicalem ecclesiam Meritonae, ubi morantes Deum merentur, in gratiam et familiaritatem recepit. Henry completed the building and endowed the place at his own cost, and once at least, if not oftener (aliquando...celebrabat...visitabat), spent the close of Holy Week there in prayer and watching with his monastic friends, and visited the poor neighbouring churches to pray in secret,—a mediaeval Saul among the prophets.

[4] Fitzst. iii. 14.

well be genuine. Gilbert came to see him at Merton. The lad made his appearance, and the father bent low in humble obeisance to his son. The prior remonstrated on this reversal of the due order of things, but his objection was met by a quiet rejoinder from Gilbert: "I know what I am doing: that boy will be great in the sight of his God."

From Merton the lad was removed to the schools of London[1], which had no mean reputation. Fitzstephen gives a welcome glimpse of these institutions in the prefatory account of London with which his life of Thomas opens[2]. There were three schools, he says, attached to the leading churches in the city, and famous for their privileges and ancient dignity, though the list was sometimes extended to include other schools as a concession to the personal merits of an eminent teacher. On the ecclesiastical festivals which were observed as holidays, the magistrates

(3) London.

---

[1] Fitzst. iii. 14: annis igitur infantiae, pueritiae et pubertatis simpliciter domi paternae et *in scholis urbis* decursis, Thomas adulescens factus studuit Parisius. Grim, ii. 359: literarum primordiis puer traditur imbuendis. quibus decursis ad artes missus multa in brevi comprehendisse memoratur. Freeman (*Contemp. Review*, vol. 32, p. 120, note) takes '*literarum primordia*' to cover both Merton and London, and refers '*artes*' to Thomas' studies at Paris.

[2] Fitzst. iii. 4, 5: In Londonia tres principales ecclesiae scholae celebres habent de privilegio et antiqua dignitate. Plerumque tamen favore personali alicujus notorum secundum philosophiam plures ibi scholae admittuntur. Diebus festis ad ecclesias festivas magistri conventus celebrant. Hook (*Archbps.* ii. 609) takes *magistri* to mean the *magistrates* who visited and feasted the schools, but it may mean the *masters* who brought the schools to the place of meeting.

visited these schools. The scholars gave proof of their training in logic and rhetoric by syllogistic disputations and declamatory speeches; and the boys of different schools met in friendly rivalry on the familiar ground of verse composition or examination in the "principles of grammar and the rules of preterites and supines." Free play was given to wit and humour; jest and epigram flowed unchecked; and masters and boys, great men and small, had to run the gauntlet of fun and sarcasm. It is a scene worth recalling, if only as the germ of two later institutions, speech day at school and degree day at the university. Fitzstephen's account of their recreations is startling enough. One illustration must suffice. On Shrove Tuesday each boy brought a fighting cock of his own to his master; the school resolved itself into a cockpit; and the whole morning was devoted to the spectacle of boys and masters intent on the death or glory of their crested favourites. "Nous avons changé tout cela." After dinner the youths of London crowded to the suburban fields to play football. Students took sides according to their respective studies, city-officials according to their respective offices; and the game waxed fast and furious in the sight of the city fathers who rode out to see the fun and wish themselves at school again[1].

Richer de l'Aigle.

It was about this time apparently that Thomas made the acquaintance of a wealthy nobleman, Richer de l'Aigle, who frequently stayed at Gilbert's house. There was nothing abnormal in this intimacy

[1] Fitzst. iii. 9.

between the baron and the citizen; for the citizens of London ranked on a level with the minor barons[1]. Thomas, during his temporary absence from school[2], often accompanied his noble friend to the chase with hounds and falcons, and either developed or acquired that liking for sport which he indulged so freely in his chancellor days. On one occasion it nearly cost Thomas his life. He fell from his horse in taking a short cut across a narrow foot-bridge over a mill-stream which Richer had passed in safety, and was only rescued from a terrible death by the unexpected stoppage of the mill-wheel[3]. Thomas spent part of

[1] Hook, *Archbps* ii. 359, n. and 611, n. Fitzst. iii. 4: habitatores aliarum urbium *cives*, hujus *barones* dicuntur. Cp. the language which William of Malmesbury puts into the mouth of Henry bishop of Winchester at the Council of Winchester in 1141: Londonienses, qui sunt *quasi optimates*, pro magnitudine civitatis, in Anglia, nunciis nostris convenimus. It is noteworthy that the French biographer Garnier calls Thomas' parents "baruns de la cit."

[2] Auct. Anon. i. iv. 6: cum per dimidium annum a scholis vacaret. (1) It might mean during the holidays, but they would scarcely last half the year. (2) "At the end of the half-year" would not be exactly a translation of "per dimidium annum." (3) Freeman takes it to mean that Thomas was away from school for half a year at some particular time and so was thrown more into Richer's way.

[3] Auct. Anon. i. iv. 6. The story is given in Thomas Saga on the authority of prior Robert of Cretel (Cricklade), who wrote a life of Thomas in Latin (Thomas Saga, i. 32). The Saga represents Thomas as attached to Richer at the close of his education in the capacity of secretary; "Thomas becomes his notary and in his fellowship cometh for the first time into the king's court amid courtly manners." According to Grim's version of the above accident (ii. 360) Thomas had plunged into the stream to save his hawk from drowning, and was carried away by the current.

his time, it seems, in town with his father and part in the country with his friend the baron[1]. Richer's home was Pevensey Castle in Sussex, and perhaps it was this early introduction to the pleasures and pursuits of a country life which had something to do with the interest that Thomas afterwards took in the archiepiscopal manors in Sussex, particularly in the one at West Tarring, where the site of his menagerie and his brewhouse are still pointed out, and tradition still preserves the memory of Thomas the archbishop in the capacity of landlord[2].

(4) *Paris.* Thomas had not yet completed his education. From the schools of London he passed to the University of Paris. His biographer simply states the fact of his residence there as a student[3]. Modern

Freeman (*Contemp. Rev.* vol. 32, pp. 116, 117) identifying the anonymous biographer with Roger of Pontigny, and regarding this version of the story as perhaps originating with Thomas' own reminiscences, traces the growth of the miraculous element in the hands of Grim, who made the acquaintance of Thomas only a few days before his death, and would naturally view his early days through an atmosphere of the marvellous. Auct. Anon. I. iv. 6: homo qui molendinum curabat, nihil penitus de his quae agebantur sciens, aquam subito a rota exclusit. But Grim (ii. 360) says: stetit rota nec se movit semel. In the earlier version the miller happens to stop the wheel at the right moment; in the later the wheel stops of itself. "The providential delivery becomes a miraculous one." There is no wilful falsification; it is simply the natural, unconscious tendency of the hagiographer's mind.

[1] Grim, ii. 360.

[2] Hook, *Archbps* ii. 359, 360, refers to the *Sussex Archaeological Journal* and Warter's *Appendicia et Pertinentia* for a full account of West Tarring and Sussex traditions relating to archbishop Thomas.

[3] Fitzst. iii. 14. Thomas adulescens factus studuit Parisiis.

historians have found a reason for the fact in his anxiety to get rid of the obnoxious English accent which recalled his Saxon origin[1]; but this seems merely a gratuitous assumption which falls to the ground along with the theory of his English descent, by which indeed it was probably suggested. Very little is known of Thomas' student days in Paris. The Icelandic Saga is the only life that dwells upon this stage of his career. From that source (i. 22, 23) we learn that he composed " praises of our Lady both for private reading and for proses in the church," and wrote meditations on the Psalms. Two sacred compositions were attributed to him by general opinion—*Imperatrix gloriosa* and *Hodiernae lux diei*. But this information, even if credible, is unsatisfactory. It only goes a little way, and that in a doubtful direction. The name of one fellow-student has been preserved in a mediaeval chronicle. Everlin,

---

[1] Thierry, *Norm. Conqu.* ii. 54, and Lord Campbell in his *Lives of the Chancellors*. Thierry makes Thomas utilise his Parisian accomplishments (to which the historian gives a very modern look) for the purpose of insinuating himself into the familiar friendship of a wealthy baron (evidently Richer de l'Aigle), whose stud and pack he is permitted to use in the pursuit of "amusements forbidden to every Englishman who was not either the servant or the associate of a man of foreign origin." Milman (*Latin Christianity*, iii. 446), though absolutely free from the fallacy of the Saxon origin, seems to imply the same linguistic motive. "His accomplishments were completed by a short residence in Paris, the best school for the language spoken by the Norman nobility." It may have been that, but it was considerably more than that, to judge from the picture drawn by Joh. S. *Metalogicus*, bk ii. Cp. Stubbs, *Mediaeval and Modern History*, p. 138.

abbot of S. Laurence, Liège (1161—1183) dedicated an altar to S. Thomas in memory of their affectionate intercourse when they were students together at Paris[1]. It is said that Ludolf, who became archbishop of Magdeburg in 1194, was once a pupil of Thomas at Paris, where he spent twenty years[2]. But it is hard to picture Thomas at his age playing "guide, philosopher and friend," or seated in the master's chair; his stay in Paris was short, and ended before he reached man's estate. It is just possible that Thomas, like John of Salisbury, eked out his allowance from home by taking private pupils at Paris; but perhaps the chronicler made a mistake, and should have said that Ludolf and Thomas were fellow-students[3]. It would be tempting to hazard a similar conjecture with regard to John of Salisbury, whose twelve years of student life at Paris, so vividly sketched in the second book of his *Metalogicus*, began in 1136 and must have coincided with Thomas' briefer residence at the same seat of learning. But there seems no trace of any intercourse between the

[1] Hist. Mon. S. Laur. Leodensis (*Materials*, iv. 260, 261): ex amore quem erga eum (Everlinus) habuerat cum secum studeret Parisiis.

[2] Bothonis Chron. Brunsvicensium (*ib.* iv. 261): ...Parys, dar wart he sunte Thomas van Kantelber scholer, unde was dar twintich jare.

[3] Robertson (*Materials*, iv. 261 n.) mentions another name, Conrad bishop of Würzburg (murdered in 1202), who is described in an old MS. (in the *Fontes Rerum Germanicarum* of Böhmer) as "contemporaneus et combursalis beati Thomae de Kandelberg in studio Parysiis." But, as Robertson points out, the statement is a historical error. Conrad was not born till after 1153—the year of his mother's marriage.

two friends until they met in the service of archbishop Theobald, whose secretary John became on his return to England in 1150. As with fellow-students, so with masters. The names of the particular doctors whose lectures Thomas attended are not recorded. Of all the brilliant roll of eminent teachers that Paris boasted at this time[1], not one can be specified with certainty as responsible for any part of Thomas' education. But there is one name that provokes conjecture. Robert of Melun, who was invited back by Henry II. to his native England at the suggestion of Thomas the chancellor[2], and consecrated bishop of Hereford by Thomas the archbishop[3], had "taught dialectic and the sacred page for more than forty years at Paris[4]," where John of Salisbury had figured among his pupils. Thomas' student days at Paris must have fallen somewhere within that period; and Robert's promotion to an English see is perhaps a second instance of a grateful tribute from a former pupil to his old

[1] Joh. S. *Metalogicus*, bk ii. Stubbs, *ibid.* pp. 138, 139.
[2] Fitzst. iii. 24: cancellario Thoma suggerente pauperes Angligenas morantes in Galliis quos fama celebrabat bonos, vel monachum in religione vel magistrum in studio, rex revocabat et tales in regno suo plantabat personas, ut magistrum Robertum de Meliduno, in episcopali ecclesia Herefordiae.
[3] Herb. iii. 260: Robertum de Meliduno, et saecularium et sacrarum litterarum in scholis magistrum praeclarum...cujus et ille sacerdos magnus, de quo proxime sermo, prius consecratus, in scholis discipulus fuerat. This would be decisive if it referred to Thomas, but the 'sacerdos' seems to be Roger (mentioned by Herbert on pp. 258, 259), newly consecrated by Thomas to the see of Worcester.
[4] Fitzst. iii. 60.

master. Robert of Merton and Robert of Melun may be parallels in more than name.

The order of events at this point is by no means clear. Thomas' mother died when he was twenty-one; but it is not certain whether her death occurred before he went to Paris or during his residence there or after his return. It has been suggested[1] that perhaps he was recalled from Pevensey by the sad news, and then decided, instead of returning to Pevensey, to complete his education in the schools of Paris. But this is after all mere conjecture. The scanty notices in the biographers point rather to his mother's decease as coming after his studies at Paris had begun. One anonymous writer says distinctly that it was his mother who had insisted upon the necessity of a thorough education, and that after her death his enthusiasm for learning subsided[2]. But

[1] Hook, *Archbps* ii. 361. Hook is inclined to regard Thomas' choice of Paris as due, partly to a disinclination for merely theological studies which kept him away from Oxford (then rising in reputation as a theological school), but mainly to the social attractions which Paris offered in addition to the more solid benefits of dialectic, rhetoric, grammar, and divinity.

Prof. Froude in his *Short Studies* (iv. 22) omits the Oxford career with which he credited Thomas in the original essay in the *Nineteenth Century* for 1877, and which drew down the scathing criticism of Freeman in the *Contemp. Review* for 1878 (vol. 32, pp. 118, 119). There is certainly not an atom of original authority for the statement, though Lingard (vol. ii. p. 56, 6th ed.) inserts it after the London schools (which Froude still ignores) and before the Parisian studies of Thomas.

[2] Auct. Anon. I. iv. 8: cum autem Thomas annum aetatis vicesimum primum implevisset, mater, quae sola ut erudiretur instabat, defuncta est, et ex inde circa studia Thomas se remissius coepit habere.

there was another cause which might of itself have cut his stay in Paris short. His father had sustained loss after loss through fires in the city[1]; and his diminished purse, if it did not necessitate his son's speedy return from Paris, seems at least to have made immediate work of some kind compulsory for Thomas on the completion of his studies. His twenty-second year was spent without definite employment[2]; but at last, tired of his lonely motherless home, he entered the service of Osbern Huitdeniers, a kinsman of his, a man of property and high standing in official circles as well as in citizen society[3]. For three years Thomas was busily em-

Osbern and the sheriffs of London.

---

[1] Grim, ii. 359, places these losses before the mother's death. Parentes frequentibus incendiis ceterisque infaustis incursibus rerum non mediocriter attenuati, minorem noscuntur in instruendo filio diligentiam adhibuisse...Sed et filii desolationem geminavit interitus genetricis...Pater quippe senuerat nec ad filii sumptus sufficere poterat substantia quae remansit. Grim then goes on to mention Richer and his kindness to Thomas, and lastly the mill-stream incident. But this is evidently out of its place here, for Auct. Anon. I. iv. 7 describes the mother's joy over her rescued son. It must have happened in her lifetime. Grim's chronology is badly involved, to judge from the more business-like arrangement of the facts in other biographers.

[2] Will. C. i. 3: matre defuncta, sibi patrique relictus, quem incendia crebra civitatis attenuabant, vigesimum secundum annum quem jam agebat otio impendit, et tandem civi vice tabellionis adhaesit.

[3] Auct. Anon. I. iv. 8: paternam igitur domum quasi vacuam et desolatam sublata matre fastidiens, ad quemdam Lundrensem cognatum suum, qui non solum inter concives verum etiam apud curiales grandis erat nominis et honoris, se contulit; apud quem ferme per triennium consistens...etc.

Robertson calls him a merchant; but Freeman doubts the

ployed in keeping Master Eightpenny's books[1]. That is one account, but there is a serious discrepancy among the original authorities on this point. Fitzstephen omits the name of Osbern, and simply says that Thomas on his return from Paris began to enter into the responsibilities of municipal government as clerk and accountant to the sheriffs of London[2]. John of Salisbury, whose life of Thomas only professes to be a brief summary of his career, throws no light upon the difficulty. He merely states that Thomas passed from the scholastic to the official world, and threw himself heart and soul into the round of business and pleasure with a vigour that outstripped all competitors, his only fault being an overweening passion for popularity[3]. Various attempts have been made to reconcile the discrepant details. Osbern, it is suggested, may have been a

accuracy of the title. "No words are used of him which necessarily imply trade; and it is most important for a full understanding of the true position of the London 'barons'...to grasp the fact that many citizens were not traders and that many citizens were Normans" (*Contemp. Review*, vol. 32, p. 121).

[1] Grim, ii. 361 (the only Latin biography which gives the name): 'Osbernus Octonummi cognomine.' The MS. reading was Octonumini; but the correct reading was suggested by Garnier's French life, which in one MS. describes Osbern as "dit Deniers" and in another "wit Deniers" (i.e. huit deniers).

Grim speaks of Thomas as employed "in breviandis sumptibus reditibusque" of Osbern, who was "vir insignis in civitate et multarum possessionum."

[2] Fitzst. iii. 14: reversus in partem receptus est sollicitudinis reipublicae Londoniensis et *vicecomitum clericus et rationalis* effectus.

[3] Joh. S. ii. 303: liberalium vero disciplinarum scholas egrediens ad curiarum se transtulit occupationes.

sheriff himself[1] or clerk to the sheriffs[2]; in either case the two accounts will coincide, and the sphere of Thomas' work will have been one and the same. On the other hand, the two employments may have been quite distinct. Thomas may have passed from the desk in Master Eightpenny's office to the service of the municipal authorities[3]. But the main point to notice in any case is the importance of this stage in Thomas' career. It was his first introduction to

[1] Freeman, *Cont. Rev.* vol. 32, p. 121.
[2] Hook, *Archbps* ii. 362.
[3] Robertson, *Becket, a biography*. Both Robertson and Hook lay stress upon the political importance of the business that passed through the sheriffs' office. Froude, in his *Short Studies* (iv. 23), omits Thomas' employment under the sheriffs, and dismisses him vaguely on his return from Paris to a place "in a house of business in the city," apparently taking Osbern for a merchant and ignoring Fitzstephen's statement altogether. His whole treatment in fact of Thomas' early career is scrappy, eked out with a picture of the startling things that were happening during his youth and may have come to his hearing. The sketch is apparently drawn from one or two biographers to the exclusion of the rest. In places he seems to have followed Grim's unmethodical arrangement. He has now omitted the remarkable statement (made originally in the *Nineteenth Century* for 1877) that Thomas "was left ill provided for to the care of his father's friends" by the death of both parents when he was still young, and was taken up by one of these friends, Richer de l'Aigle, and sent to school at Merton Abbey and then to Oxford. But he still replaces Gilbert by Richer de l'Aigle. "Gilbert," he says, "survived his wife for several years, but appears to have left his son to the care of others, as he is mentioned no longer in connexion with him." He then proceeds to mention Richer's fancy for Thomas. But the idea that Gilbert neglected his son's welfare is surely contradicted beyond a doubt by Fitzstephen's testimony to Gilbert's share in the introduction of Thomas to archbishop Theobald (Fitzst. iii. 15).

questions of national interest. The citizens of London played no mean part in the contest for the crown between Stephen and Matilda. It was an education in itself to live at such a historical crisis, still more to occupy a position however subordinate in the service of men who were situated at the very centre of the conflict, and had a share in the making of their country's history. Such was the situation of the sheriffs of London whose service Thomas had entered[1]. It was an epoch in his life. To the intellectual training of the schools, and the social advantages of the baron's acquaintance, Thomas now added what was the coping stone of his education, a practical experience of the world of politics.

[1] Thomas entered the service of Osbern (according to Will. C. i. 3) at the close of his twenty-second year, i.e. at the end of 1140, if his birth is placed, as seems most probable, in 1118. It is possible then, even if Osbern's office was distinct from that of the sheriffs, that Thomas was already in the employ of the municipal authorities at the time of the famous ecclesiastical synod of Winchester in April 1141 (described in detail by William of Malmesbury, *Hist. Novellae*) at which Henry bishop of Winchester presided as papal legate,—when Matilda was elected queen of England by the English clergy,—when further decision was postponed to await the arrival of the Londoners who had been summoned by the legate's nuncios,—and when the Londoners, on their introduction to the Synod, describing themselves as a deputation—missos a communione quam vocant Londoniarum—boldly requested the release of their lord the king. London, it seems, was already recognised in Stephen's reign as a *communio*, though it did not gain the legal status of a perpetual corporation before the reign of Richard I. (Stubbs, *Select Charters*, pp. 107, 117.)

CHAPTER II.

THE SERVANT OF THEOBALD.

FROM the close of his political apprenticeship in the sheriffs' office to the day of his consecration, the life of Thomas of London falls into two clearly marked periods, the earlier of the two spent in the service of Theobald archbishop of Canterbury, the latter in the service of king Henry II. Hitherto a close spectator, Thomas now became an actor in the busy scene, first as the faithful minister of the Church, then as the equally faithful minister of the Crown.

The transition from the sheriffs' office to the archbishop's household was not so violent a change as at first sight it seems to us with our modern ideas of the division of labour between church and state. In those days the ecclesiastic was often merged in the statesman and sometimes in the soldier. Especially was this the case in England during the reign of Stephen. Two causes contributed to throw the secular and political influence of the day into the hands of the Church. It had a practical monopoly of talent; and it was the one stable and constant element in the midst of a kingdom given over to anarchy. Theobald archbishop of Canterbury and Henry bishop of Winchester were the two greatest powers in the country. Combined they were masters of the political situation; and the compromise which ended the battle for the crown in 1153 was the immediate result of their co-operation. It was not therefore an absolute change of life, a clean break with the past, for Thomas to cross from the service of the city magistrates to the service of the archbishop. New ties of friendship, new associations were formed; new traditions and ideals inherited, new duties undertaken; but there was one phase of his new position which recalled the old, and that was the diplomatic work of his new master, the primate's constant intervention in the struggle for the crown. The political crisis was still the same, except that it was viewed and approached from a different standpoint. Thomas was now to thread this "mazy labyrinth of events," as William of Malmesbury calls it, from the ecclesiastical side.

Introduction to Theobald.   Thomas had spent something like three years in the municipal service when his promotion came. The exact circumstances of his introduction to the primate's court are not clearly known. Fitzstephen attributes it to two brothers of Boulogne, Archdeacon Baldwin and Master Eustace, who were frequent guests at Gilbert's house on their visits to London and at the same time friends of the archbishop. It was at their joint instance that Theobald found Thomas a place in his household, though their influence was apparently backed by a request from Gilbert himself, who laid great stress on the resemblance, if not the connexion, between his own antecedents and those of Theobald, like himself a Norman by birth and a native of the neighbourhood of Thiersy in Normandy[1]. A very different account is given by one of the anonymous biographers. This writer says that a certain official of Theobald's household, who used to stay with Gilbert when transacting his master's business in London, and had watched with interest the fulfilment of Thomas' early promise, urged him to come to the archbishop's palace. Thomas hesitated. He was not sure of the reception that might await an uninvited candidate for the primate's patronage; but at last he yielded to the man's arguments, and was introduced by him to the archbishop himself, with whom he found favour at first sight[2]. It is not easy to harmonise the two

[1] Fitzst. iii. 15: per duos fratres Bolonienses, Baldewinum archidiaconum et magistrum Eustachium, hospites plerumque patris ejus et familiares archiepiscopi, in ipsius notitiam introductus: et eo familiarius, quod praefatus Gilebertus cum domino archipraesule de propinquitate et genere loquebatur; ut ille ortu Normannus et circa Tierrici villam, de equestri ordine, natu vicinus. Horum, inquam, et patris introductu, archiepiscopus sui gregis scripsit Thomam. 'Loquebatur' may refer to conversations which took place during the early acquaintance of Theobald and Thomas, or it may refer to a reminder from Gilbert on the occasion of his son's recommendation. The words in parenthesis—'de equestri ordine'—may apply to Gilbert only; otherwise another point might have been added to the resemblance, "and a member of the same social class,—the knightly order."

[2] Auct. Anon. i. iv. 9. Cp. Grim, ii. 361, invitatus a quodam ministro domus Theobaldi.

accounts; but perhaps the key to the solution lies in Fitzstephen's concluding statement that Thomas came to the primate's court at Harrow with a single companion whom he describes as an "armiger"— Ralph of London by name. This man may be the "officialis quidam" of the anonymous biographer, and the "minister domus" of Grim's version. Thomas' original acceptance by Theobald may have been due to the recommendation of the two learned brothers of Boulogne and the reminder of his own father Gilbert, but perhaps his first actual appearance in person at the archbishop's palace was made under the humbler auspices of the household official whose menial duties pointed the sarcasm of Thomas' rivals there. Roger de Pont l'Evêque, we are told, fastened the epithet Baille-hache as a nickname upon Thomas himself[1].

Two of the other biographers deal with Thomas' motive in taking this step. Herbert of Bosham describes it as a deliberate choice on the part of Thomas. Unable to reconcile his religious professions with the views and practices of his lay masters, he decided to forsake his secular surroundings for a place in the service of some prominent ecclesiastic[2].

---

[1] Auct. Anon. I. iv. 10: aliquotiens palam in contumelias et improperia erumpebat, ita ut Thomam *clericum Baille-hache* plerumque vocitaret: sic enim cognominabatur vir ille *cum quo ad curiam venerat*. Cp. Grim, ii. 362, clericum cum ascia sive securi (= the clerk with the hatchet) faceta contumelia crebrius appellavit, cognomento videlicet illius, a quo ad curiam archiepiscopi fuerat invitatus. Garnier says,—le clerc Baille-hache plusieurs fois le nomma.

[2] Herb. iii. 167.

We might dismiss this assertion lightly as one of the many instances in which this diffuse biographer has read his own views of Thomas' saintly character as archbishop into the facts of his early career. But it is supported by a remark of John of Salisbury, a fairly impartial witness, judged by the frankness with which he admits the faults and failings of his hero. He credits Thomas already with the resolve to lead a religious life, and attributes his anxiety to enter Theobald's service to his disapproval of much that he saw in the life and conduct of the secular officials[1]. It is true that a marked change is recorded in his manner of life after his admission to the primate's household. He set himself soberly and resolutely to benefit by the society of those older and wiser men with whom he was thrown into contact[2]. But while we admit the sincerity of this motive, we are not bound to exclude the working of all other motives. The single eye is proverbially rare, and it is at least probable that the young layman, earnest-minded perhaps but certainly ambitious, and not yet launched upon any permanent calling, was as fully alive to the fact that the surest way to eminence for a commoner lay through the Church as he was to the difficulty of living a religious life in a secular environment.

[1] Joh. S. ii. 303 : cum vero in curiis procerum plurima contra honestatem cleri geri conspiceret, et convictum eorum proposito cui addictus erat perniciosius adversari...se ad Theobaldum... contulit.

[2] Grim, ii. 361: ubi, ludis et levitate postposita, seniorum sapientiumque sermonibus ad meliora semper animum informabat.

The archbishop's court.

His footing once gained, Thomas made rapid progress in the archbishop's favour[1], and soon won his way to the front. The competition was keen, for Theobald had gathered round him the most promising ability of the younger generation. His court was a veritable nursery of talent, "a substitute in England for the as yet undeveloped universities[2]," a training ground for future bishops and archbishops at home and abroad. Six years had yet to elapse before the arrival of the scholarly John of Salisbury[3], the faithful secretary of Theobald, afterwards bishop of Chartres. But Richard—Thomas' successor in the primacy—was already Theobald's chaplain[4]; and there were three young aspirants to fame, singled out by William of Canterbury for special mention, who made no secret of their ambition. Their names were Thomas of London, Roger of Neustria, and John of Canterbury, afterwards bishop of Poictiers and archbishop of Lyons. The two last-named lost no time in securing the goodwill and cooperation of

[1] Grim, ii. 361: consiliis archiepiscopi negotiisque et causis publicis et privatis interesse jubetur.

[2] Stubbs, *Mediaeval and Modern History*, pp. 130, 142.

[3] John went, after his twelve years' study in Paris (1136–1148), to act as secretary or chaplain to Peter, abbot of Celles, and in 1150 was recommended to Theobald by S. Bernard (Stubbs, *ib.*, p. 130). It was apparently late in 1143 or early perhaps in 1144 when Thomas joined the little band of budding scholars and ecclesiastics under Theobald's care. He was born in 1118, and was twenty-two (Will. C. i. 3) at his entrance into the London offices, where he spent the next three years.

[4] Gervase, *Chron.* (quoted by Hook in his *Life of Richard, Archbps* ii. 509): Theobaldi capellanus effectus una cum beato Thoma eidem sedulo ministravit.

the favourite, and all three bound themselves by an ingenuous compact to help each other in the quest of preferment. One or other of the three was present at most of the primate's business, and each worked for the rest as well as for himself[1]. But this harmony of purpose was soon broken by the discord of jealousy. The worst offender seems to have been Roger, surnamed 'de Pont l'Évêque[2],' whose contemptuous nickname for Thomas has been already noticed. His envy, ill-concealed at the outset, broke out at last into open opposition. Twice on some pretext or other he procured the dismissal of Thomas from the palace. But on both occasions his triumph was short-lived. Thomas, conscious of his innocence, took refuge with the archbishop's brother Walter, then archdeacon of Canterbury, who was staying in the palace at the time, and, thanks to his intercession, regained to the full the favour of Theobald[3].

[1] Will. C. i. 4: qui videntes eum in necessitatibus expediendis prudenter agentem et consilio providum, cum eo sociale foedus inierunt, condicentes ut in petendis sibi beneficiis ecclesiasticis suffragium suum communicarent.

[2] Rogerius (Rogerus) de Ponte-Episcopi is the name given by Auct. Anon. I. iv. 9, and Fitzst. iii. 16; cp. Grim, ii. 362. It is sometimes translated 'Bishop's-bridge,' but Brompton (Twysden, col. 1057) calls him a Neustrian; cp. Will. C. i. 3. Probably Pont l'Évêque in Normandy is meant.

[3] Fitzst. iii. 16 is the only authority for this twofold dismissal and reinstatement. Grim, ii. 362, and Auct. Anon. I. iv. 9 speak only in general terms of Roger's jealous opposition. They style Roger 'Cantuariensis archidiaconus,' and Milman follows suit (*Lat. Christ.* iii. 447). But Fitzstephen distinctly says, '*Walterum tunc archidiaconum Cantuariae*, postea episcopum Roffensem.'

Ecclesiastical services of Thomas.

It is difficult to estimate exactly the extent or the value of the services which Thomas rendered to Theobald at home and abroad. The actual evidence at our disposal is only very slight. Thomas is rarely mentioned in the authorities for the reign of Stephen, but the omission is no proof of his inactivity. Judging from the historical importance of those occasions on which Theobald is said to have found his help valuable, it seems quite permissible to infer that in other cases also, where he was not the agent employed in the execution of a task, he was perhaps responsible for the policy adopted. He seems to have been Theobald's right hand, and it is quite possible, for instance, that during Theobald's informal regency[1] between the death of Stephen and the arrival of Henry (Oct. 25 to Dec. 20, 1154) Thomas had a considerable share in the transaction of current affairs of state.

Legal studies at Bologna and Auxerre.

It will be convenient to deal first with Thomas' legal studies in Italy and France, though they may not have come first in the actual order of events. Fitzstephen states that Thomas, having obtained the archbishop's permission to go abroad, spent a year at Bologna and some time at Auxerre afterwards in the study of law[2]. John of Salisbury,

It was not until 1147, the date of Walter's promotion to the see of Rochester, that Roger became archdeacon; whereas this double downfall and restoration evidently came soon after Thomas' introduction to the archbishop's circle.

[1] Gervase, 1376 (Twysden), describes the peace as kept 'nutu divino et cooperante Theobaldo Cantuariensi archiepiscopo.'

[2] Fitzst. iii. 17: tunc impetrato (? impetrata) a domino suo archiepiscopo transfretandi licentia, per annum studuit in legibus

while omitting all mention of time and place, is more definite as to the subject of these studies. They included both the civil and the canon law; and he regards them as a providential training in judicial and educational work for the future primate[1]. But this visit to the home of the new jurisprudence was more than a finishing touch to Thomas' own training. It was part of a great legal movement in England which owed its rise to archbishop Theobald. A brief retrospect will make this clear. The separation of the ecclesiastical from the civil courts of justice at the Conquest had thrown into the hands of the bishops more judicial work than they were able to discharge in person. The demand was met by the subdivision of their dioceses into archdeaconries, the archdeacon standing in the same relation to the bishop as the sheriff to the king. "There

---

Bononiae, postea Autissiodori. This notice, coming as it does between a list of his earlier preferments and the notice of his ordination and appointment as archdeacon, would seem decisive in favour of a later date for his foreign studies. The length of time given may include his stay at both places, or it may apply only to Bologna, leaving the length of his residence at Auxerre to conjecture. Hook (*Archbps.* ii. 363) makes it a shorter period.

[1] Joh. S. ii. 304: ut vero in causis perorandis et decidendis et populis instruendis facultas a Deo praedestinato pararetur antistiti, juri civili et sacris canonibus operam dedit. Cp. Auct. Anon. I. iv. 10: interim autem quantum licuit juri civili et sacris canonibus studium adhibuit ut per haec in causis perorandis seu decidendis (i.e. as advocate or as judge) instructior haberetur et ecclesiasticarum rerum notitiam plenius consequeretur. It is not clear whether 'quantum licuit' refers to the time and opportunities at his disposal, or hints at the prohibition of legal studies in England.

was a vast increase," writes Dr. Stubbs on Canon Law, "in ecclesiastical litigation, great profits and fees to be made out of it; a craving for canonical jurisprudence and reformed jurisprudence analogous to the development of constitutional machinery; and with it the accompanying evils of ill-trained judges and an ill-understood system of law.......The archdeacons were worldly, mercenary and unjust; the law was uncertain and unauthoritative; the procedure was hurried and irregular[1]." The twofold need of regular procedure and substantive law seemed to be supplied about the middle of the twelfth century, the one by the revival of Roman jurisprudence, which was now being studied eagerly at Bologna and other Italian schools, the other by the codification of the canons which was issued in 1151 by Gratian, a Benedictine monk of Bologna. A generation elapsed between these two movements in Italy, but they nearly coincided in their influence upon the English Church. It was Theobald who was responsible for their introduction. In 1149 he placed Vacarius at Oxford to teach the Roman civil law[2]; and, nothing daunted by the royal opposition

[1] Stubbs, *Mediæval and Modern History:* 'Canon Law in England,' pp. 300, 301, closely followed in the sketch in the text above.

[2] Joh. S. *Polycraticus*, viii. 22: tempore regis Stephani a regno jussae sunt leges Romanae quas in Britanniam domus venerabilis patris Theobaldi Britanniarum primatis adsciverat: ne quis etiam libros retineret edicto regio prohibitum est et Vacario nostro indictum silentium. Theobald's household was the only "inn of court," as Hook remarks, for the lawyers of the new school (*Archbps.* ii. 337–339).

which silenced Vacarius and the conservatism of the Church which suspected and resisted the new learning, he set his heart on the foundation of an Anglican school of canon law as soon as the "*Concordantia discordantium canonum*" of Gratian made its appearance. Long before the close of the twelfth century Bologna was the recognised training school for the archidiaconate, which was essentially a legal and judicial office. Archdeacons *in praesenti* and archdeacons *in futuro*, English and continental, crowded to its lectures[1]. Thomas, it is true, was not yet archdeacon of Canterbury, but he had already taken a subordinate part in the judicial labours of the archiepiscopal court[2]; and it is more than probable that Theobald had kept Thomas in view long before the promotion of Roger to the see of York threw the archdeaconry open. Viewed in this light, Thomas' legal studies at Bologna and Auxerre acquire a new significance. They look like a definite provision on the part of the lawyer-archbishop for the reform of the judicial work of his see, for the improvement of legal education, and for the growth of the new ecclesiastical jurisprudence on English soil.

The date of Thomas' residence at Bologna under

---

[1] Stubbs, *Med. and Mod. Hist.*, p. 139 ('Literature and Learning at the Court of Henry II.'), gives a graphic description of their adventures and temptations at Bologna.

[2] Grim, ii. 361, immediately after describing his reception by Theobald and his efforts at self-improvement, adds: cognitaque in brevi vivacitate viri per verba prudentiae...consiliis archiepiscopi negotiisque et *causis publicis et privatis* interesse jubetur. This probably refers to the legal and judicial work of the archbishop.

the recognised master of canon law is not certain. Gervase places it after the diplomatic mission to Rome which resulted in the transference of the legatine office from Henry of Blois to Theobald[1]. But the date of this mission is another open question. It is not even certain whether Thomas' visit to Bologna preceded or followed the actual publication of Gratian's Decretum in 1151, but it probably falls in close proximity to that important event in the history of ecclesiastical law.

Connexion with Rome.

With regard to Thomas' share in the intercourse between the Church of England and the Papacy during Stephen's reign, the two biographers upon whom we can best rely—John of Salisbury and William Fitzstephen—speak only in vague and general terms. We learn from them nothing beyond the fact that Thomas paid several visits to Rome on ecclesiastical business, and succeeded not only in carrying out Theobald's wishes but also in winning the favour and esteem of the papal court[2]. But

---

[1] Gervase, *Act. Pontif. Cant.* s. v. Theobald. Hook (*Archbps.* ii. 339), apparently converting the "post hoc" of Gervase into a "propter hoc" says: "the study of canon law seemed to be a necessary consequence of the introduction of the legatine jurisdiction." He might have gone further back: it was the natural outcome of the separate episcopal jurisdiction which the Church had exercised since the days of the Conqueror.

[2] Joh. S. ii. 303: quotiens pro expediendis necessitatibus ecclesiasticis apostolorum limina visitaverit, quam felici exitu quae sibi injuncta fuerant expedierit, nequaquam dicta facile est. Cp. the similar language of Gervase (*Act. Pontif. Cant.*). John adds, by way of apology for this dismissal of the subject, that a detailed account is impracticable in a compendious summary such as his biography of Thomas is intended to give. Fitzst. iii. 16:

from the evidence of one anonymous biographer, from incidental notices in the chronicles of the period, and from the letters of Thomas himself, we are enabled to single out three distinct occasions on which he played an important part. The first of these was the transference of the legatine commission from Henry of Blois, brother of king Stephen and bishop of Winchester, to Theobald himself[1]. This *legatio* was a standing difficulty in the way of the primate The 'legatus apostolicae sedis,' acting as the representative of the papal jurisdiction, which was at this time accepted *de facto*, even if not recognised *de jure*, by the bishops and the king, claimed precedence of the primate of England, and held ecclesiastical courts in England from which the appeal lay not to the primate but to the Pope. A deadlock was almost inevitable unless the legatine office and the primacy coincided in the same person[2];

(1) *The papal legation.*

intellecta mox ipsius industria, mittebat eum archiepiscopus aliquotiens Romam pro negotiis ecclesiae Anglorum; ubi, Domino favente, sapienter se gerens in plurimam *summorum pontificum et sanctae ecclesiae Romanae* gratiam receptus est. Evidently Thomas visited more than one of the succession of Popes from 1143 to 1153.

[1] Joh. S. *Epist.* 89 (ed. Giles) calls bishop Henry's commission 'primum legationis officium,' i.e. the first in England during Stephen's reign. William of Malmesbury (*Hist. Nov.* ii. 22) fixes its date: Theobald was consecrated in January, 1139, and Henry was appointed legate early in March that same year.

[2] The archbishop of Canterbury was the obvious person to represent the papal authority, to whatever extent it was exercised or acknowledged, in England; but it was part of the Roman policy to reserve the alternative of appointing a special 'legatus a latere,' such as Winchester in this case, to supersede the 'legatus natus,' as the archbishop might be styled (Hook, *Archbps.* ii. 341).

and the deadlock came. Gervase of Canterbury—
our sole authority for Thomas' share in the matter—
says that Henry of Blois pushed his rights as legate
too far. He daily cited his fellow-bishops and his
own archbishop to attend upon him in his capacity
of papal legate. Theobald at last refused to submit
to such claims and took steps to reverse the position.
Aided by the efforts of 'Thomas a clerk of London,'
says Gervase, he so managed the matter with Pope
Celestine II. (who had succeeded Innocent II., the
original source of this particular commission) that
Henry was removed from his legatine office and
Theobald substituted. Hence arose bitter disputes
and appeals on either side. That is Gervase's
account[1]. But his chronology is doubtful. Celes-

After the public indignation roused by the conduct of John of
Crema, the 'legatus a latere' in England in 1125, William
Corbeuil, archbishop of Canterbury, solved the difficulty of exercis-
ing the papal jurisdiction without offending the national spirit of
the English Church by accepting the formal 'legatio' himself.
Theobald now procured the same official recognition, partly to
secure his own precedence over the rival archbishop of York,
partly to thwart the ambition of the scheming prelate of Winchester. The Winchester annalist under the year 1143 describes
the continual disagreement between the legate and the primate
briefly but forcibly: iste enim major videri voluit quam archiepiscopus, ille quam legatus. Winchester's schemes for the exaltation
of self and see are given in detail by the writer of the *Historia
Pontificalis* (Pertz, xx. 542): elaborare coepit ut ei pallium daretur
et fieret archiepiscopus occidentalis Angliae, vel ut ei legatio
regni concederetur, vel saltem ut ecclesia sua eximeretur a
jurisdictione Cantuariensis. The Pope refused his requests.
Winchester was not erected into an archbishopric, Henry was not
reappointed papal legate in England, and his see was not eman-
cipated from the jurisdiction of Canterbury.

[1] Gervase (*Act. Pontif. Cant.* s. v. Theobald).

tine II. was Pope from September 1143 to March 1144, while the first notice of Theobald's *legatio* occurs some seven years or more after this date. Henry may have ceased to be legate at the time stated by Gervase; perhaps, if his commission expired with Innocent II., the Pope who granted it, Theobald and Thomas may have prevented its renewal by Innocent's successors[1]. But Theobald himself is not styled papal legate by Gervase or Henry of Huntingdon till the year 1151. That is at all events the date assigned to the council summoned at London by Theobald as "archbishop of Canterbury and legate of the Apostolic See[2]," a

---

[1] John of Hexham under A.D. 1144 remarks that Celestine, who was prejudiced against Stephen by his own early Angevin associations, took a dislike to Henry, bishop of Winchester. The same writer notes under A.D. 1145 that Henry fared better in winning the favour of the next Pope, but nevertheless did not continue to hold the office and title of legate. Evidently the commission had lapsed; it is hardly likely that, if it had been withdrawn by a definite act on the part of Celestine, the chronicler would have omitted to mention such an important fact.

On the supposition that Thomas was born in 1121 (1122), Celestine's papacy would have been past and gone before Thomas in his twenty-fifth year was introduced to Theobald, i.e. 1146. If we accept the more probable date for his birth, 1118, and so place his introduction to Theobald late in 1143 or early in 1144, it will fall within the limits of Celestine's papacy; but it is scarcely possible that Theobald would have employed Thomas on such a confidential mission so soon after his entrance upon his new service. Inett (*Orig. Angl.* ii. 203) on the former supposition places Thomas' mission to Rome in the papacy of Lucius II. (1144-1145) or Eugenius III. (1445-1153).

[2] Gervase (*Act. Pontif. Cant.* s. v. Theobald). Wilkins (*Conc.* i. 424) dates the council 1151. Lyttelton, i. 358, notes the fact that Lucius II. sent a cardinal legate into England as an

council at which Stephen and his son Eustace were both present, and the discussion was broken by new and unaccustomed appeals, partly no doubt the expression of Winchester's disappointment.

(2) *Council of Reims*, 1148.

The second occasion on which Thomas comes out clearly as the faithful servant of Theobald in his negotiations with the Papacy was the council held at Reims by Eugenius III. in 1148[1]. The objects of the council, though nominally ecclesiastical, bordered closely on the political. One of the questions for settlement was the validity of the election of William, Stephen's nephew, to the see of York, an election which Eugenius had declared void on the ground that it was carried by Stephen's nomination. Stephen rose to the occasion. He met the papal summons to this council with a royal prohibition which kept all the English bishops at home, except three sent by Stephen to explain the absence of the rest. But Theobald went in defiance of his lord the king. With Thomas in attendance, he stole across the Channel at the risk of shipwreck, and earned the warm thanks of his friend the Pope for a journey

indication that Theobald was not yet in possession of the legatine office. Stubbs (*Const. Hist.* i. 330, note) attributes the commission of Theobald to Eugenius III. "who acted under the advice of S. Bernard and was generally opposed to Stephen," and dates the grant in or before the year 1150.

[1] The writer of the *Historia Pontificalis* (possibly John of Salisbury) gives the list of persons present at the Council of Reims. "Affuerunt etiam bonae memoriae Theobaldus Cantuariensis...et qui adhuc supersunt Thomas Cantuariensis et Rogerus Eboracensis archiepiscopi" (Pertz, xx. 523). Roger was at the time archdeacon of Canterbury (1147–1154).

which, as Eugenius wittily remarked, had been "more of a swim than a sail." We have Thomas' own evidence directly and indirectly for the fact of Theobald's visit to Rome. In a letter written in 1166 to Cardinal Boso (an old acquaintance, as we learn from this very letter, whom he had introduced to Theobald), he mentions this incident as a signal proof of the loyalty of Canterbury to Rome at all costs[1]. And Herbert of Bosham says that in his defence before Pope Alexander III. and his cardinals at Sens in 1164, Thomas cited Theobald's fearless escape to Reims in defiance of king Stephen as a justification of his own flight from England in defiance of king Henry[2]. The council adopted the resolution of Eugenius confirming the deposition of William from the see of York and electing Henry

[1] *Epist.* 250 (vi. 57, 58): bis a sede et patria pro fide et obedientia exclusus est, rege Stephano hoc in eo persequente, quod contra prohibitionem ejus vocatus a domino papa Eugenio ad concilium Remense venerat, ceteris episcopis domi contra obedientiam remanentibus, exceptis tribus qui de mandato regis venerunt ut aliorum absentiam excusarent. The second occasion was Theobald's refusal to crown Eustace in 1152. In this letter Thomas himself gives the *ipsissima verba* of the witticism of Eugenius,—ut verbis ejus utamur, "natando potius quam navigando venerat" (vi. 58). It reappears in Herbert's version of Thomas' defence, but shorn of its alliterative vigour, "magis natando quam remigando."

[2] Herb. iii. 356: et ita pater meus hic ob causam fugit tunc sicut et nunc ego. Herbert puts a vivid description into the mouth of Thomas, who, as he calls himself the 'comes individuus' of Theobald in that adventure, would no doubt give the conference at Sens the full benefit of his recollections. The passage was made stealthily by night, with two or three followers unused to the sea, in a little boat, 'quasi absque nauclero et remigio.'

Murdac, abbot of Fountains, in his place. Apparently also it was on this occasion that Theobald and Eugenius began to lay their plans for the accession of Henry of Anjou by way of retaliating upon Stephen, who had offended the primate by supporting his brother Henry's appeal to Rome for the renewal of his legatine commission, and had lost the favour of the Pope by upholding the claims of his nephew William to the see of York[1]. Theobald however paid dearly for his disloyalty. His suffragans were suspended by Eugenius for absenting themselves from the council; but Stephen punished the archbishop by confiscating his property and forcing him into temporary exile from England[2]. There is one other notice which perhaps should be referred to this event. It is very probable, though not certain, that the Council of Reims is the occasion described by the anonymous biographer who is identified by some modern authorities with Roger of Pontigny. He says that Theobald had occasion "to visit the Roman Church," and took with him in his retinue the faithful Thomas, whose services he found so valuable on the journey and in the execution of his plans that he rewarded him on his return with the living of Otford, and afterwards employed him more than once to transact ecclesiastical business at Rome[3].

---

[1] Lyttelton, *Henry II.* (vol. i. p. 320).

[2] Ralph de Diceto, *Hist. Archiep. Cant.* (s. v. Theobald), and *Abbreviationes Chronicorum* (i. 362, Rolls Series).

[3] Auct. Anon. I. iv. 10: exstitit causa qua Cantuariensis antistes Theobaldus Romanam ecclesiam visitare disposuit.

One other crisis is recorded in which Thomas comes to the front. He is said to have been Theobald's agent in procuring the papal veto which forbade the coronation of Stephen's son Eustace. Gervase gives the following brief account of the incident. Stephen summoned bishops and nobles to an assembly at London, and requested their consent to his son's coronation. The archbishop of Canterbury was opposed to the project, and on the withdrawal of the bishops, who refused to commit themselves, prudently departed for Canterbury and crossed from Dover to the Continent. Stephen confiscated the temporalities of his see, but Eustace lost the crown which his father coveted for him. The whole of this affair was the work of the subtle foresight of a certain Thomas, a clerk, a Londoner by birth, says Gervase in conclusion[1], though he does not specify the steps taken by Thomas to procure the desired result. A fuller light however is cast upon the transaction by the *Historia Pontificalis*, a valuable fragment of ecclesiastical history which may perhaps have come from the pen of John of Salisbury[2]. From this record we learn that Henry,

(3) *Papal prohibition of Eustace's coronation,* 1152.

Robertson, in a foot-note on this passage, takes it to refer to the Council of Reims. There is one difficulty in the way of this explanation. The writer proceeds: profectusque est, ut dignum erat, cum honesto et copioso comitatu, assumpto etiam secum Thoma, etc. This is scarcely reconcilable with the pitiful story of the voyage told by Thomas in Herbert, iii. 356.

[1] Gervase (*Act. Pontif. Cant.* s. v. Theobald): subtilissima providentia et perquisitione cujusdam Thomae clerici natione Londoniensis.

[2] Stubbs, preface to R. de Diceto, i. xxiv. (Rolls Series).

archbishop of York, now reconciled to Stephen, promised to exert his influence to procure the papal sanction for the coronation of Eustace. This sanction, as the chronicler remarks, was considered indispensable. The validity of Stephen's title, he adds, had been questioned more than once on the ground that he had won the crown in 1135 by breaking the oath of allegiance to the empress which had been exacted from him by Henry I.[1]. The case had already been discussed before the papal court in the days of Innocent II. On that occasion Matilda's claim was represented by Ulger, bishop of Anger, while Stephen's interests were defended by Roger, bishop of Chester, Lupellus, a clerk who had been in the service of William (Theobald's predecessor in the see of Canterbury, who had consecrated Stephen), both specially despatched by Stephen for the purpose, and Arnulf, afterwards bishop of Lisieux. Innocent cut the matter short. In defiance of the advice of his cardinals and in consequence of a bribe from Stephen, he wrote a letter to the king confirming his title to the crown of England and the duchy of Normandy[2].

---

[1] *Hist. Pontif.* (Pertz, *Mon. German. Hist.* xx. 542): Henricus Eboracensis archiepiscopus, cum Stephano rege Anglorum faciens pacem, promisit se daturum operam et diligentiam ut apostolicus (i.e. Eugenius, to whom Henry owed his promotion to York) Eustachium filium regis coronaret. Quod utique fieri non licebat nisi Romani pontificis venia impetrata. Regi enim saepe quaestio mota fuerat super usurpatione regni, quod contra sacramentum Henrico regi praestitum dinoscitur occupasse. Querimoniam imperatricis ad papam Innocentium Ulgerius detulit, etc.

[2] *Hist. Pontif. ib.* p. 543: non tulit ulterius contentiones eorum dominus Innocentius, nec sententiam ferre voluit aut

Afterwards his successor Celestine, who as Cardinal Guido had headed the opposition to Innocent's decision, reversed it in favour of the empress, and wrote to archbishop Theobald forbidding any change in the succession to the crown, as its transference to Stephen had been duly condemned. His successors on the papal throne, Lucius (1144–1145) and Eugenius (1145–1153), renewed the prohibition. Consequently the archbishop of York was unable to obtain the consent of the Pope to the coronation of Eustace[1].

causam in aliud differre tempus, sed contra consilium quorumdam cardinalium et maxime Guidonis presbyteri Sancti Marci, receptis muneribus regis Stephani, ei familiaribus litteris regnum Angliae confirmavit et ducatum Normanniae. Arndt (the editor of the *Historia Pontificalis* in Pertz' collection) prints this passage in italics as the conclusion of Ulger's reply to Arnulf. This is surely a mistake. The passage is evidently part of the narrative, a statement from the chronicler's own pen; for he proceeds: Ulgerius vero cum cognitioni causae supersederi videret, verbo comico utebatur, dicens, "de causa sua querentibus intus despondebitur," et adjiciebat, "Petrus enim peregre profectus est, nummulariis relicta domo,"—a telling sarcasm directed against the venality of Innocent's procedure.

[1] *Hist. Pontif. ib.* p. 543: postea cum praefatus Guido cardinalis promoveretur in papam Celestinum, favore imperatricis scripsit domino Theobaldo Cantuariensi archiepiscopo inhibens ne qua fieret innovatio in regno Angliae circa coronam, quia res erat litigiosa cujus translatio jure reprobata est. Successores ejus papa Lucius et Eugenius eandem prohibitionem innovaverunt. Unde contigit ut praefatus Eboracensis archiepiscopus promotionem Eustachii non potuerit impetrare. Arndt prints the passage from *postea* to *innovaverunt* in italics, apparently attributing it to Ulger, whose jest it follows in the text. But this cannot be right. The passage deals with events that happened years after the trial of the case before Innocent in 1135. Celestine II. was Pope from Sept. 1143 to March, 1144.

Such is briefly (omitting the arguments of Arnulf and Ulger before the papal court under Innocent) the account given in the *Historia Pontificalis*[1]. Thomas is not mentioned at all. Nor does he mention his own share in the transaction in the letter to Cardinal Boso already quoted in reference to the Council of Reims[2]. He alludes to Theobald's refusal to crown Eustace—a refusal based on the papal prohibition—but there is not a word of allusion to his own services. The omission may perhaps be

---

[1] The case is discussed by Freeman, *Norman Conquest*, vol. v. App. DD. p. 857. I hesitate to contradict such an authority as the late Professor Freeman, but he seems to me to have misread the *Historia Pontificalis*. He quotes this collision between Ulger and Arnulf before Innocent as having taken place at the time when Stephen was trying to procure the papal consent to Eustace's coronation. In other words, he regards the whole passage (pp. 542, 543) as referring to the discussion of the case in 1152. But the date of the trial described on pp. 542, 543 is fixed by the fact that the letters of confirmation despatched to Stephen on the conclusion of the case are assigned by John of Hexham and Richard of Hexham to the year 1136. All the evidence points to the early date of this trial. Innocent died in 1143, Roger of Chester in 1148 (Robt. de Monte, A.D. 1148). The whole passage is really a retrospective account of the history of the dispute from Stephen's accession in the time of Innocent to the time of Eugenius, when Henry of York, who owed his see to Eugenius (Joh. Hexh. A.D. 1148, Gervase, A.D. 1147), offered his services to Stephen and went to Rome in person to ask Eugenius' consent to Eustace's coronation (Joh. Hexh. A.D. 1152). We therefore know practically nothing of the negotiations of 1152.

[2] Epist. 250 (vi. 57): alia autem, ut scitis, causa persecutionis ejus exstitit quod contra prohibitionem Romanorum pontificum filium regis Eustachium noluit coronare. The plural *pontificum* is explained by the evidence of the *Historia Pontificalis*. It includes Celestine II., Lucius II., and Eugenius III.

explained by the supposition that he is only dealing
there with one aspect of the case. Throughout the
letter it is Theobald's loyalty to Rome in opposition
to Stephen that he is dwelling upon as a precedent
for his own resistance as archbishop to the policy of
Henry II. He does not mention his own association
with Theobald in the adventurous journey to Reims,
which is the first instance that he cites in proof of
Theobald's devotion to Rome; yet we know from
other sources that he was in attendance upon Theobald on that occasion. The omission of his own
name is therefore no proof of his inactivity in the
matter. The fact however remains that the vague
language of Gervase is our only clue to Thomas'
action in 1152. He may have been merely responsible for the suggestion that the necessity of the
papal sanction to the coronation of Eustace opened
the way for a decisive check upon Stephen's ambition. He may only have insisted on referring the
question to Rome in view of the prohibition already
issued by Celestine II. and renewed by Lucius II.
In other words, it may have been his insistence on
this point that called forth Henry of York's offer to
mediate between the king and the Pope. Or he
may have done more; he may have actually gone to
Rome on Theobald's behalf to oppose the petition of
the rival archbishop. His biographers speak of
several visits to the papal court[1]; this was perhaps

[1] Fitzst. iii. 16: mittebat eum archiepiscopus *aliquotiens*
Romam pro negotiis ecclesiae Anglorum. Joh. S. ii. 303:
quotiens apostolorum limina visitaverit, etc. Auct. Anon. 1. iv. 10:
postea vero (i.e. after the visit to Rome or Reims in company with

one of the occasions which they dismiss *en bloc* with such disappointing brevity. Lyttelton, taking the visit as a fact, enlarges upon the difficulty of the task which Thomas had accomplished at Rome. Stephen, he remarks, was in ill odour at the papal court, but still there were serious obstacles in the way of Theobald's plan for the succession of Henry of Anjou. On the one hand, Stephen's election had been ratified by the papal see in the person of Innocent II. in 1136; on the other hand, Henry, coming as he did of a family that had shown scant respect for ecclesiastic authority, scarcely seemed a likely king to tolerate any papal encroachment upon the prerogatives of the English crown. The success therefore of Thomas' negotiations in the face of such difficulties speaks highly for his diplomatic skill[1]. But the evidence of the *Historia Pontificalis* proves that the obstacle presented by Innocent's ratification of Stephen's title had already been removed by the action of his successors in prohibiting the permanent transference of the crown to the line of Blois; and the danger of high-handed policy on the part of the young duke of Anjou was to say the least hypothetical at this stage of affairs.

Stephen did everything in his power to reverse the decision of the Roman Curia. Theobald was inflexible, and Roger, archdeacon of Canterbury, Thomas' old rival, was sent to Rome on behalf of the

---

Theobald) *aliquotiens* ecclesiasticorum negotiorum causa eum Romam direxit (Theobaldus), in omnibus ejus industriam merito collaudandam experiens.

[1] Lyttelton, *Henry II.* vol. ii. pp. 20, 21.

king and his partisans to get the papal prohibition withdrawn[1]. But his efforts were all in vain; and Stephen's persecution of Theobald, as Thomas calls it, was met by a papal sentence of excommunication against the king and an interdict on the whole country, to be carried into execution by all the bishops, which terrified Stephen into reluctant acquiescence[2].

The precise share, however, which Thomas had in the confirmation of Henry's claim to the English crown (for that was the practical result of the failure of Stephen's project in 1152) cannot be determined.

---

[1] Thomas himself states the fact in his letter to Boso, *Epist.* 250 (vi. 58): nonne recolitis quomodo ille qui nunc Eboracensis est Romam profectus sit, regis illius et procerum procurans negotium, ut, quia Cantuariensem archiepiscopum non poterant flectere, saltem prohibitionis apostolicae solutionem a domino papa Eugenio impetrarent? Thomas does not spare his old opponent, whom he accuses of deliberately fomenting the enmity between Theobald and Stephen, as he afterwards did between Thomas and Henry II. In the preceding sentence he writes, et quosdam eorum qui nos persequuntur ille rex habuit hujus fomitis incentores.

[2] *Epist.* 250 (vi. 59): nam et rex Stephanus ab antecessoris nostri persecutione non destitit antequam....Eugenius, omni cessante appellationis obstaculo, in caput ejus anathematis et in terram interdicti sententiam praecepit ab omnibus episcopis auctoritate apostolica exerceri. Gervase (*Act. Pontif. Cant.* s. v. Theobald) mentions an interdict against the royal demesnes issued by Theobald during the short exile which followed his visit to Reims in 1148. Hook (*Archbps.* ii. 343), omitting the interdict of 1152, seems inclined to recognise in the earlier one the hand of Thomas, always so ready to wield the weapon of excommunication in his own exile. Lingard (x. 46) is not certain whether the second sentence was a new one or only a confirmation of the first; but the distinction is immaterial.

It was evidently considerable, to judge from the emphasis which Gervase lays upon his intervention. But little more can be said with certainty, except that in this case, as in all his public actions while in the service of Theobald, he fully recognised and insisted upon the recognition of the papal claims in Church and State.

Preferment: pluralities of Thomas. Preferment in the meantime had been coming thick and fast from the hands of the grateful archbishop, partly as a reward for the services of Thomas at home and abroad, partly as a definite means of providing for his maintenance. He had already been admitted into the minor orders of the Church, apparently to facilitate his holding ecclesiastical benefices, the revenues of which went to make his income, while the spiritual duties were performed by a paid substitute. A grave doubt is cast upon the existence of any real spiritual motive by the fact that his promotion to the orders now recognised in the Church of England coincided with his elevation to high ecclesiastical dignity. He was not ordained deacon, it seems, until the archdeaconry of Canterbury fell vacant[1]; and his ordination to the priesthood—the Rubicon of the sacred calling—was postponed

---

[1] Herb. iii. 168: Theobaldus Thomam, quem prius secundum formam canonum ad alios inferiores ordines, *postea in levitam, simul etiam et ecclesiae suae archilevitam* in illa sancta et humili monachorum congregatione ordinavit. Cp. Fitzst. iii. 17, where the churches of St Mary-le-Strand and Otford and the prebends are mentioned first, then the legal studies at Bologna and Auxerre, and then the writer adds: processu temporis et meritorum ejus, ordinavit eum archiepiscopus diaconum et fecit Cantuariensis ecclesiae archidiaconum.

until it was necessitated by his election to the primacy.

The only full account of Thomas' preferments while in the service of Theobald is given by Fitzstephen. His first benefice[1] was the church of St Mary-le-Strand, London—the gift of John, bishop of Worcester. Next came the living of Otford in Kent as a present from Theobald in recognition of his services on that memorable journey to Reims in 1148. Gradually his acquisitions rose in the scale of importance. One prebend at St Paul's, London, fell into his hands, and another at Lincoln. Last of all came the archdeaconry of Canterbury, which ranked next in dignity to the bishoprics and abbacies of the English Church, and was estimated at the monetary value of a hundred pounds a year in the currency of that day. It was a suggestive appointment, indicating as it did the career marked out for its recipient in the mind of his patron. The biographers regard it in that light unmistakably. John of Salisbury describes it as an opportunity of gaining a thorough experience of ecclesiastical administration[2]. William of Canterbury hints that Theobald had an eye to the prospect of his archdeacon succeeding him as archbishop[3]. Whatever his ulterior motive was, Theobald gladly seized the opportunity which helped his

---

[1] Fitzst. iii. 17: primum *reditum* habuit. The word is suggestive.

[2] Joh. S. ii. 304: quo per experientiam rerum facilius dispensationis ecclesiasticae usum consequeretur...a praefato archiepiscopo...archidiaconus institutus est.

[3] Will. C. i. 4: forsan ut tempore suo, gradu suo locoque suo archidiaconus in archiepiscopum promoveretur.

favourite clerk into a post of eminence and at the same time gave the see of Canterbury an archdeacon who knew his canon law. The see of York was left vacant in 1154 by the death of its archbishop, William. Theobald procured the appointment of Roger, then archdeacon of Canterbury, and thus opened the way for the promotion of Thomas, on whom he conferred the vacant archdeaconry and the provostship of Beverley, which Roger had held, along with other pieces of preferment[1]. In the October of that year the death of Stephen removed the last obstacle to the accession of Henry of Anjou. During the three months that elapsed before his coronation the maintenance of law and order rested with Theo-

[1] Auct. Anon. I. iv. 10, 11: Eboracensi itaque sede vacante Theobaldus...modis omnibus sategit qualiter archidiaconum suum Rogerium...eidem sedi praeficeret, quatenus per hoc et dignitati ecclesiae Cantuariensi et honori suo et in clerico suo prospiceret et Thomae ad majora viam aperiret. The king's consent was obtained, Roger was consecrated by Theobald (in his capacity as papal legate, by special request of the chapter of York, according to Walter of Hemingburgh, i. 79, quoted by Freeman, *Norm. Conqu.* v. 315 n.), and, absque mora archidiaconatum Cantuariensis ecclesiae et praeposituram Beverleiae, quae Rogerius obtinuerat, cum aliis ecclesiis pluribus Thomae assignavit. Foss (*Lives of the Judges*) is uncertain whether the provostship followed or preceded the archdeaconry, but the above quotation seems decisive enough: they were both of them (*quae* neut. plur.) resigned by Roger and both transferred to Thomas together. The chroniclers are unanimous in dating the appointment 1154 (e.g. *Chron. of Holyrood, and Melrose; Annals of Winchester,* etc.). Thierry (*Norm. Conqu.* ii. 54) makes Thomas archdeacon already at the time of his negotiations with the Roman Church on the question of Eustace's coronation, and puts "a few years" between this event and Henry's accession, and "a few years" more between the accession and Thomas' appointment as chancellor!

bald, and it is more than probable that Thomas helped his patron in the work of government. But the next recorded fact in the career of the new archdeacon is his appointment as chancellor under the new king[1]; and this chapter of his life may fitly close with a subsequent allusion of his own to his worldly position at this date. The bishops and clergy reminded him in their letter of remonstrance in 1166 that his rise in the world had been one series of royal favours from the very outset. Thomas met the charge by pointing simply to the long roll of preferments which were already his before the king gave him the chancellorship. "If you look back," he said in his reply to Foliot[2], "to the time at which

---

[1] The Icelandic *Saga* (i. 47) represents Thomas as acting as the king's chamberlain for some time before his promotion to the chancellorship; but there is no mention whatever of this earlier office in any of the other contemporary authorities.

[2] *Epist.* 224 (v. 515). It was a conclusive reply to his opponents' insinuation that he was a nonentity until he was taken up by the king. But it has found a severe critic in the author of *Short Studies on Great Subjects* (iv. 26). "It is noticeable," says Prof. Froude, "that afterwards, in the heat of the battle in which he earned his saintship, he was so far from looking back with regret on his accumulation of preferments that he paraded them as an evidence of his early consequence." It is hard lines that in repudiating the character of a needy place-hunter, Thomas should have incurred the opposite charge of being an unscrupulous pluralist. As Freeman long ago pointed out in his criticism of Froude's sneer at Thomas' expense (*Contemp. Review*, vol. 32, p. 124), no expression of regret was called for. Thomas had merely to answer a "misstatement of fact"; and the answer involved a frank avowal of his early pluralities, in which anything like an apology would have been an inappropriate digression from his point. Robertson, in his *Becket, a Biography*, is much fairer than Froude, but still has a grievance against Thomas. "The

the king promoted me to his service, the archdeaconry of Canterbury, the provostship of Beverley, churches in plenty, prebends more than one, and other benefices not a few, then in my possession, prove that I was not so poorly furnished with this world's goods as you say I was."

circumstance," he remarks, "that he was only a deacon was no hindrance to the accumulation of benefices on him; for in those days a prosperous ecclesiastic would seem to have regarded his parishes merely as sources of income, while he complacently devolved the care of each on some ill-paid priest. Nor, when Becket afterwards appeared as an ecclesiastical reformer, did he make any attempt to remedy this, which to modern apprehensions may perhaps seem the most crying abuse of all." Robertson's mistake in fact lies in measuring Becket by modern standards, and in ignoring the principle which underlay the system of mediaeval pluralism. The whole question of pluralities has been treated by Freeman in an exhaustive manner which leaves nothing to be said (*Contemp. Review*, vol. 32, pp. 126–128). He points out how the older view of a spiritual office, which placed the duties first and regarded the emoluments as a maintenance for the man holding the office while he fulfilled the duties in person, gave way to the feudal idea of a possession in which "the duties were attached to the benefice rather than the benefice to the duties. So that the duties were discharged, it was not necessary that the holder of the benefice should always discharge them in person." Towards the close of the eleventh century the principles of feudalism stamped themselves on Church preferment, and the pluralism so prevalent in the case of temporal benefices seemed to warrant pluralism in ecclesiastical benefices. The baron had his many manors on condition of doing duty to his lord for each, and so the ecclesiastic might have his many livings. "The average conscience of the time," says Freeman in conclusion, "was fully satisfied if the holder of several benefices provided a competent person to do the duties of each. If Thomas did this at Beverley and Otford and wherever else he held preferment, he would not reach the standard either of primitive or of modern morality; but he would fully satisfy the morality of his own age."

CHAPTER III.

THOMAS THE CHANCELLOR.

THE archdeacon of Canterbury now became the *His introduction to the king.* chancellor of England, and Thomas exchanged the service of the archbishop for the service of the king. The appointment seems to have been mainly the work of Theobald. It is quite possible that Henry had himself recognised the value of Thomas' share in the semi-ecclesiastical, semi-political negotiations to which he owed in part his acceptance as king of England, and was more than ready to find a place in his court for a servant whose ability was enhanced by his evident devotion to the aims of his master. But the biographers lay greater stress on the archbishop's share in his favourite's promotion. It was Theobald's recommendation that won Thomas the chancellorship, a recommendation seconded by Henry, bishop of Winchester[1], who had decided to forgive

---

[1] Fitzst. iii. 17: commendatione et obtentu archiepiscopi et hortatu actuque nobilis Henrici Wintoniensis episcopi, regis factus est Thomas cancellarius.

and forget, and not only joined his old rival Theobald in welcoming Henry of Anjou, but also lent a hand to lift the young diplomatist who had thwarted his ambition in the past. One of the anonymous biographers lets us further into the secret workings of the royal favour. Theobald consulted Philip, bishop of Bayeux, and Arnulf, bishop of Lisieux, two Norman ecclesiastics on whose advice the young king relied at the outset of his reign, and persuaded them, it seems, to support him in urging the claims of Thomas upon the royal notice[1].

Theobald's motives.

The early biographers have not quite done justice to the motives of Theobald in procuring the appointment of Thomas. He seems to have had a double purpose in view, the restoration of law and

[1] Auct. Anon. I. iv. 12: adscitis igitur ad se Cantuariensis antistes Philippo Baiocensi et Arnulfo Lexoviensi episcopis, quorum consiliis rex in primordiis suis innitebatur, coepit de Thomae prudentia, strenuitate, et fidelitate atque morum laudabili et admirabili mansuetudine inferre sermonem, memoratisque episcopis secundum voluntatem et suasionem archiepiscopi annuentibus, Thomas regiam ingressus curiam cancellarii nomen officiumque suscepit. It is interesting in this connexion to notice the subsequent relations between Arnulf and Thomas. There is an undated letter from Arnulf to the chancellor (Epist. i. in the *Materials*, v. 1–3) written in the most complimentary terms, warning him at the same time against the dangers of a courtier's life with its scanty opportunities for true friendship, and closing with the request that the chancellor would watch over the interests of a friend of Arnulf's and keep Arnulf himself in evidence before the king. In 1162 Arnulf writes (*Epist.* 12, v. 20) to congratulate Thomas on his consecration. For a time at least they were good friends, though at a later date Arnulf wavered between his friendship for Thomas and his loyalty to the king, siding generally with the latter.

order throughout the country, and at the same time the maintenance of the privileges of the Church. The reign of Stephen had bequeathed to England a legacy of civil anarchy and ecclesiastical predominance, the latter the natural result of the former; and it was apparently Theobald's aim to ensure the suppression of the disorder without losing the advantages which it had given to the Church. The first claim upon the energies of the new king was undoubtedly the substitution of rule for misrule, law for licence, throughout the realm; but Theobald foresaw that a crisis could not long be postponed when the king turned to face the pretensions of the ecclesiastical body within his kingdom. The secular power of the Church had grown rapidly during the turbulence of Stephen's reign. It was strong in territorial resources. A large proportion of the knights' fees were in the hands of ecclesiastical holders; and the frowning castles that rose thick and fast during that reign of anarchy were many of them the strongholds of bishops militant like Henry of Winchester[1] and Roger of Salisbury, whose nephews Alexander of Lincoln and Roger of Ely were castle-builders as energetic as their uncle. It was strong in organisation. While the body politic was divided against itself, alternating between two sovereigns and torn by rival factions among the barons, the national Church had all the strength of

---

[1] Winchester's castles had to come down at Henry's bidding in 1155. Robert de Monte, A.D. 1155. Cp. Pipe Roll 2 Henry II. (1155–1156), in prosternendis castellis episcopi Wintoniensis, in Hampshire (Hunter, p. 55).

unity, though it was unity purchased by the recognition of a foreign court of appeal in the Papacy[1]. The national assembly had ceased to meet, and civil justice was in abeyance; but the synods of the Church were still held, and law was still administered in the episcopal courts. When there was not even a semblance of authority in the State, there was the reality in the Church. The pretensions of the clergy more than kept pace with their power. Gervase styles Henry of Blois, bishop of Winchester, on one occasion "Angliae dominus utpote frater regis et apostolicae sedis legatus," and at the Synod of Winchester in 1141 this "lord of all England," presiding as legate, actually claimed for the clergy the right of electing as well as consecrating the occupant of the royal throne[2]. But now the tide seemed to be turning. With a young king at the head of the State determined to be king over all his subjects in fact as well as in name and surrounded by advisers who looked with an evil eye upon the privileges and possessions of the Church, the current seemed to be setting in the opposite direction. The attitude of the court was unmistakable, that of the

---

[1] Freeman considers that the absence of any central authority in England was largely responsible for the ready acquiescence in appeals to Rome. "The pontiff seemed the sublime and dimly seen embodiment of that reign of law which had passed away from our own shores" (*Contemp. Review*, vol. 32, p. 133).

[2] William of Malmesbury, *Hist. Nov.* iii. 44: ventilata est hesterno die causa (i.e. the claims of Matilda) secreto coram majori parte cleri Angliae, ad cujus jus potissimum spectat principem eligere simulque ordinare.

king suspicious[1]; and Theobald was as anxious about the immediate interests of the Church as he was afraid for her future welfare[2]. But the Church was not his only care. It was only natural that the contemporary biographers of Thomas, all of them ecclesiastics in position and sympathy, should lay special stress on this side of Theobald's policy, but it was not the whole. The actual sufferings of the people at the hands of lawless barons, and the possibility of their suffering further at the hands of a king of semi-foreign extraction who might be tempted to treat England as a conquered nation and play the part of a conqueror by wreaking an arbitrary revenge upon his new subjects,—these were considerations which Theobald kept clearly in view, as we learn from John of Salisbury[3]. He was anxious

---

[1] Milman (*Lat. Christ.* iii. 447) notes the possibility of an hereditary bias against the Church. His father Geoffrey had been a cruel enemy to more than one ecclesiastic. Cp. Robertson, *Becket*, p. 25.

[2] Auct. Anon. I. iv. 11: erat in ecclesia regni illius non modica trepidatio, tum propter suspectam regis aetatem, tum propter collateralium ejus circa ecclesiasticae libertatis jura notam malignitatem. Nec frustra, sicut rei exitus indicavit. Cantuariensis autem antistes, tam de praesenti sollicitus quam de futuro timidus, aliquod remedium malis quae imminere timebantur, opponere cogitabat: visumque est ei quod, si Thomam regis posset inserere consiliis, maximam exinde quietem et pacem Anglicanae ecclesiae posse provenire: sciebat enim eum magnanimum et prudentem, qui et zelum Dei haberet cum scientia et ecclesiasticam libertatem totis affectibus aemularetur.

[3] Joh. S. ii. 304: erat enim ei (Theobaldo) suspecta adolescentia regis, et juvenum et pravorum hominum, quorum consiliis agi videbatur, insipientiam et malitiam formidabat: et *ne instinctu eorum insolentius ageret jure victoris*, qui sibi videbatur, etsi

62 THOMAS THE CHANCELLOR.

to place near the king a minister who would befriend the people as well as the Church,—who would help Henry to put down anarchy with a strong hand, and at the same time watch all ecclesiastical interests with a protecting eye. Thomas seemed the very man for the work, and Theobald lost no time in putting him forward. The recommendation of the archbishop and his friends and Thomas' own services in the cause of Henry's accession were both strong claims upon the royal favour, and Thomas of London became the king's chancellor.

Foliot's charge: the chancellorship saleable.

A very different light is thrown on this transaction by an assertion in a letter written by Gilbert Foliot, bishop of London, to archbishop Thomas in 1166. Foliot accuses him of having bought the chancellorship publicly with an eye to the prospect of the primacy[1]. It is true that promotion to offices of

aliter esset, populum subegisse, cancellarium procurabat in curia ordinari, cujus ope et opera novi regis, ne saeviret in ecclesiam, impetum cohiberet, et consilii sui temperaret malitiam, et reprimeret audaciam officialium, qui sub obtentu publicae potestatis et praetextu juris *tam ecclesiae quam provincialium facultates diripere* conspiraverant. Will. C. i. 5, is equally emphatic on the subject of the king's encroachment upon the rights, and the courtiers' designs upon the property of the Church, but says nothing of the sufferings of the people, actual and prospective, at which John of Salisbury hints. Cp. with regard to the danger of the Church "the dying admonitions of Theobald to the king," as Milman styles the letter written by John in Theobald's name, probably towards the last days of the archbishop's life: suggerunt vobis filii saeculi hujus ut ecclesiae minuatis auctoritatem ut vobis regia dignitas augeatur (Joh. S. *Epist.* 64, ed Giles).

[1] *Epist.* 225 (v. 525): ad ipsa siquidem recurramus initia, quis toto orbe nostro, quis ignorat, quis tam resupinus ut nesciat vos certa licitatione proposita cancellariam illam dignitatem multis

state by purchase was not unknown in those days. While the ordinary offices in the royal household, such as the stewardship, became hereditary, those which tended to develop into ministerial posts of

marcarum millibus obtinuisse, et aurae hujus impulsu in portum ecclesiae Cantuariensis illapsum, ad ejus tandem sic regimen accessisse? Froude (*Short Studies*, iv. 28) thinks it "inconceivable that the bishop of London would have thrown such a charge directly in Becket's teeth unless there had been some foundation for it," and leaves the question, evidently regarding it as settled by this off-hand remark. The charge is really two-fold, (1) the purchase, (2) the design upon the primacy. The latter is improbable, but more of this in its proper place. The simple question of the purchase cannot be settled for certain either way, in the absence of the Pipe Roll of 1 Henry II., where a transaction so public (certa licitatione proposita,—apparently competition is implied) would certainly have been recorded, if it ever took place.

Stubbs (*Const. Hist.* vol. i.) gives instances of the sale of offices. In the Pipe Roll of 31 Henry I. (1130-1131) Geoffrey Rufus, afterwards bishop of Durham, is recorded as owing £3000. 13s. 4d. "pro sigillo." In the *Annals of Margam*, A.D. 1122, it is stated that he bought the chancellorship "pro vii. millibus libris argenti." Evidently the sum in the Pipe Roll was the remainder of the purchase-money agreed upon in 1122. (Robertson, *Becket*, App. II. p. 322.) In the same Pipe Roll John the marshal appears as paying 40 marks for a post in the Curia Regis, and Richard Fitzalured pays 15 marks for the privilege of acting as assessor to Ralph Bassett "ad placita regis" in Buckinghamshire, i.e. as an itinerant justice. Bishop Nigel of Ely bought the treasurership for his son for £400 (*Hist. Eliensis*, in Stubbs, *Const. Hist.* i. 384). Under Richard I. William Longchamp, bishop of Ely, bought the chancellorship for £3000, though Reginald the Lombard had ventured to bid as high as £4000 (Stubbs, i. 497). In the 7th year of John's reign, Walter de Grey fined with the king in 5000 marks to have the king's chancery for life and to obtain a charter to that effect (Madox, *Hist. Exchequer*, p. 43).

political importance, like the chancellorship, were not unfrequently sold. No source of revenue was left untried by the Angevin dynasty. Ministers of state fined for their offices in the royal service, just as litigants fined for the administration of royal justice and boroughs for the confirmation of royal grants; and no discredit was involved in either case. But as a matter of fact there is no proof that the chancellorship was sold to Thomas. Foliot's assertion stands unsupported by other evidence. It is true that we have no extant reply from Thomas, but the argument *ex silentio* can scarcely be pressed to prove that silence in this case meant inability to disprove the charge. It might with equal probability be interpreted as the silence of contemptuous disregard. On the other hand there are two considerations which detract from the weight of Foliot's accusation. (1) The chancellorship had never yet been a stepping-stone to the primacy. It was the added greatness of the chancellorship in Thomas' hands that made his promotion straight from that office to the primacy possible; and in this light Foliot's assertion looks like an afterthought. (2) It must be remembered that this isolated charge comes from the pen of an old rival, embittered by his own disappointment and by the high-handed policy of his successful opponent. It occurs in the last of a group of letters that passed between the archbishop and the bishops of his province after his excommunication of his antagonists, and ended in a personal epistolary warfare between Thomas and Foliot, who championed the cause of his fellow-suffragans. They are essentially party pamphlets, and little reliance can be placed upon their assertions unless corroborated by evidence from more dispassionate sources.

The date of Thomas' appointment to the chancellorship has been variously given from 1154 to 1158; but anything later than 1155 seems out of the question. Gervase places the appointment "at the very outset of the reign[1]." There may have been a brief interval between Henry's accession and the promotion of Thomas. The charter of liberties, which has been assigned to the coronation (Dec. 19th, 1154), is attested not by the chancellor but by Richard de Luci the justiciar; and this may perhaps be an indication that the chancellorship was still vacant, for the chancellor's name was usually appended as a witness to all royal charters[2]. But it seems certain that Thomas was Henry's first chancellor. More than one name, it is true, has been suggested by modern historians, but no other name occurs in the original authorities[3]. Diceto

Date of the appointment.

[1] Gervase, *Chron.* (col. 1377, Twysden): "statim in initio regni" Theobald obtained the promotion of Thomas "cui anno praeterito dederat archidiaconatum." The date of the archdeaconry was October 1154.

[2] Stubbs (*Select Charters*, p. 135) takes the attestation by Luci as an indication of the date of the charter, which he describes as "probably earlier than the appointment of Thomas as chancellor."

[3] Robertson mentions an undated grant to the earl of Arundel (Rymer, *Foedera*, i. 41), at the close of which occur the following words among the list of witnesses,—Theobaldo archiepiscopo Cantuariensi N. episcopo de Ely *et* cancellario. This might be alleged, as Robertson points out, in favour of a previous tenure of

records the appointment under the year 1154, and there is only one passage in the early biographers that appears to point to a later date than 1155. Herbert of Bosham says that Thomas had served five years at court as chancellor when he was elected archbishop. This would place his appointment in 1157[1]. But against this statement must be set the evidence of another biographer whose chronology is much more reliable. Fitzstephen distinctly credits Thomas the chancellor with a share in the speedy restoration of law and order which took place within three months after the coronation (December 1154– March 1155)[2]. The one conclusive authority—the Pipe Roll of the first year of Henry's reign—is missing; but the evidence of the next year's Pipe Roll (Michaelmas 1155–1156) is practically decisive in favour of 1155 as the latest possible date. It

the chancellorship by Nigel. But Foss (*Judges*, i. 166) explains *et* as a clerical error for T, the initial letter of *Thoma*. Nigel was recalled to the Exchequer as treasurer by Henry II. at the outset of his reign.

The name of Philip, who was chancellor for a time under Stephen, has been put forward as a possible predecessor of Thomas under Henry II., but it is without evidence.

[1] Herb. iii. 185. Lingard (ii. 55) apparently dates the chancellorship of Thomas from 1156 or 1157. He makes Theobald retain "the first place in the councils of his sovereign" for two years, and then procure the promotion of Thomas to the chancellorship; but he quotes no authority in support of this assertion.

[2] Fitzst. iii. 19: miseratione Dei, consilio cancellarii, et cleri et baronum regni qui pacis bonum volebant, intra tres primos menses coronationis regis,...Willelmus de Ipra...cum lacrimis emigravit; Flandrenses omnes collectis impedimentis et armis ad mare tendunt.

contains the name of no other chancellor than Thomas, and, as the biographer of the "Judges of England" has pointed out, its evidence is largely retrospective[1]. The notices of the chancellor's exemption from certain charges on his property refer probably to charges due in the first year of the reign, though accounted for in the Roll of the second year. Similarly the payments mentioned as arising out of the pleas held by the chancellor in Essex and Kent were probably imposed in the previous year, as some time would elapse before the sheriffs could collect the money due to the Exchequer. The appointment of Thomas to the chancellorship may be fixed early in 1155 at the latest. It was perhaps made, if a conjecture may be hazarded, at the Council which Henry held at Bermondsey on Christmas Day 1154, within a week of his coronation[2].

The office of chancellor.

The chancellorship in 1154 was an important office, though its importance was potential rather than actual. The chancellor yielded a formal precedence to the justiciar[3], who acted as regent in

[1] Foss, *Judges*, i. 196, 199.

[2] Diceto's date (1154) in that case will be just correct. It was at this Council apparently that Henry concerted his plan of campaign with his new ministers. Gervase (col. 1377, Twysden): in nativitate Domini tenuit rex curiam suam apud Bermundeseiam, ubi cum principibus suis de statu regni et pace reformanda tractans, proposuit animo alienigenas gentes de regno propellere et munitiunculas pessimas per totam Angliam solo tenus dissipare.

[3] Fitzst. iii. 17: cancellarii Angliae dignitas est ut secundus a rege in regno habeatur. The author of the *Dialogus de Scaccario* (Stubbs, *Select Charters*, p. 176) describes the justiciar, "capitalis

the king's absence, and apparently to three or four other officers of the royal household, the constable, the marshal, the steward and the chamberlain; but at the same time he had functions to discharge and opportunities for active influence with the king which lent themselves readily to further development. It will be convenient here at the outset to sketch in outline the character and duties of this office of state. The full title of its holder was *cancellarius regis*[1], so called in all probability for the sake of distinction from other chancellors of inferior rank who occasionally come upon the scene, e.g. *cancellarius reginae*[2], and at a later date the chancellors of cathedral churches. The chancellor was the king's chief chaplain, entrusted with the care of the royal chapel[3]; and on this account the post of chancellor was always held by an ecclesiastic. But his ecclesiastical functions ended there. It was "a thoroughly secular office" which "must have left

---

domini regis justicia," as being "primus post regem in regno ratione fori." Bishop Stubbs accordingly explains Fitzstephen's 'secundus a rege' as meaning 'next after the justiciar' (*Const. Hist.* i. 604, n.).

[1] Madox, *Exchequer*, p. 41. Stubbs derives *cancellarius* from *cancelli*, the screen behind which the secretarial work of the royal household was done.

[2] Bernard bishop of S. David's was chancellor to Matilda, the first wife of Henry I., and Godfrey of Bath to the second. (Florence of Worcester, 1115, and Continuator Flor. Worc. 1123, Stubbs, l. c.)

[3] Madox (p. 41) notes that the chancellor is called "chef de le chapele le Roy" as late as Edward II.'s reign in an ordinance relating to the royal chapel of Windsor. Fitzst. iii. 18: ut capella regis in ipsius (cancellarii) sit dispositione et cura.

its holder very little time for ecclesiastical duties or thoughts." In fact one of its functions was scarcely consistent with the principles of a conscientious churchman[1]. It was part of the chancellor's work to receive and control the revenues of vacant bishoprics and abbeys[2], which fell to the Crown now that the ecclesiastical benefice had been assimilated to the feudal grant. The civil functions of the chancellor were many and various. He was briefly, to borrow a modern term, secretary of state for all departments[3]. As keeper of the royal seal, he supervised all charters that were to be stamped with the great seal, and all writs and orders that were issued at the Curia Regis and at the Exchequer. Like the chief justiciar and the other officers of the

[1] Freeman, *Contemp. Review*, vol. 32, p. 477.
[2] Fitzst. iii. 18: ut vacantes archiepiscopatus, episcopatus, abbatias, et baronias, cadentes in manu regis, ipse (cancellarius) suscipiat et conservet. Cp. Herb. iii. 180 (on the death of Theobald): rex dissimulat nisi quod archiepiscopatus, sicut et episcopatus et etiam vacantes abbatiae *solent*, curae cancellarii et custodiae traditur. Lyttelton (*Life of Henry II.*, Appendix on the Chancellorship) concludes from the evidence of the Rolls that the custody of vacant preferments did not fall to the chancellor *ex officio* but by personal favour of the king, and considers that the king entrusted the care of vacant benefices to whom he pleased. But he gives no reference to the particular Rolls on which his view is based, and quotes no instance of preferment entrusted to the care of any one besides the chancellor. And Fitzstephen and Herbert seem positive enough on the point.
[3] Cp. William of Canterbury's designation of the chancellorship as *scribatus* (i. 5, and elsewhere). Fitzst. iii. 18: ut altera parte sigilli regii, quod et ad ejus pertinet custodiam, propria signet mandata; ut omnibus regis adsit conciliis, et etiam non vocatus se ingerat; ut omnia sigilliferi regii, clerici sui, manu signentur, omnia cancellarii consilio disponantur.

royal household, he was *ex officio* a member of both those courts,—a justiciar of the Curia Regis and a baron of the Exchequer. Fitzstephen sums up his introductory sketch of the chancellor's position in the realm with the remark that a chancellor with a good record might die a bishop or an archbishop if he chose. *Inde est quod cancellaria non emenda est.* It was a precaution against simony. The door which led to such an avenue must open only to the key of merit. In the face of Foliot's assertion that Thomas used a baser key, and certainly in the face of the contemporary evidence as to the possibility of such an entrance, we must discount Fitzstephen's estimate of the sanctity of the office. Perhaps even his testimony to its dignity must be taken with some qualification, as the evidence of a witness who is looking at the chancellorship through the halo of magnificence which the genius of Thomas had thrown around the office. As a matter of fact, its greatness was only incipient in 1154. Various causes contributed to its growth[1]. Royal charters increased in number and importance. Pleas and cases came thick and fast for trial to the sessions of the royal justices when it was seen how superior they were to the local courts in fairness and efficiency. These changes added to the work of the chancellorship. The office of justiciar in time lost much of its early prestige, and what the justiciar lost the chancellor gained. But the personal element accounted for more than any of the above causes. The ability and influence of one chancellor

[1] Madox, *Exchequer*, p. 43.

after another clothed the office with a grandeur not originally its own. They left it greater than they found it, and their successors entered upon a wider range of power won largely by the enterprise of former chancellors in extending their influence beyond the traditional limits of their office.

Thomas of London was the first great chancellor. The civil and ecclesiastical duties which fell officially to him as chancellor form but a small part of the work with which he is to be credited during his chancellorship of seven years and a half. He was the responsible agent, if not the author, of Henry's foreign policy,—his lieutenant in time of war, his ambassador in time of peace. He was the confidential minister of the Crown at home, the practical head of the executive, the recognised approach to the royal ear, the acknowledged channel of royal favour[1]. All this was in a sense *extra ordinem*,— the result of personal influence, not official powers. It was an age of personal government. The larger Curia Regis—the great council of the Norman kings —consisting of the mass of barons summoned by royal mandate for deliberative and judicial purposes, met only at intervals. The natural result of this was that the current affairs of state came to be transacted immediately by the king and the smaller

[1] Cp. Auct. Anon. I. iv. 12: Thomas vero vices ejus et negotia strenue et potestative exsequens nunc princeps militiae loricatus exercitum praeibat, nunc vacans et expeditionibus jura populis dictabat. Solo namque nomine a rege differens regnum universum pro voluntate disponebat, principibus et magistratibus ad ejus nutum subjectis, certissimeque scientibus hoc solummodo regi gratum fore quod Thomas expedire judicasset.

72 THOMAS THE CHANCELLOR.

Curia Regis—the few officers in permanent attendance on the king. The chancellor, as the royal secretary, had practically unlimited opportunities for exerting his influence with the king; and when to these opportunities was added a personal friendship of the warmest kind, we need not wonder that the power and prestige of the chancellorship rose in the hands of Thomas to such an unprecedented height[1].

The work of Thomas the chancellor is perhaps best grouped under the different heads of foreign, civil, and ecclesiastical administration. A clearer view of the man and his work will thus be gained than from any merely chronological arrangement. It will be an additional gain in orderly sequence to take his ecclesiastical policy last of all—a position required by its obvious connexion with the climax of his career, his elevation to the primacy. But it will not be inappropriate to notice here beforehand the general views which the early biographers take of his relations with the king and with his fellow-courtiers respectively.

Relations of Thomas (1) with the king, Fitzstephen waxes enthusiastic on the subject of the confidential intimacy between the king and his chancellor, whom he styles, it may be with pardonable exaggeration, the favourite alike of king, clergy,

---

[1] Freeman remarks that "perhaps the greatest witness of all to the height to which the great chancellor had raised the chancellorship is to be found in the fact that the king thought it possible that he could hold both chancellorship and archbishopric together." (*Contemp. Review*, vol. 32, p. 476, cp. pp. 494–496.)

barons and people¹. When the serious business of the court was done, they would launch out into the wildest freaks of boyish fun. There is an oft-told story of a fight between the two for the chancellor's cape as they rode down a London street on a wintry day, while the shivering beggar for whom the prize was meant and the gay retinue of knights looked on in amazement. It may be only a fragment of court gossip, but it is at least a bit of characteristic gossip which must have had some foundation in the habits of king and chancellor. Often the king would pay an unexpected visit to the chancellor's board, partly out of curiosity to test the reality of its rumoured grandeur, partly from sheer amusement. Sometimes he would ride straight into the hall, sometimes empty a cup and disappear as hastily as he had come, sometimes vault over the table and take a seat beside his favourite. Never were seen two such friends in all Christendom². Henry's confidence knew no limits. Thomas was entrusted with powers that placed him on a level with the king in all but name. His word was law for barons

[1] Fitzst. iii. 24: Cancellarius regi, clero, militiae et populo erat acceptissimus. Pertractatis seriis, colludebant rex et ipse tamquam coaetanei pueruli in aula, in ecclesia, in consessu, in equitando. Henry was twenty-one, Thomas thirty-six in 1154; but Thomas was a boy at heart when there was sport to be had. Fitzstephen's account is probably nearer the mark than that of Auct. Anon. I. iv. 12, who makes Henry play while Thomas worked. England never had a harder worker on the throne than Henry of Anjou, scholar, linguist, lawyer, soldier, statesman all in one,—warring in France one week, the next travelling from shire to shire in England,—always on the move, never resting, never tired.

[2] Fitzst. iii. 24, 25.

and magistrates, his favour the one thing needful for suitors at court. Grim styles him "a second Joseph in Egypt[1]."

(2) *with the court.*   There is however another side to the picture. It was not all plain sailing for Thomas. There were serious difficulties to contend with at court, as we learn from the other biographers. The secret envy of his rivals[2] had its share in creating opposition now in the royal household as it had before in the palace of the archbishop. But the language of the biographers indicates that it was Thomas' policy rather than his promotion that made his enemies. John of Salisbury credits him with a threefold responsibility, the task of contending daily (1) for the welfare and dignity of his lord the king against the enemies of the Crown, (2) for the needs of Church and people against the king, and (3), last but not least, against "the wild beasts of the court." In pursuance of his own line of action Thomas was harassed by plots and intrigues until, as he tearfully confessed to his archbishop and his other friends, he was often weary of existence, and ready enough to break away from the complications of court life, if he could but withdraw without

---

[1] Grim, ii. 363: novus itaque erigitur super Aegyptum Joseph, praeficitur universis regni negotiis post regem secundus.

[2] Herb. iii. 177: aulicorum vermis, per aulam serpens jam sed adhuc latens invidia.

[3] Joh. S. ii. 305: nec conditionis nec oneris sui immemor erat, qui quotidie hinc pro domini sui regis salute et honore, inde pro necessitate ecclesiae et provincialium tam contra regem ipsum quam contra inimicos ejus contendere cogebatur et variis artibus varios eludere dolos. sed hoc praecipue perurgebat quod indesinenter oportebat eum pugnare ad bestias curiae.

disgrace[1]. According to the Icelandic Saga (i. 59) it was only Theobald's refusal to allow his resignation and Theobald's entreaty to him to persevere for the sake of the Church that kept Thomas at his post at court. There is not a word of these difficulties in Fitzstephen's glowing account of his chancellorship, full and detailed as that account is. But the language of John of Salisbury and the anonymous biographer who tells the same tale is too strong to be ignored. It probably relates only to the early days of Thomas' chancellorship, when he was yet feeling his way into the royal favour, and perhaps making his first attempts to check the rapacity of barons and officials; but it points unmistakably to the fact that Thomas had to work hard and fight hard at the outset for the universal goodwill and gratitude which Grim describes as the reward of his conduct as chancellor[2].

[1] Joh. S. ii. 305: *in primis cancellariae suae auspiciis* tot et tantas variarum necessitatum difficultates sustinuit, tot laboribus attritus est, tot afflictionibus fere oppressus, tot laqueis in aula expositus a malitia inhabitantium in ea, ut eum, *sicut archiepiscopo suo et amicis sub lacrimarum testimonio referre solitus erat*, saepe in dies singulos taederet vivere, et post vitae aeternae desiderium super omnia optaret ut absque infamiae nota posset a curiae nexibus explicari. Cp. Auct. Anon. I. iv. 12: *in primordiis suis* tantos aemulatorum assultus pertulit tantaque delatorum lacessitus est protervia...ut a curia recedere disponeret. The writer then proceeds to describe Thomas' rapid rise in the king's estimation. Verum rex, fide illius et industria citius cognita, tanta eum dilectione carissimum habuit, ut neminem aliquando aeque dilexisse putetur.

[2] Grim, ii. 365: tantam quoque gratiam adeptus est a rege et regno universo ut hos solum beatos reputaret opinio qui in ejus oculis complacere et regis consiliario et cancellario obsecundare in aliquo potuissent.

CHAPTER IV.

FOREIGN AFFAIRS.

Henry of Anjou and Louis of France.

THE foreign interest of Thomas' chancellorship centres in France. Fitzstephen, in his picture of the chancellor's magnificence at home and abroad, alludes to the generous welcome which Thomas gave to an embassy from the kings of Norway[1]; and it is probable that he had a share in the reception of more than one of the complimentary embassies which came from the Emperor[2], the king of Jerusalem and

---

[1] Fitzst. iii. 26. The date of the embassy is fixed by its mention in the Pipe Roll of 2 Henry II., 1155-1156 (Hunter, pp. 4, 15). Cp. Stubbs, *Mediæv. and Mod. Hist.* pp. 124, 125, on the intercourse between the Churches of Norway and England under Stephen and Henry II. There is also a notice in the Pipe Roll of 3 Henry II. (1156-1157) relating to the reception of an embassy from Sweden (Hunter, pp. 101, 108).

[2] The signature of Thomas is appended to a letter from Henry II. to the Emperor Frederic Barbarossa, which was conveyed with an oral message by Herbert of Bosham and a royal clerk named William: "De manu beati Jacobi super qua nobis scripsistis, in ore magistri Heriberti et Guilhelmi clerici nostri verbum posuimus. Teste Thoma cancellario apud Norhant(onam)": quoted by Robertson from Radevic's *Life of Frederic*, i. 7 (*Materials*, vol. v. addenda, opposite to p. xxvi), and dated by him about 1156.

the Moorish princes of southern Spain, to pay their respects to the new king of England who was building a second empire in Western Europe. But we have no record of any intervention in foreign affairs on the part of Thomas beyond his share in the relations between England and France. Those relations were precarious in the extreme. The position of Louis VII. of France was peculiar. He was the titular head of that conglomeration of small states between the Channel and the Pyrenees, all owning allegiance to him as their feudal lord. But circumstances had thrown one after another of these fiefs into the hands of Henry of Anjou, until at last he was practically master of the situation. He was duke of Normandy and count of Anjou and Maine by inheritance. By his marriage with Eleanor, the divorced wife of Louis, in 1152, the earldom of Poitou and the duchy of Aquitaine, which she inherited from her father William, were transferred from the French to the English Crown, from the lord to his vassal; and Louis was left "cribb'd, cabin'd and confined" on the north, the west and the south by the territories of a powerful prince over whom he had no hold beyond his oath of feudal allegiance. Henry was already a continental sovereign before he became king of England, and during the first eight years of his reign (1154–1162) he was only in England twice, and that merely for a year or more at a time. His foreign dominions required his immediate attention, and Thomas was frequently on duty abroad with him.

The first call to action came with the aggression

Campaign against Geoffrey, 1156. of Geoffrey, the king's brother, who had laid claim to the provinces of Anjou and Maine under the pretext that Henry had only received them on the express condition of resigning them to his younger brother on his own accession to the throne of England. Henry crossed the Channel in January 1156, reduced the strongholds of Chinon, Mirabeau, and Loudon, which had taken Geoffrey's side, and compelled Geoffrey to resign his claim on the receipt of an annuity by way of compensation. Henry then exacted the homage of all Aquitaine, and prepared to return to England. Thomas' share in this short campaign is mentioned, though not distinctly specified, by Gervase, who describes Henry at the outset as "relying on the valuable help of Thomas his chancellor[1]." Apparently Thomas was not abroad long, for the evidence of the Pipe Roll of 1155–1156 proves that he was busy with judicial work at home before Michaelmas 1156.

Henry's policy in France. Henry spent part of 1157 and 1158 in expeditions against the Welsh, and in a progress through the northern shires of England; but the August of 1158 saw him once more engaged in the extension of his

---

[1] Gervase, *Chron.* A.D. 1156 (Twysden, col. 1378): Thomae cancellarii sui magno fretus auxilio. Joh. S. *Epist.* 128 (ed. Giles) connects the first scutage of the reign with this campaign: scutagium remittere non potest (rex) et a quibusdam exactionibus abstinere, quoniam fratris gratia male sarta nequidquam coiit, sed ob hoc perniciosissime scissa est, quod domino regi frater totam haereditatem paternam, nominatim terram cujus ei vis major possessionem abstulit, noluit abjurare, quum tamen munitiones et regi cedere et obsides dare paratus esset, ut terram quam dono patris habuerat recuperaret.

power on the continent. He had at least three distinct objects to secure. (1) The fortresses of the Vexin, the military frontier between his Norman duchy and the dominions of Louis, were in the hands of the French king, and Henry was bent on their recovery. (2) The death of Geoffrey, whom the citizens of Nantes had accepted as their earl, made Henry anxious to secure the earldom for himself. (3) The lordship of Brittany was just now a subject of dispute between two claimants, and Henry was determined to assert his authority in that quarter also. Every gain to Henry in territory or influence was a clear loss to Louis, who could ill brook any addition to the power of a vassal that had already robbed him of his wife and half his dominions. There was one insuperable obstacle to a policy of naked aggression on Henry's part, and that was the feudal relation between the vassal and his suzerain lord which remained "the dominant and authoritative fact of the political morality of that day[1]." Open war was the last policy to which Henry or Louis wished to resort. The only alternative for Henry was diplomacy, and in Thomas the chancellor he had a diplomatist who had already won signal triumphs in the sphere of papal negotiations. How far the continental policy of Henry during the years 1158—1160 was the fruit of Thomas' influence in the private counsels of his king, we cannot say. In the light of their difference of opinion before the walls of Toulouse in 1159, when Thomas showed himself as impetuously regardless as Henry was

[1] Mrs J. R. Green, *Henry II.* p. 32.

cautiously observant of feudal honour, we might be inclined to credit Henry rather than Thomas with the authorship of a policy which aimed at finding a technical justification in the sight of the feudal world for every act of aggression, and sought to avoid war wherever peace would suffice for its purpose. But perhaps some allowance must be made for Thomas on that occasion. The sword was already drawn, and the diplomatist lost in the soldier wild with excitement over his first campaign. Thomas in 1158 may have been as keenly alive as Henry was in 1159 to the need of wary walking. But whatever doubt there is as to the chancellor's share in the origination of this policy, there is no doubt that he was the responsible agent in its execution.

Thomas the ambassador, 1158.

Before the close of 1158 a marriage had been arranged between Louis' infant daughter Margaret and little Henry, the eldest surviving son of Henry of England, and the Vexin secured as Margaret's dowry; Henry had quelled the disturbances in Brittany, and added the earldom of Nantes to his dominions. The marriage alliance and Louis' consent to the extension of Henry's influence in the West are distinctly described by one authority or another as the work of Thomas, and the connexion between the two is obvious. Louis had been disarmed, his threatened opposition to Henry's plans in Brittany changed into a formal sanction, and his fortresses on Henry's frontier neutralised, by a successful visit from Henry's ambassador—Thomas the chancellor.

Fitzstephen dwells with lingering delight upon

the magnificence of this embassy. Its splendour was
part of its policy. It was Thomas' aim not only to
make his own mark upon the French world, but
also to leave a still more distinct impression of his
master's greatness, and this he succeeded in doing[1].
The inhabitants of the districts through which he
passed took the glory of the chancellor as an indication of the still more wonderful glory of his lord
the king. It was a grand sight, Fitzstephen tells
us,—a mounted retinue of two hundred members of
the chancellor's own household, knights, clerks, attendants, budding slips of English and foreign
nobility, learning the arts of knighthood under his
supervision; hounds and hawks to beguile the journey;
eight five-horse cars, with a new-liveried groom to
each horse's head, one of them the chancellor's chapel,
another his private chamber, another his wardrobe,
another his kitchen, two of them laden with iron-
bound casks of a bright wholesome beverage like
wine in colour but superior in taste, which found
great favour with the men of France (now com-
monly known as beer); twelve sumpter horses, each
with a groom at its head and a monkey on its back;
eight coffers to carry the chancellor's gold and silver
plate and miscellaneous utensils, chests containing
cash for current expenses, and one sumpter horse
preceding the rest, laden with the sacred vessels and
altar ornaments and books. At the head of the

---

[1] Fitzst. iii. 29-33. The double motive which prompted this
splendour comes out clearly in the language of Fitzstephen:
"ut honoretur persona mittentis in misso et missi sua in se",—
personal vanity and national pride both had their share.

whole procession came two and fifty footmen in companies of six or ten, singing as they went in English fashion. Behind the cars came the knights and clerks, riding two by two; and the chancellor with a few personal friends brought up the rear.

The magnificence of the chancellor on the way was only equalled by his munificence at the end of his journey. On landing he had sent word of his arrival to the king of France, and had received a reply appointing the time and place of meeting at Paris. Louis, bent on giving his guest a royal welcome, had forbidden his subjects to sell anything to the chancellor or his agents; but Thomas was equally bent on keeping up his reputation. He baffled the king's precautions by sending his men in disguise under a false name to buy provisions in the neighbouring markets of Lagny, Corbeil, Pontoise, and S. Denys. His stratagem was successful. When he entered Paris to take up his abode at the Temple, his attendants met him with the news that he would find ready stored there three days' provisions for a thousand men. The extravagance of his table is almost incredible. A hundred pounds sterling for one dish of eels is literally a fabulous price; and it is hard to avoid a suspicion that the amount was exaggerated as the story passed from mouth to mouth. But Thomas' generosity was not confined to the court and retinue of his royal host. The quondam student of Paris gave practical proof of his interest in the university to which he had once owned allegiance by extending his bounty to the scholars, the doctors, and (significant touch of human nature) the hungry creditors of the English students.

Thomas had not spent in vain. The embassy was a success, and Thomas returned in triumph, winning fresh laurels on his way home by a less peaceful exploit, the capture and imprisonment of Wido de la Val, a notorious robber-chief, whom he left in chains at Neuf-marché[1]. Fitzstephen's graphic narrative however fails just where a trustworthy guide is most wanted. He throws no light upon the progress of the negotiations. He merely states at the outset that the king had discussed the project of the marriage alliance with the chancellor and other magnates of the realm, and that the chancellor was chosen to conduct the negotiations and accepted the responsibility[2]. The result he dismisses with the brief statement that Thomas got what he asked at Paris[3]. The only biographer who refers to this mission at all is Herbert of Bosham, and he only mentions incidentally the fact that Thomas won from the king of France by a marriage alliance five strongholds on the confines of France and Normandy, which were considered to belong by

---

[1] Fitzst. iii. 29–33.

[2] Fitzst. iii. 29: deliberavit quandoque rex Anglorum cum cancellario et aliis quibusdam regni sui magnatibus petere a rege Francorum filiam ejus Margaretam matrimonio copulandam filio suo Henrico. Placuit consilium...Ad tantam petitionem tanto principi faciendam quis mittendus erat nisi cancellarius? Eligitur, assentitur.

[3] ibid. 33: legatione sua feliciter functus est; propositum assecutus est; quod petiit, ei concessum est.

right of old to the Norman duchy,—namely, Gisors and four other fortresses[1].

It is the evidence of the contemporary chroniclers that enables us to piece together the facts of the case. Henry crossed into Normandy in August, 1158, met Louis at the river Epte to discuss the question of peace and this alliance, paid a visit to Louis at Paris, and returned with the infant Margaret. So says the Norman chronicler Robert of Mount S. Michael[2]. But Ralph de Diceto distinctly asserts that it was Thomas who procured the consent to the marriage and went in state to Paris to fetch the little bride-elect[3]. The language of Fitzstephen and

---

[1] Herb. iii. 175: quam industrie munitiones quinque munitissimas, in Franciae et Normanniae sitas confinio, domino suo regi, ad cujus tamen jus ab antiquo spectare dignoscebantur, a rege Francorum per matrimonium, sine ferro, sine gladio, absque lancea, absque pugna, in omni regum dilectione et pace revocaverit, Gizortium scilicet, castrum munitissimum, et alia quattuor. The Icelandic *Saga* speaks vaguely of some occasion on which "by his wisdom and law-pleading, Thomas brought about a settlement as to what line of landmark had been laid down of old between France and Normandy" (i. 57). The rectification of the frontier thus attributed to Thomas must be the arrangements made by him with Louis in 1158-1160 as to the possession of the Vexin.

[2] Robert de Monte, A.D. 1158 (Twysden, 994): rex mense Augusto transfretavit in Normanniam et locutus est cum rege Francorum Ludovico super Eptam de pace et de matrimonio contrahendo inter filium suum Henricum et filiam regis Francorum Margaretam, &c.

[3] Diceto: Thomas regis cancellarius procuravit ut Henricus primogenitus regis Anglorum Margaritam...sponsam acciperet (Capitula "Imaginum Historiarum," A.D. 1158). Thomas regis cancellarius in apparatu magno venit Parisius Margaritam...

Herbert also points to a distinct mission entrusted to Thomas and executed by him alone. It may have preceded and paved the way for the conference between Louis and Henry in August, 1158; or it may have followed that conference and dealt with the details of an alliance which had been already agreed upon in general terms by the two kings in person. The former solution of the difficulty seems preferable, for Fitzstephen speaks of Thomas as landing on the French coast, in words which seem to imply a special mission direct from England[1]. It is quite possible that the two alternatives may be combined. Thomas may perhaps have been responsible both for the first overtures and for the final settlement of the conditions, the conference between Henry and Louis coming between the initial and the final stages of the negotiations[2]. In whatever way the alliance was arranged, its terms were distinctly to Henry's advantage. Thomas succeeded in inducing Louis to send his infant daughter into Normandy to live under Henry's charge until she reached a marriageable age; and she was entrusted to the care of Robert de Neubourg, one of Henry's vassals[3].

accepturus uxorem Henrico, &c. ("Imagines Historiarum," A.D. 1158).

[1] Fitzst. iii. 31: appulsus in transmarinis, statim praemiserat domino regi Francorum cancellarius mandans quod ad eum veniret. Lingard (ii. 57) sends Thomas to Paris first to lull Louis' suspicions of Henry's plans against Nantes, and makes the king follow "to ratify the engagements of his minister," including the marriage alliance.

[2] Lord Lyttelton seems to take this view in his *Life of Henry II.* (ii. 82–84).

[3] John Brompton, 1050 (Twysden). William of Newburgh,

With regard to her dowry—the Vexin with its castles, Gisors, Neufle, and Neuf-châtel—Thomas had to be content with a compromise. The coveted fortresses were sequestrated in the hands of certain Knights Templars nominated by the two kings, to be surrendered to Henry at the time of the marriage[1]. But the neutrality of these strongholds, which commanded Henry's frontier, was a distinct gain second only in importance to their actual possession. Thomas had done good work for his royal master. Even Louis' anxiety for the alliance could scarcely have led him to make such substantial concessions without the most skilful diplomacy on the part of Thomas.

The reversion of the Vexin was only a distant prospect; but there were other benefits to be derived immediately from this alliance. Gervase[2] distinctly states that it was through the agency of Thomas that Henry obtained Louis' permission to enter

bk. ii. ch. 24. It is Robert de Monte who gives the guardian's name.

[1] Brompton, 1050. Ralph de Diceto, A.D. 1160. Robert de Monte, A.D. 1158. William of Newburgh says that Henry managed all this through a man of great ability, his chancellor Thomas (bk. ii. ch. 24).

[2] Gervase, *Chron.* A.D. 1158: 'eo tempore per industrium Thomae,' Henry obtained Louis' permission 'ut quasi senescallus regis Francorum intraret Britanniam et inter se inquietos et funebre bellum exercentes coram se convocaret et pacificaret.' This was Henry's first entrance into Brittany, he adds, and it ended in an accession of territory,—civitatem de Nantes ad jus suae dominationis inflexit. Cp. William of Newburgh, bk. ii. ch. 8.

Brittany as seneschal[1] of France and quell the disturbance then rife in that practically independent province by the assertion of his authority as representative of the suzerain of France, enforced, if necessary, by an appeal to arms. The whole army of Normandy was summoned to Avranches, to advance against Conan earl of Brittany in the event of his refusing to submit; but in September Conan surrendered the city of Nantes, which he had seized, and acknowledged Henry as earl of Nantes and overlord of Brittany. In November Henry escorted Louis in state through Normandy and Brittany, "not now as a vassal requiring help but with all the pomp of an equal king[2]," and ended by paying him a visit and accepting the hospitality of his palace at Paris[3].

Campaign of Toulouse, 1159.

It was however a precarious peace, and it proved short-lived. The summer of 1159 found Louis and Henry in collision, with Thomas once more to the front, this time as an impetuous and energetic

---

[1] The Count of Anjou was hereditary seneschal of France, according to Robert de Monte. Giraldus Cambrensis mentions Geoffrey of Anjou as seneschal. But the office was usually executed by a deputy (Stubbs, *Const. Hist.* vol. i.). See especially Miss Norgate, *England under Angevin Kings*, i. 450 n.

[2] Mrs J. R. Green, *Henry the Second*, p. 34.

[3] Gervase, A.D. 1158. Robert de Monte and Ralph de Diceto, A.D. 1158. Among the list of persons mentioned by Robert de Monte as present on the occasion of the charter granted by Henry to his own abbey, Mount S. Michael, occurs the name of "Gervase, a clerk of Thomas the chancellor" (identified by some with Gervase the chronicler, but without sufficient evidence,—see Stubbs, preface to Gervase in the Rolls Series). Apparently the chancery clerks were on the spot in attendance upon the king, and the chancellor was possibly not far away.

soldier. Henry was determined to enforce the claim of his wife Eleanor to the earldom of Toulouse, now in the possession of Count Raymond de S. Gilles. Louis had himself asserted and followed up this claim when Eleanor was his wife, but had been compelled to desist. He had come to terms with Raymond and given him his sister Constance in marriage; and now Raymond looked to his royal brother-in-law for support in his resistance to Henry's aggression. Louis responded to his appeal, and for once broke through the meshes of the net in which the diplomacy of Thomas and Henry had involved him. The two kings met twice in conference, but failed to come to terms; and in June Henry marched south from Poictiers with a magnificent army at his back and a goodly array of princes and nobles in his train, including his ally Malcolm king of Scotland[1]. But Chancellor Thomas outshone them all, as he rode at the head of a picked body of seven hundred knights raised from his own household. If we may credit the panegyrical language of John of Salisbury in the closing passage of a work dedicated to the chancellor at this very time, Thomas was the moving spirit of the whole expedition[2]. It is probable that, if his advice had

Thomas the soldier.

---

[1] Robert de Monte, A.D. 1159.

[2] Joh. S. *Polycraticus*, viii. 25: rex illustris Anglorum Henricus secundus, maximus regum Britanniae, si initiis gestorum fuerit exitus concolor, circa Garunnam et (ut dicitur) *te auctore te duce fulminat* et Tholosam felici cingens obsidione non modo provinciales usque ad Rhodanum et Alpes territat, sed munitionibus diruptis populisque subactis, quasi universis praesens immineat, timore principes Hispanos concussit et Gallos. John

been followed, the war might have been ended by one bold stroke. The king of France had thrown himself into Toulouse with a handful of troops, and the impetuous chancellor suggested a sudden attack upon the city, with the almost certain prospect of taking Louis prisoner. The immediate advantage of such a prize was great; but Henry looked beyond to its ultimate consequences. Louis was his suzerain lord, and to violate the principle of feudal allegiance by drawing the sword against the person of Louis was to set a dangerous precedent for his own discontented vassals. Perhaps too Henry had an eye to the possibility of his son's succession to the French throne through his future bride. The chancellor contended that Louis had forfeited the privileges of a feudal lord by lending open assistance to Henry's enemies in contravention of the existing alliance between the two. But Henry held resolutely to his decision[1], and refrained from attacking the city. Reinforcements had arrived for Louis in

implores the chancellor to keep his character unstained: in tantis rerum tumultibus, quaeso, custodi innocentiam, et vide *et dicta et praedica aequitatem*, nec amore nec odio, timore vel spe, declines a via recta. The words in italics evidently refer to Thomas' voice in the royal counsels.

[1] Fitzst. iii. 33, 34: vana superstitione et reverentia *rex tentus consilio aliorum*, super urbem in qua esset dominus suus rex Francorum irruere noluit; *dicente in contrarium cancellario*, quod personam domini rex Francorum ibi deposuisset eo quod supra pacta conventa hostem se ibidem ei opposuisset.

Robert de Monte, A.D. 1159, says that Henry, *acting upon the advice of his council*, did not besiege the king of France, but beleaguered the surrounding castles. Evidently Thomas was not the only trusted adviser at Henry's side.

the meantime, and Henry withdrew his army. The expedition had proved a failure as far as concerned its primary purpose, the conquest of Toulouse[1]; but minor successes had been already won. Cahors and other strongholds in the neighbourhood of Toulouse —some the original possessions of its earl, others conquests made from the partisans of Henry—had fallen into the hands of the English army; and the chancellor remained behind, with his own contingent and Henry earl of Essex the royal constable, to keep a firm hold on these acquisitions, the rest of the English barons declining the task. Thomas more than fulfilled his commission. He stormed three other strongholds in helmet and cuirass at the head of his men, and did not rejoin his royal master until after he had crossed the Garonne and exacted the submission of the province in the king's name[2].

Thomas again figured prominently in the later

---

[1] Fitzst. iii. 34: impos voti et inefficax propositi rediit. There is a marked discrepancy between the original authorities as to the extent of Henry's forbearance. Most of the chroniclers (William of Newburgh, Robert de Monte, Ralph de Diceto, John Brompton) represent him as refraining altogether from an actual siege. Herbert of Bosham is not quite clear; he says, rege differente obsidionem (iii. 176). But Gervase (*Chron.* A.D. 1159, col. 1381, Twysden) and Roger of Hoveden say that Henry lay before the city besieging it for four months (from S. John the Baptist's Day, June 24, to All Saints' Day, November 1), and merely refrained from any attempt to take it by storm. The former statement seems better supported.

[2] Fitzst. iii. 34,—the fullest account throughout of Thomas' share in the campaign. Robert de Monte, A.D. 1159, mentions his being left in charge of the garrisons of the newly acquired fortresses.

campaign on the Norman frontier in the neighbourhood of Gisors, where Henry was winning and fortifying new castles at the expense of Louis' northern domains. In addition to the seven hundred knights of his own following, the chancellor now brought into the field twelve hundred mercenary troops, and four thousand men besides, the latter enlisted in the service of his knights. The cost of their maintenance was a heavy drain on his purse. Each knight received three pounds a day for the keep of his men and horses, and dined himself at the chancellor's mess. They were the very flower of the king's army[1],—none so brave in action as they were, none so prompt to obey orders. The chancellor was himself the foremost in the fray. Deacon as he was, he rode to the charge at the head of his men, and distinguished himself by unhorsing a famous French knight, Engelram de Trie, whose war-horse he carried off as the prize of victory[2]. In fact

The campaign in Normandy.

[1] It can scarcely be called the English army except as being the army of the king of England. It was a motley host drawn from various countries,—England, Normandy, Anjou, Aquitaine, Brittany, and Scotland. The English barons were in their places under the flag of their lord the king, but the knights, townsmen, and yeomen, who should have followed their lords the barons, were left at home and replaced by mercenaries bought with the proceeds of the scutage now levied for the first time as a commutation for personal service. Robert de Monte, A.D. 1159.

[2] Fitzst. iii. 35. Cp. the evidence of the French monk Garnier—an eye-witness of his exploits in Normandy:

      En Guascuingne fu-il lung tens pur guerreier
      As Guascins; kovint de lur chasteus lesser.
      En Normendie r'ont sun seinur grant mester,
      Et *jo l'vi sor Franceis plusur feiz chevaucher.*
      De ses bensuignes fist le Rei mult avauncer.

Thomas fought as to the manner born: soldiering might have been his destiny. Even his devoted and partial biographer Grim dwells with regretful emphasis on the change from the man of peace to the man of blood which came with his elevation to the chancellorship. "Who can tell," writes Grim, "how many suffered death at his hands, how many the loss of all their wealth? Surrounded by a valiant body of knights, he attacked whole states, destroyed cities and towns, gave villages and farms to the greedy flames without one thought of pity, and proved merciless to the enemies of his lord the king, in whatever quarter they rose[1]."

[1] Grim, ii. 365. The passage has been taken to refer to Thomas' share in the expulsion of the Flemish free-lances from England in 1155; but it falls in much better with what we know of his action in the French campaigns of 1159. Froude in the *Nineteenth Century* for 1877 took a strange view of the passage and its application. "Such words," he wrote, "give a new aspect to the demand afterwards made that he should answer for his proceedings as chancellor, and lend a new meaning to his unwillingness to reply." Freeman disposed of this insinuation by pointing out that Froude had ignored Grim's distinct statement that the severity of the chancellor was directed against the king's *enemies*. In the reprint of Froude's articles in his *Short Studies* (iv. 30, 31) the above quotation is omitted, and Grim's language is explained as referring to "the war of Toulouse or the suppression of a revolt which followed in Aquitaine." But Froude's argument against the application of Grim's words to the expulsion of the Flemings is a flagrant inaccuracy. "The work of suppressing the Flemings," he says, "is distinctly said to have been completed by Henry within three months of his coronation, and *before Becket became chancellor*." Fitzstephen is the authority in question, and his exact words are,—*consilio cancellarii* et cleri et baronum regni qui pacis bonum volebant, infra tres primos menses coronationis regis, &c. (iii. 19).

The war was not of long duration. It ended in *The peace*
a truce which lasted from November 1159 to May *of 1160.*
1160, when a formal peace was concluded[1]. A copy
of the treaty is now extant, and Thomas appears
among the list of witnesses. The terms were de-
cidedly advantageous to Henry. The possession of
the Vexin was guaranteed to him as soon as ever
the marriage of Henry and Margaret should take
place; and his acquisitions in the south of France
were confirmed. In October the two kings met
again on friendly terms, and the boy Henry did
homage to Louis for the duchy of Normandy[2]. In
November 1160 Henry reaped the fruits of Thomas'
labours in 1158. Alarmed by Louis' remarriage
with Adelais of Blois, a niece of Stephen the late
king of England, Henry obtained a dispensation
from the cardinal legates, Henry of Pisa and
William of Pavia, had the marriage of the two
children solemnised at Neubourg on the 2nd of

---

[1] Robert de Monte, A.D. 1159, 1160. The treaty is preserved
in the Harleian MSS. at the British Museum, and is reproduced
by Lord Lyttelton in an appendix to his *Life of Henry II*. It is
connected in the MSS. with a selection of Thomas' letters—an
indication perhaps that he was regarded as responsible for the
negotiation of the treaty.

John of Salisbury, writing to Thomas some time in 1160,
alludes to his influence in suggestive language: *si enim vera sunt
quae dicuntur a redeuntibus...rex et tota curia adeo pendent
de consilio vestro ut nec spes pacis immineat nisi eam vestra
prudentia praefiguret* (Ep. 9, v. 13). This can scarcely refer to
anything but the relations between Henry and Louis.

[2] Robert de Monte, A.D. 1160. Joh. S. Ep. to Bartholomew,
bishop of Exeter (Ep. 461, vi. 507).

November, and promptly relieved the Templars of the long-coveted castles in the Vexin[1].

The Flemish marriage: opposition of Thomas.

There is one other incident in the dynastic annals of this period in which Thomas plays a prominent part, this time in decided opposition to Henry. A project was set on foot for the marriage of Matthew (a brother of Philip count of Flanders, and a cousin of Henry) with Mary the daughter of Stephen of Blois. The intended bride was abbess of Romsey in Hampshire, bound by her vows to the religious life of maiden sisterhood. Henry was bent on the marriage for political reasons. Thomas opposed it on religious grounds, but Henry ignored the chancellor's protest and insisted on having his own way. The marriage took place in May 1160[2].

---

[1] Ralph de Diceto, A.D. 1160 (*Imag. Hist.*), says the bride was three years of age, the bridegroom seven.

[2] Robert de Monte, A.D. 1160. Diceto, A.D. 1160. Robert calls it "inauditum exemplum." Herbert of Bosham (iii. 328) refers to the fact in detail by way of explaining the enmity between Thomas and Philip which made Thomas afraid to set foot in Flanders as an exile. Causa etiam qua in illis partibus prodi metuerat, eo quod domino rege Anglorum procurante, Matthaeus, frater comitis Flandrensis Philippi, tunc Boloniae comes, cum abbatissa quadam, filia Stephani quondam regis Anglorum, matrimonium profanum et omnibus post futuris saeculis detestandum contraxerat, *archipraesule, tunc regis cancellario, propter facti enormitatem contradicente et quoad potuit reclamante;* unde et comes Boloniae ex tunc perfecto eum odio oderat. Robert de Monte explains that the earldom of Boulogne fell to Matthew as his wife's dower. Lyttelton (*Life of Henry II.* ii. 105–107) says that the papal schism made it difficult to obtain a dispensation, and the lady was conveyed secretly from her convent with Henry's consent and apparently her own too. But I cannot find any authority for these particulars.

It is a significant incident for two reasons. It is the only recorded occasion on which Thomas distinctly avowed his ecclesiastical scruples while he was chancellor[1]; and it is the second occasion on which Thomas opposed Henry in a matter of political importance and found his opposition vain[2].

[1] Fitzstephen (iii. 142) tells how Le Breton, one of the archbishop's murderers, dealt a brutal blow at his victim with the words: "Take that for the love of my lord William, the king's brother." Thomas had opposed and prevented the marriage of William and the countess of Warenne on the ecclesiastical ground of consanguinity, as Fitzstephen explains; but the date of his opposition is not known. Miss Lambert (*Nineteenth Century*, Feb. 1892, "The Real Thomas Becket") places it between 1159 and 1163 at the outside,—very soon after his consecration, if not during his chancellorship. Fitzstephen says, 'archiepiscopus contradixerat...et omnes sui (i. e. friends of William) archiepiscopo inimici facti sunt.'

[2] The first occasion was before the walls of Toulouse (p. 89).

CHAPTER V.

JUDICIAL ADMINISTRATION AND GENERAL REFORM.

Suppression of anarchy.

THERE can be no doubt that the foundations of Henry's later reforms were laid during the first eight years of his reign, while Thomas was chancellor. But the first task that lay before the new king was the suppression of the anarchy that was rife throughout the realm. The very idea of law and justice had to be restored before the methods of its administration could be improved. The work of clearance had first to be carried out before the work of reconstruction could begin; and Henry with the chancellor at his side lost no time in attacking the disorder. The chroniclers paint a vivid picture of the sufferings of the nation. One sample will suffice from the pages of the biographer who records so distinctly the fact of the chancellor's co-operation in the good work of restoring peace and order. The storm of war had swept over the whole realm. In almost every third township was a newly fortified castle, the den of a robber-baron. The native nobles of English and Norman birth had been driven from their inheritance, and the strange mercenaries, the Fleming and his foreign comrades, had fastened upon Kent and a large part of the kingdom besides. The anarchy of well-nigh twenty years had left little hope that the foreigner would ever be expelled, and the peace and dignity of the realm restored. It was a desperate task for a new king who was yet a youth. But "by the merciful providence of God, by the wise counsels of the chancellor, the clergy, and those barons of the realm who longed for the blessing of peace, within three months of the king's coronation" the thing was done. "William of Ypres, whose hand lay so sore upon Kent, withdrew in tears; the Flemings sailed away, every man of them, bag and baggage; the castles throughout England all came down with a rush, except the old towers and fortresses that served to keep the peace; the crown of England regained all that it had lost; the disinherited were restored to their fathers' rights; the brigands forsook their forest dens for the open town, and, sharing gladly in the universal peace, beat their swords into ploughshares and their spears into pruning-hooks. The lesser thieves, frightened into honesty by the sight of the gallows, put their hands to farming or mechanic trades. There was peace on every side; shields were no longer made at home, but fetched from abroad, while the wares of England once more poured into the foreign mart; the merchant left the shelter of town and fortress to wend his way to the market fair, and the Jew to find his creditors, without a thought of danger."

"Thanks to the energy and wisdom of this same chancellor, with the help of the clergy, and earls, and barons, the noble realm of England renewed its life like the freshness of spring. Holy Church received the honour that was her due; vacant sees and abbeys were bestowed upon deserving men without a taint of simony; the king prospered in all his doings by the favour of the King of kings; the realm of England was rich in plenty; the hillsides were cultivated; the valleys were thick with corn, the pastures full of oxen and the folds of sheep[1]."

Some allowance must no doubt be made for the rhetorical and poetical element in this picture of the golden age restored to "merrie England." But the main facts,—the suppression of the turbulent barons, the destruction of their castles, the expulsion of the mercenaries, the summary execution of justice,—stand out clearly in the more sober language of the chroniclers[2]. Six months sufficed to work the change, and convince barons and people that the sceptre was once more wielded by a strong-minded and strong-handed king, whose efforts were ably seconded by a little band of men after his own heart. We know no details of the chancellor's share in the work; in fact the chroniclers do not mention his name in connexion with the restoration of law and order; but Fitzstephen's distinct assertion cannot be explained away, and even after admitting that Fitzstephen

[1] Fitzst. iii. 18, 19.
[2] Gervase, *Chron.* A.D. 1154. Robert de Monte, A.D. 1154. William of Newburgh, bk. ii. ch. 1.

may have credited him with too large a share, enough will remain to account for the fact that the chancellor won the favour of all classes alike, king, clergy, barons, knights, and people[1].

Peace once restored, the judicial and financial machinery of the kingdom was set working on the old lines. The administrative system of Henry I.'s last years was resumed as a preliminary step to further development. Nigel bishop of Ely was recalled as treasurer to the Exchequer, from which Stephen had driven him in 1139. Richard de Luci and Robert earl of Leicester were appointed justiciars, and Thomas of London was made chancellor.

The chancellor's share in the civil administration gained both in extent and in importance in the hands of Thomas. It falls mainly under the two heads of judicature and finance, but not entirely. The scutage assessed on all tenants *in capite* of the king in 1159, as a commutation for personal service, owes its importance in constitutional history not so much to its financial aspect as a source of revenue for military purposes as to its political results at home. It may have been merely an expedient suggested by the exigencies of a possibly long campaign, which made it advisable to substitute standing mercenary forces for the brief service of the English feudal levy, which was at liberty to return home at the end of forty days. The chroniclers attribute the

Scutage of 1159 anti-feudal.

---

[1] Fitzst. iii. 20: cancellarii summus erat in clero, militia et populo regni favor. This passage follows close on the panegyric translated above. Cp. Fitzst. iii. 24: cancellarius regi, clero, militiae et populo erat acceptissimus.

measure to Henry's consideration for the prosperity of his people. He was unwilling, says Robert de Monte, to disturb the country knights or the citizens of the rising towns or the yeomen of the land[1]. But whatever its real or apparent motive was, in its results the measure was more or less fatal to the power of the barons at home, and it is scarcely possible to avoid the conclusion that it was part of "the anti-feudal policy which was hereditary in our kings since the Conqueror dealt the greatest of all blows to feudalism at Salisbury[2]." The question of Thomas' share in this institution of scutage will be considered more fully under the head of ecclesiastical affairs; it is sufficient here to note that the exaction was attributed to him by some of his contemporaries, who regarded him as either the author or the instrument of the scheme.

Municipal charters.
The chancellor's name is connected with one other branch of national development which can only be regarded as financial in this respect, that it was made to contribute to the royal treasury[3],—

[1] Robert de Monte, A.D. 1159: rex igitur Henricus iturus in expeditionem praedictam et *considerans longitudinem et difficultatem viae, nolens vexare agrarios milites nec burgensium nec rusticorum multitudinem*, sumptis LX solidis Andegavensibus in Normannia de feudo uniuscujusque loricae, et de reliquis omnibus tam in Normannia quam in Anglia sive etiam aliis terris suis secundum hoc quod ei visum fuit, *capitales barones suos cum paucis secum duxit*, solidarios vero milites innumeros.

[2] Freeman, *Contemp. Review*, vol. 32, p. 137.

[3] Gilds were continually fining for the retention or extension of their privileges. In the third year of Henry II.'s reign the citizens of York pay 40 marks for the temporary privilege of not pleading causes outside the county till the king's return. The

and that is the growth of the municipal system. Several of the borough charters granted by Henry II. bear the signature of "Thomas the chancellor" at the head of the list of witnesses. Winchester, Lincoln, Nottingham, Oxford, all had the privileges of their merchant gilds confirmed and extended during the chancellorship of Thomas[1]; and it is only natural to suppose that he had a voice in the granting or drawing up of the charters to which he set the royal seal and his own signature.

The incidental notices here and there of Thomas' activity in the sphere of judicature and finance will be best explained by a preliminary sketch of the constitutional framework into which the chancellorship fitted. In addition to the great Curia or national council of the early Norman kings, which met regularly three times a year and on certain special occasions besides, and consisted theoretically of all tenants in chief, though practically only the greater barons as a rule attended, we find from the reign of Henry I. onwards a central system of administration consisting of two supreme courts of judicature and finance, called respectively the Curia Regis and the Exchequer[2]. The anarchy of

Financial and judicial system.

weavers (*telarii*) of London, Nottingham and Lincoln pay various sums *pro gilda sua* in the 2nd, 3rd and 4th years of the reign. Pipe Rolls 2, 3, 4 Henry II. pp. 29, 39, 137, 153, etc. Madox (*Exchequer*, ch. xi.) gives a full list of liberties acquired by fine under Henry I.

[1] Stubbs, *Select Charters*, pp. 164–168.

[2] Their early development is to a great extent a matter of conjecture. They have been regarded from one point of view as "committees of the national council," from another as "mere

Stephen's reign paralysed the executive powers, and no official records of the administration of that period have survived. The extant rolls of the Exchequer begin with the 31st year of Henry I., and the next is the 2nd year of Henry II., when law and order once more prevailed. Our knowledge therefore of the administrative machinery as restored at the outset of Henry II.'s reign is largely derived by inference from the records of its procedure at the close of his grandfather's reign[1].

The Curia Regis or supreme court of judicature and the Exchequer or supreme court of finance were practically identical in their personal staff. The Exchequer consisted of the great officers of the royal household,—the justiciar (its president), the chancellor, the constable, two chamberlains, the marshal and the treasurer, with certain other persons specially appointed by the king on the ground of their legal ability, sometimes nobles, sometimes churchmen,—

---

sessions of the king's household ministers." The former theory emphasizes the English element, the latter the Norman; but it is almost impossible to trace with certainty the fusion of the two elements in the new organisation. Stubbs, *Const. Hist.* i. 376, 377.

[1] The Pipe Rolls of the Exchequer give the particulars of work done, but their evidence would be almost unintelligible without the light thrown upon the development of the administrative powers by the *Dialogus de Scaccario*, an exhaustive treatise begun in 1178 by Richard bishop of London, treasurer of the Exchequer, the son of Nigel bishop of Ely (his predecessor at the treasury) and the great-nephew of that Roger bishop of Salisbury whose genius it was that shaped the original organisation of the Exchequer under Henry I. The Dialogus is reprinted in Stubbs' *Select Charters*, pp. 168-248.

all entitled "barons of the Exchequer," and each having a definite place and definite functions of his own. The Curia Regis similarly consisted of the same great household officials with a few other persons chosen by the king for their knowledge of law. But in this court there was no rigid division of labour such as existed in the Exchequer, and the president was the king himself, the justiciar presiding only in the king's absence. The rest of the members of the Curia Regis were also called 'justitiarii,' the president being distinguished by the epithet 'summus,' 'magnus,' or 'capitalis.'

There was also a close connexion between the business of the two courts. The fines paid or remitted in the Curia were recorded in the Exchequer. In fact the work of the Exchequer was to a large extent judicial. The fines from the local courts were an important item in the sheriffs' accounts which were audited by the Exchequer, and in the readjustment of taxation questions of ownership frequently came before the barons of the Exchequer for legal decision. "So intimate is the connexion of judicature with finance under the Norman kings," and, it may be added, the early Plantagenets, "that we scarcely need the comments of the historians to guide us to the conclusion that it was mainly for the sake of the profits that justice was administered at all[1]."

The Curia Regis was the instrument through which the judicial power of the Crown was exerted. It was a supreme court of appeal from the decision

[1] Stubbs, *Const. Hist.* i. 386, 387.

of the local courts, and a court of primary recourse in the case of tenants in chief of the Crown who were powerful enough to intimidate the local authorities, and also in the case of suits which called for a more equitable method of procedure than was afforded by the strict customary process of the provincial courts. In addition to this, it exerted a direct control over the action of the local judicature, by the visits of its itinerant justiciars.

Judicial work of the chancellor. The revival of the judicial system[1] was one of Henry's first anxieties. It followed immediately or perhaps accompanied the active measures of repression that marked the first months of his reign; and even without positive evidence of the fact we might reasonably have concluded that the chancellor whose help proved so valuable in the suppression of anarchy would have had some share at least in the restoration and administration of the long-forgotten forms of justice. But we are not left to conjecture. There are ample indications of the chancellor's judicial activity. They fall under three heads, (1) his place as a member of the Curia Regis, (2) his work as an itinerant justiciar, and (3) a group of less precise allusions which were at one time regarded as establishing the existence of a distinct court of judicature presided over by the chancellor.

(1) The Curia Regis in the earlier years of

[1] William of Newburgh, bk. ii. ch. 1: publicae quoque disciplinae in primis sollicitudinem (rex) habuit; et ut legum vigor in Anglia revivisceret qui sub rege Stephano exstinctus sepultusque videbatur, cura propensiore satagebat.

Henry II.'s reign seems to have been little more than what it was under Henry I., "a tribunal of exceptional resort to which appeals though increasing in number were still comparatively rare, and the action of which is scarcely distinguishable from that of the national council¹." The king is its nominal and frequently its actual head²; and the chancellor appears in attendance as an officer of the royal household³. A remarkable example of the working of this court is preserved in the chronicle of Battle Abbey,—an instance of royal intervention in an ecclesiastical dispute. It will recur again in estimating the chancellor's ecclesiastical policy; but it is interesting at this point as a glimpse of the Curia Regis in action, and an indication of the chancellor's position in the court. The case was briefly as follows. Hilary bishop of Chichester claimed the right of exerting his episcopal jurisdiction over Battle Abbey, which lay within his diocese; but Walter the abbot of Battle (a brother of Richard de Luci the justiciar) resisted the bishop's claim on the ground that the original privileges granted by its founder, William the Conqueror, included exemption from all episcopal authority. Early in this reign Henry II. had himself granted a charter confirming the privileges

(1) The Curia Regis: case of Battle Abbey.

---

¹ Stubbs, *Const. Hist.* i. 598.

² *Dial. Scacc.* I. iv.: Regis curia, in qua ipse in propria persona jura decernit. Henry II. frequently heard cases in person.

³ Fitzstephen (iii. 18) says that it was one of the chancellor's privileges, ut omnibus regis adsit conciliis et etiam non vocatus se ingerat.

of the abbey; but the bishop procured from Pope Adrian IV. (the only Englishman that ever sat in the Papal chair) a brief requiring the abbot to submit to the episcopal jurisdiction. The two parties met to discuss the question at Chichester, but without any decisive result; and both appealed to the king, who resolved to hear the case in person on his return from Normandy. The trial was held in May 1157. The king had kept Whitsuntide at Bury S. Edmund's, wearing his crown in solemn state, surrounded by court and council. Owing to the pressure of other business he postponed the trial until his visit to Colchester, where the attendance was even greater. On the Friday the king heard the case in the chapter-house after mass. Only those summoned by personal invitation of the king were present,— Thomas the chancellor, Henry of Essex the king's constable, Richard de Luci the justiciar, Richard de Humez the constable, Warren Fitzgerald, Nicolas de Sigillo, Ralph the physician, and William the king's brother. Richard de Luci opened the proceedings by a brief statement of his brother's case. The king then required the abbot to produce his charters, and the chancellor read them out one by one,—the original charter of William I., then those of William II. and Henry I., and last of all the charter granted by Henry II. himself. The king carefully inspected them all. The chancellor called upon the abbot to reply to the bishop's assertion that he had made a profession of obedience at Chichester; and the abbot denied that he had yielded any of his privileges. His brother Richard then spoke on behalf of the abbey as a memorial of Norman prowess. Robert of Leicester supported this argument, and the king pronounced himself so far distinctly in favour of the abbey. The court then adjourned.

The case was resumed on the following Tuesday in the presence of the king and a council augmented by the attendance of several ecclesiastical dignitaries, the two archbishops Theobald and Roger, the bishops of London, Exeter and Lincoln, and the abbots of S. Augustine's and Holme. Richard de Luci again dwelt upon the Norman associations of the abbey, and urged the strong feeling of the Norman nobles in favour of the maintenance of its privileges. The chancellor again recited the charters at the abbot's request, and then called upon the bishop of Chichester to state his case. Hilary enlarged upon the spiritual jurisdiction of the Church, her independence of the secular authority and the necessity of papal sanction before a layman, even the king, could confer any ecclesiastical dignity or exemption, in language that drew a sturdy protest from the king, to which the chancellor added a sharp remonstrance of his own[1]. The bishop disclaimed the idea of disloyalty, but did not succeed in satisfying the offended king. He went on to allege various acts of submission to his authority on the part of the abbot, and referred in a tone of complaint to the futility of the conference which met to revise the abbey charter at the royal

---

[1] Battle Abbey Chronicle (*Materials*, iv. 248): [pecca]tis enim in dominum nostrum regem, cui fidei sacramentum vos fecisse nulli dubium est.

command in the presence of Thomas the chancellor and Theobald the archbishop. The king insisted that the question must be left to his own determination. Eventually Richard de Luci requested that the abbot might retire and consult his friends[1]. The king assented, and Richard invited Roger archbishop of York, Thomas the chancellor, John treasurer of York, Robert earl of Leicester, Patrick earl of Salisbury, Henry of Essex, Reginald de Warenne, Warren Fitzgerald, and a number of other Norman nobles and knights, along with his brother, and asked their opinion in another part of the chapterhouse. The king went to mass, and then resumed his seat in court. Richard de Luci and the abbot's supporters now returned, and the chancellor delivered their opinion in a long and able speech[2], dealing with each alleged act of submission to the bishop, and finally convicting the bishop of having obtained letters from Rome against the abbot. In answer to the king's indignant enquiry the bishop denied the accusation on oath, and persisted in his denial, though the chancellor pointed to the papal letters now in the abbot's possession. Archbishop Theobald, knowing the facts, crossed himself in holy horror at the bishop's perjury, and at last requested that the king would entrust the whole case to his care, to be settled in accordance with the canon law of the

[1] Battle Abbey Chron. iv. 249: abbati de Bello fratri suo super his respondendi consilium cum amicis suis secretius habere liceret.

[2] iv. 250: Ricardus de Luci cum abbate et omnibus sibi junctis consilio communicato rediit, impositoque responsionis sermone Thomae cancellario regis, omnibus audientibus facunda oratione hoc modo idem responsum reddidit heros.

church. But the king, whose dissatisfaction with the bishop had been visibly increasing during the progress of the trial, and had culminated at the disclosure of the appeal to Rome, insisted on pronouncing on the case himself[1]. He rose and withdrew to the monks' cemetery, attended by all the council. The bishop and the abbot alone were left behind. The matter was discussed, and then the bishop was summoned to the royal presence. Further discussion followed, and Henry of Essex was sent to fetch the abbot and his three monks in attendance. On their arrival the bishop, at a sign from the king, publicly announced that he withdrew all claims upon the abbot, adding, by express command of the king, that he did so voluntarily and not under any compulsion[2]. At the request of Archbishop Theobald, the king gave the kiss of peace to the bishop, and by the king's command the bishop exchanged the same token of reconciliation with the abbot and his brother the justiciar.

[1] iv. 255: the archbishop speaks, "praecipiat excellentia vestra nos super his quid faciendum sit consilio retractare atque ordine judiciario consuetudinis ecclesiasticae determinare." "Non ita" inquit rex, "haec per vos determinari praecipiam; verum ego vobis comitantibus consilio super his habito fine recto concludam."

[2] iv. 256: ad haec rex: "non coactus sed voluntarie hoc te fuisse et protulisse constans est." Episcopus: "verum est me hoc voluntarie justa ratione cogente fecisse necnon et protulisse." Thomas the archbishop, in a letter to Pope Alexander in 1168, called it an act of coercion: eidem (abbati) coram omnibus communicare (Cicestrensis episcopus) *compulsus est* sine absolutione, et eum recipere in osculo pacis. Probably Thomas was right: it was practical compulsion.

The court before which this case was tried was evidently the Curia Regis in the later and narrower sense, the inner circle of the great national council, a royal selection from the barons and knights who had met to honour the king at his coronation festival at S. Edmund's. It included the chancellor and other household officials, and a few nobles and ecclesiastics invited by the king. The chancellor's share in the trial is important. As secretary to the king he reads and takes charge of the documentary evidence, and as clerk of the court calls upon the litigants in turn to state their case. At a later stage of their proceedings he appears in a new light as the chosen advocate of the abbot's rights[1], the

---

[1] Dean Hook (*Archbps.* ii. 372) seems to have mistaken Thomas' speech for the judicial verdict of the Curia. "An adjournment," he says, "took place for a short time. *On the return of the court Becket* in a long and able speech *gave judgment* against the bishop. He stated that the abbot sought to retain the privileges conceded to his abbey by William the Conqueror, and among them an exemption from all episcopal jurisdiction. *In those privileges he was now confirmed by the command of the king*, 'not for the purpose,' said Becket in conclusion, 'of setting you at nought but with the intention of defending by sound reason as royal rights, things which you have been pleased in our hearing to call *frivolous*.'" The chancellor is really referring here to the abbot's attitude at the conference which met at Lambeth in 1155 to revise the abbey charter in accordance with the royal mandate (praecepto domini regis, *Mat.* iv. 249), which Dean Hook has apparently transferred to the trial of 1157. For the real bearing of this passage (*Materials*, iv. 249) see ch. VII. of this Essay, and the note A on the word *peremptorius*, here translated '*frivolous*.'

Canon Robertson makes a similar mistake. In his biography of Becket (p. 61) he describes the chancellor as "delivering the

mouthpiece of the great body of Norman feeling in favour of the abbey. Finally he is merged as an ordinary member in the Curia which the king deigns to consult before pronouncing his decision. The details of that consultation are not recorded in the Abbey Chronicle. The omission may be simply explained by the fact that the abbot and his attendant monks were only summoned at its close to hear the bishop resign his claims. Otherwise we might be tempted to regard the silence of the chronicler as an indication that the deliberation of the Curia amounted to little more than a statement of the king's intention, accepted without much, if any, room for variety of opinion on the part of his councillors[1].

(2) The judicial work of the chancellor, in the strict sense of the word, stands out distinctly in the records of the itinerant judicature preserved in the Pipe Rolls of the Exchequer. Already under Henry I. the officers of the Exchequer had travelled from

(2) The chancellor and the itinerant judicature.

judgment of a great assembly before which the question was tried." Father Morris is not quite clear: "Thomas the chancellor was called upon to deliver judgment—as, from its effect, we suppose we must style what certainly reads more like the speech of an advocate" (*S. Thomas*, p. 546). As a matter of fact it was not the court that adjourned; it was Richard de Luci and his brother's partisans. When the court did adjourn later to consider its verdict, it was the king who headed its deliberations; and the chancellor is not mentioned at all in connexion with the conclusion of the case. Thomas' speech is simply a masterly statement of the abbot's case; it is the pleading of a party-counsel, not the verdict of the court.

[1] Cp. Thomas' letter to the Pope in 1163: sic placuit regi et curiae, quae ei in nullo contradicere audebat.

county to county to assess the revenue, and as officers of the Curia Regis had held pleas in the local courts, as the Pipe Roll of 31 Henry I. amply proves. This system of financial and judicial inspection was resumed, perhaps on a less extensive scale, at the very outset of Henry II.'s reign[1]. It is true that it was not until 1166 that the duties of "the Curia Regis in progress" were marked out by legislative enactment in the Assize of Clarendon. It was not until 1176 that the country was systematically divided into six circuits with a detachment of three judges to each circuit, on the lines of the fiscal circuit of 1173. And it was not until 1176 that the name "justitiarii itinerantes" was applied in the Pipe Rolls to these travelling justices[2]. The "errantes justitiae"—erring as well as errant—who are singled out for condemnation in John of Salisbury's *Polycraticus*[3] (dated 1159) are still the sheriffs, the original representatives of royal justice. But the Pipe Roll of the 2nd year of Henry II. (1155–1156) proves that one or two officers of the Curia Regis were already busy in the provinces, however vague

---

[1] Stubbs, *Select Charters*, p. 141: "Everything of the kind ceased under Stephen: and in the earlier years of Henry II. the visitation was apparently made only by either the great justiciar or some other great officer of the royal household, as the constable or the chancellor."

[2] Cp. their designation in the *Dialogus de Scaccario* (I. iv.): fiunt interdum per comitatus communes assisae (i.e. the general assessment of revenue in each country) *a justitiis itinerantibus* quos nos *deambulatorios* vel *perlustrantes judices* nominamus.

[3] Joh. S. *Polycraticus*, v. 15. Stubbs, *Const. Hist.* i. 604, 605.

their title, however undefined their duties. In that year for the first time in English history the chancellor is mentioned as an itinerant justice, sitting in judgment with other members of the Curia Regis in different counties. In Lincolnshire Thomas was acting in conjunction with the chief justiciar, Robert Beamont earl of Leicester[1]. In Essex the sheriff (Richard de Luci) accounts for £14. 2s. arising from an assize held by the chancellor and Henry earl of Essex, the constable[2]. In Kent three items of revenue are mentioned in the sheriff's account as arising from pleas held by the chancellor and the earl of Essex[3]. In the same shire Hugh Pincerna accounts for 40s. *pro placitis sigilli*—apparently pleas held by the chancellor alone. In the third year it was the earl of Essex who was most busily engaged: his name occurs in three counties, Sussex, Wiltshire and Somerset. The chancellor is not actually mentioned as holding pleas in that year, but his name is found in the Shropshire accounts associated with the earl of Leicester, who was

[1] Pipe Roll, 2 Henry II. p. 26: de placitis cancellarii et comitis Legecestriae. It is interesting by the way to note that the very next item of royal revenue accounted for by the sheriff arises from the ecclesiastical courts of the diocese: de placitis episcopi Lincolniensis.

[2] Pipe Roll, 2 Henry II. p. 17: de assisa cancellarii et Henrici de Essexia. Stubbs (*Const. Hist.* i. 573, note) tabulates the meanings of the word *assisa* as follows: (1) a legal enactment, e.g. Assize of Clarendon, (2) a special form of trial prescribed by legal enactment, e.g. Assize d'Ancester, (3) the court holding the trial, e.g. the modern Assize. The meaning in this entry in the Pipe Roll is apparently the original meaning, prior to all these, = *session*.

[3] Pipe Roll, 2 Henry II. pp. 65, 66.

holding pleas in that shire[1]. The last item of expenditure in the sheriff's account is sanctioned *per cancellarium et comitem Legecestriae*. Perhaps the two had been acting in concert as officers of the Exchequer, even if the earl had been acting singly as an officer of the Curia Regis. The Pipe Roll of the fourth year reveals the chancellor acting alone in Middlesex and Huntingdonshire. The men of Laleham in the former county are responsible for two marks *de placitis cancellarii*[2], while the sheriff of Huntingdon accounts for ten marks due from the fines for *murdrum* and from the chancellor's pleas[3].

From the fifth year of the reign (1158–1159) to the eighth (1161–1162) there is no further record in the Pipe Rolls of judicial work done by the chan-

---

[1] Pipe Roll, 2 Henry II. p. 89: de placitis comitis Legecestriae. Foss (*Judges*, i. 196) speaks of the chancellor as holding pleas with the earl of Leicester in Shropshire in this year; but this is scarcely a justifiable statement. Perhaps after all the entry 'per cancellarium et comitem Legecestriae' merely means that the two tested and passed this item in the sheriff's account when it came up at the Exchequer.

[2] Pipe Roll, 4 Henry II. p. 114: homines de Laleham reddiderunt compotum de II m. argenti *de placitis cancellarii*. Homines in the Pipe Rolls has a technical meaning. It is a term applied to those "feudatory tenants who claimed the privilege of having their causes and persons tried only in the courts of their lords" (Glossary, Introduction to Pipe Rolls, p. 84). This explains the second half of the above entry,—the remission of the sum to the abbot of Westminster: in perdonis per breve regis abbati de Westmonasterio II m. argenti et quietus est. Laleham was evidently a manor in the possession of the abbot.

[3] Pipe Roll, 4 Henry II. p. 164: de placitis cancellarii et murdro.

cellor in the provinces. The reason is obvious. In the autumn of 1158 came the famous embassy to Paris, and from that date until his election to the primacy in 1162 Thomas was abroad most of his time, engaged in attendance on the king or winning fresh laurels in the field of diplomacy or war.

(3) So far we have been on the safe ground of well-authenticated facts. The Chronicle of Battle Abbey supplies definite information as to the chancellor's work as a member of the Curia Regis in session under the king. The Pipe Rolls speak for his activity in provincial judicature. There still remain for consideration the vaguer references to the chancellor's judicial labours in the pages of contemporary writers, which seem on the first glance to point to the chancery under Thomas as a separate court of judicature with an equitable jurisdiction. *(3) Equitable jurisdiction of Chancery.*

(*a*) Fitzstephen in the prologue to his life of Thomas tells us that he was remembrancer in his chancery; that he acted as subdeacon in his chapel when Thomas was celebrating mass; and that when Thomas sat to hear causes, he read out the letters and documents produced as evidence, and sometimes at the suggestion of Thomas took charge of a case as advocate[1]. At first sight this notice seems to refer to the chancellor's court. But weighty reasons have been urged in favour of its interpretation as referring to the time when Thomas was archbishop. In the

---

[1] Fitzst. iii. 1: fui in cancellaria ejus dictator; in capella, eo celebrante, subdiaconus; sedente eo ad cognitionem causarum, epistolarum et instrumentorum quae offerebantur lector, et aliquarum, eo quandoque jubente, causarum patronus.

first place, the later date is required by the allusion to the celebration of mass. Thomas was not ordained priest until the day before his consecration as archbishop. Secondly, Fitzstephen's reference to himself as a *patronus* shows that it is an ecclesiastical court which he is describing. The clergy were not allowed to plead in the secular courts[1]. Evidently the *cancellaria* in question is not the chancellor's court but the office where the archbishop transacted the judicial and administrative work of his see[2].

(*b*) Still more vague are the eulogistic allusions to the chancellor as a source of justice which occur in the Latin poems dedicated to him by John of Salisbury. In one place, speaking of Theobald's desire to have Thomas for his successor in the primacy, he pays the chancellor a marked tribute of praise. The passage is worth quotation.

[1] Robertson, *Becket*, Appendix I. Dean Hook (*Archbps.* ii. 375) infers the possibility of the later date from the description of Fitzstephen as subdeacon in Thomas' chapel. As chancellor, he remarks, Thomas had no chapel of his own, but "officiated in the king's chapel." He suggests however that "the king's chaplain, though only a deacon, may have had a subdeacon," and argues that "if causes were heard in a bishop's chancery, we may be sure they were not unheard in the king's." If the word *celebrante* merely means "officiating" in general, Hook's explanation of the reference to the *capella* may hold good. But if the word is used strictly, it settles the question: it can only refer to the celebration of the office of mass, i.e. to the time when Thomas was priest and archbishop.

[2] Robertson, *Becket*, App. I. Roger Wendover's statement that Thomas was often busy *in causis perorandis et decidendis* is explained by Robertson as relating to his legal services at the court of archbishop Theobald.

Ille Theobaldus, qui Christi praesidet aulae
  quam fidei matrem Cantia nostra colit,
hunc successurum sibi sperat et orat ut idem
  praesulis officium muniat atque locum.
hic est *carnificum qui jus cancellat iniquum*,
  quos habuit reges Anglia capta diu,
esse putans reges, quos est perpessa tyrannos;
  plus veneratur eos qui nocuere magis[1].

In the preface to his *Polycraticus* he rises to a still higher flight of eulogy. The chancellor is described as the king's right hand, the living embodiment of all that was good, the refuge of the oppressed, the light of the Church, the glory of the nation.

Ergo quaeratur lux cleri, gloria gentis
  Anglorum, regis dextera, forma boni.
quaerendus regni tibi cancellarius Angli,
  primus sollicita mente petendus erit.
hic est *qui regni leges cancellat iniquas*
  et mandata pii principis aequa facit.
si quid obest populo vel moribus est inimicum,
  quicquid id est, per eum desinit esse nocens[2].

These lines have produced quite a wealth of conjecture by way of explanation. Dean Milman[3], taking the word *carnificum* and the expressions which follow it to refer to the oppressive rule of the Norman dynasty, hazards the query,—"did Becket decide against the Norman laws by the Anglo-Saxon?"—though he confesses himself baffled by the enigma. There may be some truth in the suggestion. The development of the external

---

[1] Joh. S. *Enthelicus de Dogm. Philosoph.* 1295-1302.
[2] Joh. S. *Enthelicus in Polycrat.* i. 2 (ed. Giles).
[3] *Latin Christianity*, iii. 453, note.

machinery of justice during the Norman and early Angevin periods was one long process of fusion between Norman and English institutions; and there seems to have been a corresponding bi-legalism, if the expression may be used, in the principles of current law, which made the administration of justice a complicated task[1]. Canon Robertson, dealing with the same passage from another point of view, suggests that Thomas is here regarded not as a judicial power but as "reversing by legislation and administration what had been done under Stephen, who, notwithstanding the defectiveness of his title and the disorders of his reign, had been generally popular[2]." This conjecture certainly provides a plausible meaning for the last couplet of the former extract,—the reference to the misplaced loyalty of the English people. But it attributes too much to the chancellor. The

[1] Mrs J. R. Green in her *Life of Henry the Second* (pp. 50, 51) gives a vivid picture of the state of English law at this time. "A new confusion and uncertainty had been brought into the law in the last hundred years by the effort to fuse together Norman law and English custom. Norman landlord or Norman sheriff naturally knew little of English law or custom, and his tendency was always to enforce the feudal rules which he practised on his Norman estates. In course of time it came about that all questions of land-tenure and of the relations of classes were regulated by a kind of double system. The Englishman as well as the Norman became the 'man' of his lord as in Norman law, and was bound by the duties thus involved. On the other hand the Norman as well as the Englishman held his land subject to the customary burdens and rights recognized by English law." The whole chapter on "The government of England" is well worth studying (ch. iii. pp. 39–68).

[2] Robertson, *Becket*, Appendix III.

early administration of the reign of Henry II. is well attested by the accounts which the chroniclers and the Pipe Rolls give of the suppression of a turbulent baronage and the restoration of the judicial and financial system of Henry I. But there is no record of substantive legislation during the chancellorship of Thomas.

In the absence of sober evidence as to the precise way in which the chancellor went to work in his judicial capacity, we cannot build upon the rhetorical exaggerations of these laudatory poems in which John of Salisbury sank the historian in the panegyrist. Their language is too vague to be pressed in any technical sense[1]. Lord Lyttelton in his life of Henry II. had already suspected the existence of an element of literary humour in these lines, and taken them as a punning compliment to the "cancellarius" and little or nothing more. As he pointed out, with special reference to the lines

"leges cancellat iniquas
et mandata pii principis aequa facit,"

the language will not bear the strain of the explanation which supposes that it was already at this

[1] There is an interesting but indecisive passage in one biographer which deals in general terms with the chancellor's judicial services to his country. Auct. Anon. I. iv. 12: vices regis et negotia exsequens nunc...exercitum praeibat, nunc vacans ab expeditionibus *jura populis dictabat*. Cp. iv. 13. Thomas was always accessible to the oppressed,—faciebatque studiose judicium inopis et vindictam pauperum. There is however no reason why this should not refer merely to his services as an itinerant justice. The plural *populis* seems rather to lend itself to this explanation.

time an essential function of the chancellor's office to mitigate the rigour of common law by principles of equity. The play on the word "cancellarius" is only "a curious anticipation of the chancellor's equitable jurisdiction as developed at a later period[1]." In the earlier part of Henry II.'s reign it was the Curia Regis that was the "court of remedial and equitable jurisdiction[2]." It was not till after the later subdivision of the Curia Regis into different courts of judicature that the judicial supremacy of the king, which still remained unimpaired, came to exert itself through the chancellor as a source of equity[3]. Throughout the reign of Henry II. the chancery was simply the office from which the royal writs were issued, and its business was transacted either at the Curia Regis or at the Exchequer, mainly at the latter[4]. It was not sepa-

---

[1] Stubbs, *Const. Hist.* i. 352, note.

[2] William of Newburgh, bk. ii. ch. 1: quoties autem, judicibus mollius indigniusve agentibus, provincialium querimoniis pulsabatur (rex), *provisionis regiae remedium adhibebat*, illorum competenter corrigens vel negligentiam vel excessum. These *judices* are apparently the sheriffs appointed early in the reign (ordinati in cunctis regni finibus juris et legum ministri). Cp. *Dial. Scacc.* I. iv.: regis curia in qua ipse in propria persona jura decernit.

[3] Stubbs, *Const. Hist.* i. 602, note: "The chancellor's close attendance on the king made him the obvious recipient of petitions for royal grace. They were entrusted to him to keep and afterwards to hear; and this was the origin of the equitable jurisdiction of the Court of Chancery, under which he was empowered to remedy the *summum jus* of common law or provide remedies in cases which the common law failed to meet."

[4] Royal writs drawn up by the chancellor and his staff were issued either at the Exchequer or at the Curia Regis. In the

rated from the Exchequer and erected into a distinct court until the end of Richard I.'s reign or early in the reign of John, when distinct Rolls of Chancery began to be made[1]. Thomas cannot therefore be regarded as the founder of the Court of Chancery as a judicial institution. All that can be said with certainty is that his share in the work of itinerant judicature, first in conjunction with another justice, and then alone, is the first recorded instance in which judicial functions of any kind were exercised by the chancellor.

The extent to which Thomas may be credited, if he is to be credited at all, with a share in the positive legal reforms of the reign is as hard to determine as the extent of the judicial powers, if any, which he bequeathed to the chancellorship. On the one hand we have the simple fact that with the exception perhaps of the Great Assize, the date of which is unknown, the legislative reforms which make the reign of Henry II. an epoch in constitutional history are all subsequent to the chancellorship of Thomas[2]. They date from Henry's return to

Legal reform.

---

former case they were distinguished by the phrase 'his testibus *ad scaccarium*.' *Dial. Scacc.* I. 6.

[1] Madox, *Exchequer*, p. 44.

[2] Stubbs, *Select Charters*, p. 124. "Whatever may have been the positive influence of Thomas Becket as the king's confidant and chancellor—and there is nothing to show that it was ever strong enough to control or guide the purposes of his master—the removal of it, which followed shortly after his consecration as archbishop, coincides in time with the origin of Henry's legal reforms." Freeman viewed the question in a very different light. "The administrative and legislative work of Henry's reign," he says, "began while Thomas was still his chief counsellor. Henry

England in 1163, after his absence of more than four years, to take the reins of government into his own hands. At the same time it seems probable that those legislative reforms were not entire innovations but rather the completion of work begun and steadily continued earlier in the reign. During those first few years when the judicial and financial system was being reorganised by the king and his ministers, practical reforms were, no doubt, initiated which bore fruit in the later legislation. The decision of cases of disputed ownership by the "recognition" of twelve competent residents in the neighbourhood, the "presentment" of criminals by the knights and freeholders of each district—both great improvements in the administration of justice —are mentioned in the Constitutions of Clarendon in 1164 in terms which seem to imply that they had been at work for some time as a regular part of the judicial procedure. But the fact remains that the years of Thomas' chancellorship are a blank as far as legislation is concerned; and we cannot with certainty attribute to the early influence of Thomas any of the tentative reforms which were afterwards fixed by the king's legislation.

showed in after-times that he could go on with the work by himself; but it was while Thomas was at his side that it began" (*Contemp. Review*, vol. 32, p. 136). It should never be forgotten however that Henry had other helpers in the work, from Richard de Luci and Robert earl of Leicester the justiciars at the outset to the great lawyer Ranulf de Glanville at the close of his reign.

CHAPTER VI.

FINANCIAL ADMINISTRATION.

THE chancellor had an important part to play in the finance as well as in the judicature of the realm. Like the other great dignitaries of the royal household, the chancellor acted *ex officio* as a baron of the Exchequer. His duties in this capacity are clearly defined in the *Dialogus de Scaccario*[1]. He ranked next to the justiciar, the president of the Exchequer, on whose left he sat, facing the chequered table (*scaccarium*) on which the game of finance was played between sheriff and treasurer. His consent was requisite in all matters of importance[2]. He was charged with the custody of the royal seal, which was usually kept in the treasury at the Exchequer, and of the *rotulus de cancellaria*, the duplicate of the treasurer's roll, though this latter duty was discharged by proxy. In the opinion of contemporary legal authorities he was responsible like the treasurer for the accuracy of the rolls.

The chancellor at the Exchequer.

The Rolls.

[1] *Dial. Scacc.* I. 5 (Stubbs, *Select Charters*, pp. 178, 179).

[2] *Dial. Scacc.* p. 179: sicut in curia sic ad scaccarium magnus est, adeo ut sine ipsius consensu vel consilio nil magnum fiat vel fieri debeat.

"The Exchequer itself was a court of supreme jurisdiction in all matters relating to the revenue of the Crown, in which (technically speaking) the king was plaintiff and his debtors defendants[1]." The greatest importance was therefore attached to accuracy in points of fact, for the evidence of the rolls in which the transactions of the Exchequer were recorded was final in all future questions. The requisite accuracy was secured by the functions assigned to the chancellor and his subordinates. The chancellor was not always present in person, but his two chief clerks were always on duty at the Exchequer. By the side of the treasurer's clerk who wrote out the great Roll of the Pipe, as the *rotulus de thesauro* was called, at the dictation of the treasurer, sat the *scriptor cancellariae*, compiling a careful transcript of the Great Roll which was called *rotulus de cancellaria*. And beside the *scriptor cancellariae* sat the chancellor's watchful representative, the *clericus cancellarii*, whose duty it was to see that the chancellor's duplicate corresponded with the treasurer's roll down to the last iota in matter and arrangement. The chancellor's powers went further. He was at liberty to challenge the accuracy of the treasurer's record as it was being compiled, and

---

[1] Introduction to Pipe Rolls, p. 44. Cp. *Dial. Scacc.* I. 4 (Stubbs, *Select Charters*, p. 177): non enim in ratiociniis sed in multiplicibus judiciis excellens scaccarii scientia consistit....At cum coeperit multiplex inquisitio fieri de his rebus quae varie fisco proveniunt et diversis modis requiruntur et a vicecomitibus non eodem modo perquiruntur, discernere si secus egerint quibusdam grave est, et ob hoc circa haec scientia scaccarii major esse dicitur.

suggest the alterations which seemed to him to be required; and if the treasurer persisted in holding to his own record, the chancellor was allowed to argue the point and insist on its being settled by a judicial verdict of the barons of the Exchequer in session[1].

The chancellor's staff had other duties also in connexion with the Exchequer[2]. All royal writs relating to payments out of the treasury, allowances made to the sheriffs in consideration of previous outlay, and remissions of debts sanctioned by the barons in session, were made out in duplicate by the *scriptor cancellariae*, who also drew up at the close of the session the forms of summons which were to be sent round to the sheriffs and other debtors of the king in view of the next session of the Exchequer. The responsibilities of the *clericus cancellarii* were still greater. He had charge of all the duplicate writs made out by the *scriptor cancellariae*[3]; he corrected and sealed the forms of summons; as each sheriff came forward with his accounts, he glanced from time to time at the roll of the previous year, until the sheriff had accounted for each item against his name; and, taking from the sheriff the writ by which he had been summoned, read out the debts there recorded, demanded satis-

Writs.

[1] Introduction to Pipe Rolls, pp. 44, 45. "A further safeguard was employed by the Crown in the designation of its chancellor to represent the equitable jurisdiction of the sovereign at the Exchequer, as a foil to official callousness or rapacity."
[2] *Dial. Scacc.* I. 5, 6 (Stubbs, *Select Charters*, pp. 187-189).
[3] The original writs made out by the *scriptor cancellariae* were handed over to the care of the marshal (*marescallus*).

faction for each one singly, and ran his pen through each item as it was paid or accounted for, in order to ascertain exactly the sums that still remained due to the king. In brief, the great bulk of the secretarial work of the Exchequer was done by the chancellor's clerks.

Transactions at the Exchequer. Two full sessions of the Exchequer were held in the year, at Easter and at Michaelmas respectively. The sheriffs produced their accounts, which were inspected by the barons and finally balanced at the Michaelmas sessions, when the roll for the year was compiled. In these accounts each sheriff stated the amount of revenue due to the king from the ferm of the shire, the pleas of the local courts, the Danegeld, and the different feudal charges, and enumerated as a set-off the sums paid away by himself in liquidation of the king's debts in his shire, the expenses of public business, the cost of provisions for the court, and the travelling expenses of the king and his guests within the limits of the sheriff's district[1]. Much of this expenditure was commanded in the first instance or sanctioned at the Exchequer by royal officers, and where this was the case the Pipe Rolls record the fact. A few examples will suffice to illustrate the chancellor's share of the work. In the Pipe Roll of 3 Henry II. (1156–1157) the sheriff of Lincolnshire is allowed £72. 19s. 10d. for the travelling expenses of the king of Scotland, *per cancellarium et comitem Legecestriue*[2]. In the roll

---

[1] Stubbs, *Constit. Hist.* i. 380.
[2] Pipe Roll, 3 Henry II. p. 83 (ed. Hunter): in corredio regis Scotiae.

4 Henry II. (1157–1158) the sheriffs of London are allowed £68. 3s. 4d. under the general head of payments[1], 40s. for the king's huntsmen and hounds, and 20s. for a palfrey for a certain clerk named Thomas, all three allowances made *per cancellarium*. In the roll 5 Henry II. (1158–1159) the sheriff of Dorset is allowed £7. 6s. 8d. for money paid away to a certain person *per cancellarium, per breve regis*, i.e. by order of the chancellor, grounded on the king's writ, in obedience to which the sheriff had paid the money. In the accounts of the sheriff of Buckinghamshire and Bedfordshire, in the Pipe Roll of 4 Henry II. (1157–1158), two persons in succession who were each responsible for 100 marks, apparently the cost of the judicial division of a certain landed estate, and had each paid 50 marks into the treasury, are set down as owing 50 marks (the remainder of their liabilities) *secundum breve cancellarii*, i.e. in accordance with a writ of the chancellor[2].

---

[1] Pipe Roll, 4 Henry II. p. 112 (ed. Hunter): *in soltis*. This may perhaps be the technical use of *solta* (= *soluta*, sums paid), i.e. restitution of the value of stolen property to the owner. If the sheriff prosecuted, all the goods of the thief were confiscated to the Crown; but if the injured person prosecuted, the value of the stolen goods (*solta*) was restored to him out of the thief's chattels, and he also received compensation (*persolta* or *prosolta*) for his time and trouble. *Dial. Scacc.* II. 10.

[2] Pipe Roll, 4 Henry II. p. 140. The first entry is: Willelmus de Buissei reddidit compotum (i.e. gave an account) de c m. argenti pro terra Walteri de Espec partienda contra Robertum de Ros. In thesauro L m. argenti. Et debet L m. argenti secundum breve cancellarii. The second entry is identical, except the name of the debtor.

Perdona.

There is one interesting class of notices in the Pipe Rolls which calls for a somewhat fuller treatment. It is the constantly recurring group of items under the head of *perdona*. The *perdonum* of the Pipe Rolls, though it is the lineal ancestor of our word pardon, has not exactly the same meaning as its philological descendant. It is strictly the remission of a debt. The debt in question might be a judicial fine imposed by the king's justices; or it might be, what it seems more frequently to have been, a financial charge upon the property or person of the king's tenants, baron, prelate, freeholder, or city-gild. The chancellor's name occurs frequently every year in the different shires as the recipient of such *perdona*—remissions of charges which in many cases he shared with the other barons of the Exchequer, who were *ex officio* exempt from the *communis assisa* (= the general taxation) of their counties, from scutage, from the *murdrum* fine, the Danegeld, and various other contributions to the royal revenue[1]. These *perdona* were granted usually by king's writ, directed to the barons of the Exchequer and tested at the Exchequer by two of the greater officials[2]; and they appear in the sheriff's

---

[1] *Dial. Scacc.* I. 8 (Stubbs, *Select Charters*, p. 198).

[2] *Dial. Scacc.* I. 6 (Stubbs, *ib.* p. 188). Cp. Intr. to Pipe Rolls, pp. 49, 50. A specimen writ is given in the *Dialogus:* "Rex baronibus de scaccario salutem. Perdono illi vel clamo quietum hunc vel illum de hoc vel de illo. Testibus hiis ad scaccarium." This is strictly an *official* writ drawn up in the king's name by order of the barons, *praecognita regis voluntate*, not an *original* writ issued by the king himself: but the official writs were reproductions of an original writ.

accounts in the Pipe Rolls as a deduction from his liabilities under the heading *in perdonis per breve regis,* followed by a list of names in the dative case, the recipients of the royal grant of exemption. Only two exceptions to this rule occur in the first four years of the reign. In the Pipe Roll of 2 Henry II. (pp. 9, 23) are two entries *in perdonis per breve reginae,*—the queen here replacing the king in the exercise of this royal prerogative. But in the fifth year (1158–1159) the chancellor's name begins to appear in connexion with these *perdona* in a way which at first sight suggests that as his influence increased he was permitted to exercise his own authority in granting the remission of debts due to the king[1]. In the Pipe Roll of 5 Henry II. (p. 12) there is an entry *in perdonis per cancellarium,* and in the Roll 7 Henry II. (1160–1161) there are six entries *in perdonis praecepto cancellarii* to persons in different counties,—in Norfolk and Suffolk (p. 4), Herefordshire (p. 20), Northumberland (p. 24), Staffordshire (p. 41) and Hampshire (pp. 57, 59). These notices certainly look as though the chancellor had been solely responsible for the *perdona* there recorded. But this impression is not borne out by comparison with other *perdona* mentioned in those two years. In the Pipe Roll of 5 Henry II. (p. 10) there is an entry *in perdonis per breve regis per cancellarium;* and in the Roll 7 Henry II. (p. 50)

---

[1] Mrs J. R. Green, *Henry the Second,* p. 80: "There are even entries in the Pipe Roll of pardons issued by him, the first instance of such a right ever used by any one save king or queen."

an entry occurs *in perdono per breve regis praecepto cancellarii*. It is evident that the phrases *per cancellarium* and *praecepto cancellarii* appended in these two last instances to *perdona* based on a writ of the king cannot be pressed to imply the independent action of the chancellor in the cases cited above where no writ is mentioned. They seem rather to imply a previous warrant of some kind from the king[1]. The question is somewhat obscure, but, as far as can be inferred from extant records, the method of procedure seems to have been as follows. The writs were issued by the chancellor in the king's name. In the cases therefore where no writ is mentioned, it is probable that no writ was issued at all, but that a verbal order for the *perdonum* in question was given by the king to the chancellor and transmitted directly *by* him (*per cancellarium*) or indirectly *through* him (*praecepto cancellarii*) to the barons of the Exchequer as a warrant to them not to claim the debt from the favoured individual. In all these cases therefore the chancellor was only the channel of royal favour, the agent by whom

---

[1] Miss Norgate, the writer of *England under the Angevin Kings*, suggested that possibly the six entries *praecepto cancellarii* in Pipe Roll 7 Henry II., compared with the entry *per breve regis praecepto cancellarii* in Pipe Roll 7 Henry II. p. 50, should be explained by the supposition of a previous *writ* from the king. In reply to my suggestion that the variation between the entries *per cancellarium* and *per breve regis per cancellarium*, which had escaped her notice, should perhaps be explained by a similar supposition, Miss Norgate kindly furnished me with the following information as to the probable procedure in granting *perdona*, for which she was indebted to Mr Salisbury of the Record Office.

the royal mandate, written or verbal, was conveyed to the officers of the Exchequer.

It is not until the eighth year of the reign, when the chancellor had become the archbishop, that we find him granting *perdona* by a writ of his own, independently of the king. In the Pipe Roll of 8 Henry II. (Michaelmas 1161–1162) occurs the following entry (p. 64): *in perdono per breve archiepiscopi Waltero filio Warini* 1 m. It is scarcely probable that in a record so accurate as the Pipe Roll a writ issued by the chancellor would be described as a writ of the archbishop because he had been made archbishop since the issue of the writ. We can hardly suppose therefore that this writ was presented at the Easter session of the Exchequer, when Thomas was still only the king's chancellor. Its presentation at the Exchequer must be assigned to the Michaelmas session of 1162, when the roll for the year was compiled. It may have been issued after Easter, during the brief interval between the consecration of Thomas in June and his resignation of the chancellor's seal; but unless it falls within that short space of time, we are left to the conclusion that it was not until after he had ceased to be chancellor that he was allowed to exercise the royal prerogative of pardon on his own authority[1].

[1] Howlett (*Chronicle of Stephen and Henry II.* vol. iii. preface, p. lvii) remarks that this entry in the Roll of 8 Henry II. "speaks eloquently of the elevation which precedes a fall." Miss Norgate adds: "In nearly all the Rolls there are plenty of *solta* and *dona per breve* or *praecepto* of the queen and of the justiciars whenever the king is out of the country: but I see only two *perdona per breve* (other than that of the archbishop above) of any one

The chancellor and the royal revenues.

The chancellor's financial powers were not confined to his seat at the Exchequer. The regular contributions twice a year from the sheriffs of the counties did not constitute the whole of the royal revenues. There were other occasional and irregular sources of income which did not fall within the cognisance of the Exchequer, but were entrusted to the control of the chancellor. While he held that office, Thomas was responsible for the receipt and evidently had a voice and a hand in the expenditure of the revenues that flowed into the royal treasury from vacant sees, abbeys, and baronies. But here we are treading on uncertain ground. It is difficult to distinguish between his expenditure of his own personal resources, and his share in the expenditure of the resources of the king which passed through his hands; and the demand which the king afterwards made for the accounts of his chancellorship has awakened in the mind of one great modern historian at least a suspicion, which seems to have

except the king, and those are of the queen in 2 Henry II. (pp. 9, 23)."

Mr Salisbury of the Record Office suggests that even this pardon *per breve archiepiscopi* may not mean all that it seems at first sight to mean. If it came between the consecration and the resignation of the chancellorship, it may be only a scribe's blunder for *per breve regis praecepto archiepiscopi*, i.e. a royal writ issued through the archbishop as chancellor. But in view of all the precautions taken to ensure absolute accuracy in the compilation of the rolls—with the treasurer's clerk writing the great Roll of the Pipe at the treasurer's dictation, and the *scriptor cancellariae* copying it word for word under the watchful eye of the *clericus cancellarii*—it is not likely that such a mistake would have been made or passed over unnoticed.

been already entertained, if not expressed, by the contemporaries of Thomas, that the two sets of money were not always kept strictly separate.

The chancellor's expenditure. The expenditure of the chancellor, if we may rely on the testimony of his biographers, must have been enormous. They are never weary of expatiating on his magnificence and liberality. His household was the centre of court society. His board was always free and open to all who came to the royal council, without distinction of rank or person. The only passport required was an honest exterior. Scarcely a day passed without a visit from earls and barons summoned by personal invitation of the chancellor. The stream of guests overflowed the limits of his table, and the mass of knights crowded out of the benches found the floor of the hall ready strewn every day with fresh straw in winter and fresh rushes in summer, by the kind forethought of their host the chancellor, while the board itself groaned beneath the weight of gold and silver plate and rare and dainty dishes[1]. This may of course be a picture of the special hospitality extended by Thomas to all comers on the occasion of the three great national councils of the year, when all tenants-in-chief of the king were entitled to present themselves at court. But the ordinary expenses of the chancellor's household were heavy enough. It was

---

[1] Fitzstephen (iii. 20, 21) dwells with enthusiastic delight upon his master's grandeur during the period of his chancellorship, taking care at the same time to remark that amid all this luxury the poor were not forgotten: "summe tamen sobrius erat in his, ut de divite mensa dives colligeretur eleemosyna."

the recognised school of chivalry for the young scions of noble houses. The magnates of England and sometimes of foreign kingdoms sent their sons to be trained in all the arts and accomplishments of a courtly life under the eye of the chancellor, and to win their spurs in his service. The king himself placed his little son and heir in Thomas' charge, to be educated in the society of the youthful knights who would be his barons if ever he succeeded his father on the throne[1]. Each of them had his little retinue in keeping with his rank, and all went to swell the lordly train of knights and attendants that was the glory of Thomas the ambassador and Thomas the soldier. His splendour was no less marked when travelling. He had a fleet of six or more ships of his own, and gave free passage to all who wished to cross the channel, and good bounty to his crews on landing. Even the king was not exempt from his persistent generosity. The royal fleet, we are told by the same informant[2], consisted of a single ship; and the chancellor presented the king with three goodly vessels fully equipped as his own gift. The magnificence of his embassy to the French court and his services in the French wars have already been described in detail; but they must not be forgotten in a review of the chancellor's expenditure. The princely grandeur of his retinue,

[1] This was Henry, born in February 1155 (Robert de Monte, A.D. 1155), usually called *primogenitus filius regis*, as his elder brother William died in infancy; sometimes described as *rex juvenis* or *junior*, sometimes actually (after his coronation in 1170) as *Henricus tertius*.

[2] Fitzst. iii. 26.

the largess which he lavished on court and city and university alike at Paris, the contingent of seven hundred knights and soldiers of his own household, the array of mercenaries, horse and foot, fully five thousand all told—all within the space of two years—represent an amount of expenditure which few baronial revenues could have sustained. It is difficult to credit Fitzstephen's statement that these expenses all came out of the chancellor's own purse. It is possible that Fitzstephen has in some cases attributed to the personal expenditure of the chancellor sums that were really expended by him as a royal official out of the king's revenues. He states, for instance, that when the Norwegian envoys came to England, Thomas sent his own representative to escort them to the king's court and supply all their wants *nomine cancellarii*[1]. But in the brief notice of this embassy in the Pipe Rolls the chancellor is not mentioned; and the phrase *per breve regis* with which the entry concludes seems rather to imply that the expenditure was authorised by the chancellor officially, if at all, not undertaken by him as an act of private hospitality[2]. Again, Fitzstephen puts down the equipment and maintenance of the chancellor's contingent in the war of Toulouse entirely to his private account; but it is at least possible that Edward Grim is nearer the mark in dividing

---

[1] Fitzst. iii. 26.
[2] Pipe Roll 2 Henry II. p. 4, in the accounts of the sheriffs of London: et in donis quae Rex misit Regibus de Norwega et *in liberatione nuntiorum Regum*, £37. 2s. 8d. *per breve Regis.* Cp. the accounts of the sheriff of Cambridgeshire (p. 15): et nuntiis Regum de Norwega, 3s.

the cost between the chancellor's private purse and the king's treasury[1].

Another suggestion has been made with a view to discounting the possibly exaggerated statements of the chancellor's expenditure. It has been suggested that the extravagant banquets described by Fitzstephen took place in the *aula regis* and at the king's cost,—that it was the policy of Thomas to attract the nobility to the court and strengthen the hands of the Crown by maintaining the traditions of royal hospitality which Henry seemed inclined to neglect,—that Thomas in other words was merely acting as deputy host, presiding in the name of the king, who was only an occasional visitor at his own royal table where earls and barons met at the great national councils. On this supposition Thomas' private establishment cost him comparatively little, and it was the resources thus economised that he lavished in the interests of his king and country on the embassy to Paris and the campaigns of Toulouse and Normandy. This idea has been well worked out by the biographer of the archbishops of Canterbury in his life of Thomas[2]. But it seems irreconcilable with the incidental allusions of contemporary writers which point to the household of

---

[1] Grim, ii. 364: larga nimirum ac liberali manu *tam proprios quam regni reditus* profudit in militum stipendiis et donariis profuturos. This is not quite clear. It may mean that besides his private expenditure on his own contingent he acted as paymaster-general in collecting and maintaining out of the royal revenues the great army of mercenaries which the scutage of 1159 enabled Henry to employ.

[2] Dean Hook, *Archbishops of Canterbury*, ii. 367–369.

Thomas the chancellor as almost a rival court. Grim notes that his retinue and guest-roll were no less imposing than the king's; in fact the king, he says, complained more than once that Thomas had emptied the royal board[1]. Fitzstephen's language[2] too seems as distinctly to prove that the grandeur of which he speaks was the hospitality of a separate establishment of the chancellor's own, not the hospitality of the royal hall administered by proxy for a king who "affected to despise almost the decencies of society."

It is quite possible however that Thomas had some aim of state policy in view, though the hospitality was his own. The magnificence of his embassy to Paris was prompted largely by a desire to impress the French court and people with the greatness of English royalty as seen in the person of its accredited representative. In a similar way the splendid hospitality of his establishment at home may have been intended partly to throw a lustre round the precincts of the court and make the royal household a social centre from which the influence of the Crown would tell upon the feudal baronage none the less powerfully because peacefully exerted. Thomas may have been led into this extravagant outlay not so much by the purely selfish motive of personal vanity as by

[1] Grim, ii. 363: nec cancellario prorsus quam regi minor comitatus adhaesit ita ut nonnunquam corriperetur a rege quod regis hospitium vacuasset. Cp. the similar language of Auct. Anon. I. iv. 13.

[2] Fitzst. iii. 25: aliquotiens ad hospitium cancellarii rex comedebat, tum ludendi causa, tum gratia videndi quae de ejus domo et mensa narrabantur.

that "expansive selfishness," as it has been well described, which made him identify himself with the cause to which he was attached by force of circumstances. If this view is tenable, then the suggestion that Thomas did not always discriminate in his expenditure between his private income and the royal revenues which passed through his hands loses something of the discredit which it involves. It would still amount, plainly speaking, to a charge of misappropriation, but not of personal aggrandisement. Thomas may have mixed up some of the king's revenues with his own; but both alike were spent as much on the glorification of the Crown as on the magnifying of himself and his office.

The chancellor's income. But the facts of the case scarcely require such a supposition. If his expenditure was enormous, his income was also enormous. His official allowance as a resident member of the royal household, which is recorded in the Black Book of the Exchequer[1], was perhaps the least part of his total income. It consisted of five shillings a day in the currency of the time, one plain simnel, two spiced simnels, a

[1] An important document of Henry II.'s reign, quoted in Madox, *Exchequer*, p. 43: haec est constitutio domus regiae, de procurationibus: cancellarius v s. in die, etc. The same allowance was made to the steward (*dapifer*), the chief butler (*magister pincerna*), the chief chamberlain (*camerarius*), the treasurer, the constable, and the chief marshal (Stubbs, *Const. Hist.* i. 345, note on *Liber Niger Scaccarii*). It was therefore no sumptuous salary, judging from the minor importance of the officials who received the same allowance. The chancellor, it must be remembered, was strictly only the secretary of the royal household until Thomas lifted the office to the higher level of a minister of state.

sextary of clear wine, a sextary of ordinary household wine, one large wax candle, and forty pieces of candle besides. It was evidently intended to meet the necessary current expenses of his household and nothing more. The bulk of the chancellor's income was derived from other sources, ecclesiastical and secular. He still retained the rich archdeaconry of Canterbury and other lucrative preferments bestowed upon him by Theobald, his prebends and his canonries, and he now held in addition the deanery of Hastings, acquired since his appointment to the chancellorship. Other posts of importance he held by royal grant. The king was as generous to his chancellor as the primate had been to his clerk; and Thomas was placed in charge of the Tower of London with its military guard, the castle of Eye with its hundred and forty knights, and the castle of Berkhampstead[1]. The permanent income of the chancellor, it will be seen, must have reached a high figure. But it was apparently augmented still further to meet the chancellor's expenses. There was a rumour afloat in 1160 that the king had

[1] Fitzst. iii. 20. Cp. the list of preferments attributed to him by the prior of Leicester (ib. p. 26).

The tower of London was, along with Windsor, in the charge of Richard de Luci at the time of the settlement of the Crown in 1153 (Rymer, *Foedera*, i. 8). Vacant baronies falling into the hands of the Crown, if not granted out again to another lord, were retained by the Crown and farmed like a shire under the title of an *honor*. Some of these *honores* were utilised as a source of income for ministers of the Crown (Stubbs, *Const. Hist.* i. 401, note).

Thomas cancellarius appears in the Pipe Rolls 2, 4, 5, 6, 7 Henry II. as responsible for the ferm due to the king from Berkhampstead.

granted the revenues of three vacant sees to swell the income of his favourite minister[1]. It was a source of grave anxiety to Archbishop Theobald and his faithful secretary John of Salisbury, who were hoping for the chancellor's influence in securing the speedy appointment of their candidate to the vacant see of Exeter. It may have been true, it may have been false; but it is at least an indication that Henry and Thomas between them took care that the chancellor's income kept pace with his expenditure.

The release from secular obligations, 1162.

The disparity therefore between his income and his expenditure proves less on inspection than it seems at first sight, even if it does not vanish altogether. But the suspicion of maladministration rests partly on another ground, the subsequent demand which the king made in 1164 for the accounts of his stewardship in the matter of vacant sees and baronies. Its date falls beyond the limits of this essay, but its retrospective bearing on the chancellorship of Thomas is too important to leave it out of consideration. The facts are as follows. After his election as archbishop at London and before his consecration, Thomas was released from all secular obligations, at the earnest request of Henry bishop of Winchester[2], by Richard de Luci

[1] Joh. S. *Ep.* 9 (v. 14): fama est apud nos quod trium vacantium episcopatuum reditus ad liberationem vestram vobis dominus rex concesserit.

[2] Auct. Anon. i. iv. 17. Bishop Henry's speech to "the young king": dominus, ait, cancellarius, electus noster, multo jam tempore in domo regis patris vestri et in omni regno summum obtinuit locum, habuitque in dispositione sua regnum, nec

the justiciar, the king's little son Henry and a number of the barons in the name of the king, who was then absent in Normandy. About the simple fact of this release there is no doubt. It was mentioned in the king's letter to the Pope requesting the transmission of the pallium for the duly consecrated archbishop[1]. It is the meaning and extent of the release that is uncertain.

Two years later this quittance was challenged at the Council of Northampton in October 1164. Our information as to the facts of this trial comes direct at first hand. Two of Thomas' biographers, Fitzstephen and Herbert of Bosham, were present at the council in attendance on the archbishop, and they have both recorded the proceedings in full, though not always in agreement on points of detail[2]. Fitzstephen mentions three distinct attacks made upon the archbishop. (1) Thomas was first required to account for £300 received by him as warden of the "honours" of Eye and Berkhampstead. He refused to recognize the charge as a formal indictment: he had been cited to defend himself against John the marshal, and had received no notice of any further

Council of Northampton, 1164.

aliquid in tempore suo in regno actitatum est nisi ad suum arbitrium; unde eum liberum et absolutum ab omni nexu et ministerio curiali, ab omni etiam querela et calumnia, omnique penitus occasione ecclesiae Dei et nobis tradi postulamus, quatenus ab hac hora et deinceps emancipatus et expeditus quae Dei sunt libere exsequatur. Cp. Grim, ii. 367. Fitzst. iii. 36.

[1] Auct. Anon. II. iv. 105.
[2] Fitzst. iii. 53 foll. Herb. iii. 298 foll. Ralph de Diceto (afterwards dean of London) was also present at the council (Fitzst. iii. 59), and collateral information of some value is given in his *Imagines Historiarum*, A.D. 1164.

proceedings. But he made an informal reply to the king's demands. The money had been spent, with a great deal more, on the repair of the Tower of London[1] and the two castles in question[2]. This, he said, was plain enough for eyes to see. The king however refused to acknowledge the fact, and claimed a judicial verdict; and the archbishop, unwilling to quarrel with the king on a matter of money, consented to pay what was demanded of him, and found lay sureties for the sum. But heavier charges were in reserve. (2) The next day the king claimed by messenger two separate sums of 500 marks each, the one lent to Thomas by the king for the expedition of Toulouse, the other borrowed by Thomas from a Jewish money-lender on the king's security. Herbert of Bosham (who mentions one sum only of £500, claimed by the king in repayment of a loan) gives the archbishop's reply[3]. He admitted the receipt of the money, but described it as a gift, not a loan, and reproached the king in person with meanness in

---

[1] Fitzst. iii. 19 dwells with admiration on the rapidity with which the repairs were effected under the chancellor's orders between Easter and Whitsuntide, though the place was almost a ruin at the outset. The accounts of the sheriffs of London in the Pipe Roll of 2 Henry II. (p. 3) contain an item of £6. 15s. 10d. *ad munitionem turris*, which perhaps should be referred to these repairs.

[2] The Pipe Rolls speak for the sums expended by Thomas on Berkhampstead: e.g. Pipe Roll 2 Henry II. p. 21: in operatione castelli 63s. et in restauratione manorii £13. 14s. Pipe Roll 4 Henry II. p. 152: in reficiendis domibus regis £10. Cp. similar entries in Pipe Roll 5 Henry II. p. 7, 6 Henry II. p. 12, and 7 Henry II. p. 68.

[3] Herb. iii. 298.

recalling his own present as a debt. Thomas however could not prove the gift, and the Curia Regis—bishops and barons alike—gave a verdict in favour of the king. The primate's property, they alleged, had been confiscated by the verdict of the previous day in the case of John the marshal; but five of his friends came forward as sureties for the payment of the sum claimed. (3) Last came the most crushing blow of all, a comprehensive demand for the accounts of all the revenues received by the chancellor from the vacant archbishopric, bishoprics, abbeys, baronies and honours which had been entrusted to his charge[1]. The total was estimated at 30,000 marks. The archbishop declared that the king had received more than once an account of these revenues, which had been spent, he said, on the king's business[2]. But his main defence was the fact that he had been released publicly in the king's name from all secular obligations at the time of his election to the primacy. He reminded the king of this fact in his own reply before the court, and it was also pleaded on his behalf by Henry bishop of Winchester, whose testimony was supported by the other bishops in a body[3]. We are not here concerned with the sequel—the king's angry persistence and the archbishop's

---

[1] Fitzst. iii. 54. Herb. iii. 299. Auct. Anon. I. iv. 49 says £30,000, quas tempore cancellariae de pecunia regia *minus caute expendisse a quibusdam deferebatur.*

[2] Auct. Anon. I. iv. 49. Will. C. i. 38.

[3] Herb. iii. 300. According to Fitzstephen, iii. 63, Thomas had to appeal forcibly to their recollection in order to confute the obstinacy of the king, who persisted in ignoring the fact of the release.

appeal to Rome in anticipation of the verdict of the king and the Curia Regis. The two points to be considered now are (1) the validity of the archbishop's plea and (2) the justice of the king's claim; in other words, (1) the question whether the release from secular obligations in 1162 covered all pecuniary liabilities and precluded any future enquiry into those liabilities, and (2) the question whether there was any ground for the charge of maladministration which was implied in this demand for the accounts of the chancellorship.

Meaning of this quittance.
(1) It is evident that Thomas and his friends on their part regarded the quittance of 1162 as a full and sufficient bar against all pecuniary claims, precluding all enquiry into the financial side of the chancellor's administration. According to one biographer, Edward Grim, that was the avowed intention of the bishop of Winchester in asking for the formal release in question; and the king's ministers interpreted it at the time in the same light as the bishop[1]. John of Salisbury, in a letter written to Baldwin, archdeacon of Exeter, two years after the Council of Northampton, brings it forward as a conclusive answer to an imaginary opponent. Some might assert, he says, that Thomas, conscious

[1] Grim, ii. 367 (the bishop's speech): "cancellarius ut primus patriae thesauros regis et reditus regni in manu habuit, et ut diversa poscebant negotia tractavit. Verum ne cui in posterum pateat exactioni vel calumniae quasi qui pro libera magis voluntate quam regni commodo dissipaverit bona domini sui, liberum eum et absolutum ab omni reclamatione suscipimus." Ad quem ministri regis, "ex ore," inquiunt, "regis liberum eum clamamus ab omni calumnia et exactione nunc et in omne tempus."

of his defalcations and doubtful of his own dexterity, had fallen back upon "an imprudent and impudent subterfuge" which amounted to a tacit confession of his guilt and a justification of his opponents' procedure[1]. In reply to this charge John simply repeats the fact of this quittance of 1162—a fact none the less certain because the king had ignored it at Northampton[2]. But that was not the view taken by everybody. Gilbert Foliot's famous letter of remonstrance in 1166 throws a different light on the question. Speaking of this very trial of 1164, he regrets that Thomas had allowed his mistaken zeal to drive him into defiance of the jurisdiction of the king's court. The king, he says, was only acting within his rights in asking for a legal settlement of a financial claim[3]. There was no danger to Thomas

---

[1] Joh. S. *Ep.* 263 (vi. 96): sed fortasse dicet aliquis,...in pecuniaria (causa) conventus, in jure sibi conscius iniquitatis et de praestigiis suis diffisus, subterfugio imprudenti et impudenti suam quodam modo, immo plane, professus est injustitiam et partem justificavit adversam. It is not clear whether the subterfuge in question was the plea of quittance or the appeal to Rome against the foregone conclusion of the case. Probably it was the latter.

[2] Joh. S. *Ep.* 263 (vi. 97): quod certum erat revocabatur in dubium, ut comicum illud fere in omnium volveretur animis, "Quod scio, nescio." Quis enim nesciebat quod rex cancellarium suum ob omni administratione et obligatione liberum reddidit ad regimen Cantuariensis ecclesiae?

[3] Foliot, *Ep.* 225 (v. 535): utinam...cum a vobis debita quaedam reposceret dominus noster rex, cum de summa pecuniae quam in manu vestra ex caducis quibusdam excrevisse memorabat, quod jus dictaret id sibi solum peteret exhiberi, ad declinandum regalis curiae judicium tunc se vester minime zelus erexisset.

involved in the trial. Then referring to this disputed quittance of 1162 he remarks: "The king wished you to be transferred from the court to the government of the Church; and by that very fact released you, as the majority consider, from the obligations of his service. If there was no reference to debts, if promotion did not carry with it any release from such debts, then the difficulty could have been met almost entirely by a formal plea to the effect that the money had been spent on the king's business; and if there was any item that could not be included in the account, then the king's claim, which was prompted by irritation rather than by deliberate avarice, might have been satisfied quietly, and this legal enquiry might have come to a peaceful and honourable conclusion without such a storm as this[1]." Foliot expressed this view of the situation on more than one occasion. At the conference of Henry II. with the cardinals and prelates at Argentan in November 1167, as we learn from a friend of Thomas who described the meeting in a letter to the archbishop, Foliot stated the case at issue from the

[1] Foliot, *Ep.* 225 (v. 535): ad regimen ecclesiae vos a curia transferri voluit, et ab ipsius nexibus hoc ipso vos (ut plures opinantur) absolvit: quod si ad debita minime referendum est, ut evectus loco sic absolvatur a debito, poterat negotium per exceptionem in rem versum plurimum expediri, et siquid compoto nequivisset includi, irate magis repetenti sua quam avide de reliquo poterat satisdari, et civilis haec causa absque hoc rerum turbine pace poterat honestissima terminari. Foliot complains that Thomas had chosen instead to create a sensation by standing upon his dignity as archbishop of Canterbury and denouncing the trial of a primate by the king's court as an unprecedented act of coercion.

same point of view that he had already taken in his letter of remonstrance quoted above. He related how the king at Northampton had demanded 44000 marks in all on account of revenues entrusted to the chancellor's control, and how Thomas had replied that in the first place he was not involved in debt to the king at the time of his elevation to the primacy, and, secondly, even if he had been so implicated, he was absolved by the very fact of his promotion. "At this point," says Thomas' informant, "the bishop of London ridiculed you, remarking that you believed that debts were remitted on promotion like sins in baptism[1]."

Foliot was not the only man who doubted the validity of this plea of quittance. Ralph de Diceto, who was present at the trial in 1164, says there were many persons who thought that an account might justly be exacted from the archbishop notwithstanding the fact of this quittance, which, he says, Thomas was unable to trace back to the king's consent[2]. There is besides an expression in Herbert of Bosham's story of the trial which has been interpreted as a proof that the idea of pleading this quittance as a bar to the king's action only came to the bishop of Winchester as a second thought—an expedient that suggested itself after, if not in consequence of, the discussion of the crisis with the rest of the bishops[3]. The question is further complicated by

[1] *Ep.* 339 (vi. 271): et ibi derisit vos Londoniensis, dicens vos credere quod, sicut in baptismo remittuntur peccata, ita et in promotione relaxantur debita.

[2] Ralph de Diceto, A.D. 1164 (537 Twysden).

[3] Herb. iii. 300: verumtamen convocatis pontificibus, post

the fact that the king, who, by mentioning the release in his despatch to the Pope, sanctioned it afterwards, whether he had previously authorised it or not, evidently expected Thomas to retain the chancellorship. It is not easy therefore to understand in what light the king regarded this quittance. Thomas on his part may have meditated or foreseen a speedy resignation of the chancellorship, in which case the quittance might stand him in good stead as a defence against vexatious charges. But from the king's point of view—the prospect of having the chancellorship and the primacy united in the hands of the same minister—this release, if it referred to financial obligations, could only mean a remission of liabilities which would at once begin to reaccumulate. It is difficult from that point of view to avoid the suspicion that Thomas and his friends strained the meaning of this formal release. Foliot and the Curia Regis clearly denied its validity as a bar against subsequent enquiry into the financial transactions of Thomas' chancellorship. Yet it could not be regarded by the king as a release from secular duties, for he was counting all the while on the continuance of Thomas' services as chancellor, and Thomas did continue to act as chancellor for some little time after his consecration. It was evidently

deliberationem multam quid respondendum agendumve ad haec... Henricus tunc Wintoniensis episcopus, qui quidem archipraesuli favit sed propter metum occultus, *tandem* recordatus est quod in electione archipraesulis, tunc Cantuariensis archidiaconi et regis cancellarii, ab omnibus curiae nexibus Anglicanae ecclesiae redditus fuerit absolutus. Robertson, *Becket*, Appendix xvii. p. 337.

something that was considered a necessary precaution in the interests of the primacy and the Church. Fitzstephen compares it to the custom of requiring an abbot to renounce all claims on the obedience of any monk who had been elected abbot of another monastery, before the abbot-elect could enter upon his new responsibilities[1]. It could scarcely be a mere recognition of the fact that in case of a conflict of interests the ecclesiastical duty of the primate must take precedence of the secular duty of the chancellor. Fitzstephen's parallel would seem to imply an absolute transference from the service of the king to the service of the Church; and if it were only certain that Thomas and his friend the bishop of Winchester had the immediate resignation of the chancellorship in view, the release would be perfectly intelligible on their side. It would be an obvious precaution against retrospective charges of maladministration; and it would involve in their intention both a quittance of all financial claims and a release from all secular duties. It is just this absence of evidence as to the intentions of Thomas and his friends and the expectations of the justiciar and the other consenting parties with regard to the tenure or resignation of the chancellorship that makes it

[1] Fitzst. iii. 54: Cantuariensi ecclesiae redditus fuerat liber a cancellaria et omni regis saeculari querela; cum quaelibet etiam abbatia vacans monachum alienum abbatem sibi electum recipere nolit, nisi immunem ab omni obedientia abbatis ejus sibi dimissum. This may be a comment of Fitzstephen's own upon the advice given to Thomas at Northampton by his friends the bishops; or it may be part of their advice, a suggestion that he should rely upon this plea of quittance.

impossible to pronounce with certainty upon the meaning attached to this formal release. It is possible that it was given without any specification of its precise bearing; but it is hardly probable that it was requested without some definite idea of what was wanted. The language of the contemporary biographers—though perhaps somewhat coloured by the turn which events had taken at Northampton—is too emphatic for us to accept with regard to Thomas and his friends the statement of a modern biographer that it is "doubtful whether the release was understood as an acquittance of all pecuniary claims until such an interpretation was devised by way of meeting claims actually made[1]."

(2) Granting however—what is by no means certain—that the king was justified in denying the financial bearing of this release, was in other words strictly within his rights in claiming the accounts of the chancellorship, as Foliot and others thought he was, a further question still remains to be discussed. Was he justified by the character of Thomas' administration in persisting in his demand? What weight are we to attach to the charge of misappropriation which his claim implied? The balance of probability inclines in favour of the integrity of Thomas. The Council of Northampton was intended from the beginning to strike a deadly blow at the archbishop. He was cited as a common offender, greeted on his arrival with studied insult, and assailed with a series of charges of which he had received no previous notice,—all evidently part of a

[1] Robertson, *Becket*, App. xvii. p. 337.

concerted plan for his humiliation. The fact that the demand for the accounts of his chancellorship was issued now for the first time, two years after his resignation of the office, looks suspicious at the outset. It bears the mark of personal enmity. It has the appearance of a demand that would never have been made if the mutual relations of king and archbishop had never been disturbed, or if there had been other means at the king's disposal of crushing the archbishop. This suspicion is confirmed by Thomas' own reply. He asserted in the first place that the king had seen his accounts, and, it must be supposed, approved of them; secondly, that he had himself expended private means of his own on royal business and thereby incurred serious debts[1]. If we may take Thomas at his word (and there is no reason why we should not), there was no ground for the insinuation that he had played the unjust steward during his tenure of the chancellorship. It has been suggested on the other hand that the evident anxiety of the bishop of Winchester to obtain the quittance in 1162 lends some colour to the idea that "no very strict account was kept of the king's moneys spent by the chancellor in the king's service and those expended by the chancellor himself[2]." At first sight this supposition seems to fall in with the fact that the bishop of Winchester's first advice to Thomas on receipt of the king's demand at Northampton was to compound with the king, and a sum of 2000 marks was actually offered to the king

[1] Fitzst. iii. 63. Will. C. i. 38.
[2] Milman, *Latin Christianity*, iii. 451.

and refused by him[1]. But a compromise is not always tantamount to a confession of guilt. It is just as probable that the bishop's advice was prompted by the conviction that Thomas' assertion of innocence would be of no avail against an infuriated king and a court that would take its cue from the king, whereas a partial concession might stave off the dreaded blow. The question resolves itself into a balancing of probabilities; and the scale is turned in favour of Thomas by the fact that the charge of pecuniary maladministration, which John of Salisbury declares to have been false, was afterwards dropped[2].

[1] Fitzst. iii. 54.
[2] Joh. S. *Ep.* 263 (written in 1166 to Baldwin archdeacon of Exeter), vi. 103: the only question, he says, now at issue between the king and the archbishop is the dispute between the civil and the ecclesiastical jurisdictions: *et de causa pecuniaria (quae tunc quidem simulabatur et in veritate nulla erat) nec mentio est.* This was only two years after the crisis at Northampton.

CHAPTER VII.

THE CHANCELLOR AND THE CHURCH.

As ambassador, soldier, justiciar and minister of state, Thomas had surpassed all expectation, and more than justified his promotion to the king's service. But it was not to win such laurels as these that he was brought within reach of the chancellorship. The intentions of his patron Theobald were obvious to the early biographers. Thomas was to serve two masters, the king and the archbishop, and maintain the balance between the conflicting claims of the Crown and the Church in favour of the latter. He was placed at the king's side as an ecclesiastic and for ecclesiastical purposes. Theobald had "discerned with prophetic sagacity his archdeacon's lofty and devoted churchmanship[1]." By his negotiations with the Papal court Thomas had thwarted both Stephen and Henry of Blois and strengthened the hands of the archbishop against an ambitious prelate and an unstable king. And when on the accession of Henry the Second the Church was threatened with

The purpose of his appointment mainly ecclesiastical.

[1] Milman, *Latin Christianity*, iii. 448.

the loss of material wealth and the loss of privilege, it was to the influence of Thomas that Theobald looked to stem the threatening tide of reaction, and even perhaps to extend the jurisdiction of the Church by securing for the canon law a wider sphere of application. When however we turn to the biographers of Thomas to ascertain how far he fulfilled the archbishop's expectations, we are met by serious discrepancies. As a rule they confine themselves to general statements more or less difficult to reconcile. William of Canterbury and John of Salisbury are both explicit enough in asserting that Thomas was frequently engaged on behalf of the Church in conflict with the king and the "wild beasts of the court," apparently a term of contempt for the anti-clerical party among the barons[1]. But William puts in a saving clause. He admits that Thomas' opposition to the king was kept within limits by his own feeling of respect and his dread of the royal anger. This qualification is borne out by one of the anonymous biographers, whose version puts Thomas in a somewhat dubious light. He says that the king had already made up his mind to assert his power as he afterwards asserted it; but in the meantime the Church remained in peace and safety under the

Its fulfilment: testimony of the biographers.

---

[1] Joh. S. ii. 305. Will. C. i. 5: memor conditionis suae et oneris sibi impositi contra bestias curiae pugnavit portans ecclesiae necessitates, et, quatenus regia severitas et reverentia permisit, contra regem ipsum contendens tamquam quodam futurorum praesagio sub pacis tempore dimicabat in acie. Freeman traces the term '*bestias curiae*' to an expression applied by Boethius to his enemies at the court of Theodoric, but wrongly attributes its use to John of Salisbury alone.

protection of Thomas, who kept king and court alike in check by a cautious opposition, partly concealed in order to preclude suspicion of his real intentions[1]. Elsewhere, in his account of Thomas' promotion to the primacy, he remarks that the king quite expected to find him a compliant archbishop, as he had deliberately adopted an attitude of severity towards all ecclesiastical persons and claims, in order to divert suspicion from himself and keep in closer touch with the royal temper which he had learned to know so well[2]. A second anonymous writer, by entering upon an elaborate apology for what he describes as the forced acquiescence of the chancellor, bears witness, all the more striking because reluctantly given, to the fact that Thomas was considered at the time responsible for much of the king's anti-ecclesiastical policy[3]. Lastly, the objections to Thomas' elevation to the primacy, so frankly stated by his most devoted biographers, reveal a strong feeling in certain ecclesiastical circles that Thomas was no friend to the claims and interests of the Church[4].

[1] Auct. Anon. i. iv. 12: ipso...caute et quasi ex occulto, ne suspicioni pateret, frustrante.

[2] Auct. Anon. i. iv. 14: Thomas namque ex industria circa personas et res ecclesiasticas quasi severissimum se exhibebat, ut tali occasione omnem a se suspicionis notam excuteret, et regis voluntati, quam intime noverat, melius sub hac palliatione conveniret. The *Saga* (i. 47) attributes this design to Theobald!

[3] Auct. Anon. ii. iv. 87.

[4] Herb. iii. 183. Auct. Anon. ii. iv. 85. Cp. John of Salisbury's letter to the archdeacon of Exeter in 1166 (*Ep.* 263, vi. 101), in which he contrasts ironically the popularity of the chancellor with the enmity roused by his stricter conduct as archbishop. Certe dum magnificus erat nugator in curia, dum

To say the least, the chancellor had not distinguished himself as an ecclesiastic in the opinion of his fellow-churchmen.

The facts to be considered in estimating the chancellor's relation to the Church fall under four heads: (1) his share in the financial oppression of the Church, (2) his disposal of church preferment, (3) his attitude towards the claims of ecclesiastical jurisdiction, (4) his personal relations with the veteran archbishop of Canterbury.

(1) Financial exactions.
(a) The chancellor and the scutage.

The chief ecclesiastical grievance in the earlier part of the reign was the exaction of scutage from the lands of the Church in 1159 to provide Henry with funds for the war of Toulouse. Gervase calls it an unprecedented exaction[1], but it was not the first

legis contemptor videbatur et cleri, dum scurriles cum potentioribus sectabatur ineptias, magnus habebatur, clarus erat et acceptus omnibus, et solus dignissimus summo pontificio ab universis conclamabatur et singulis. At first sight this seems a flat contradiction of the statement in his life of Thomas (ii. 305) that Thomas was obliged incessantly "pugnare ad bestias curiae." Freeman has attempted to reconcile the discrepancy (*Contemp. Review*, vol. 32, p. 481). "There is no real contradiction," he says. "John of Salisbury speaking with different objects in the two passages not unnaturally gave each a different tone and colour. But there is no contradiction as to fact. Thomas led the life of a layman; he did not stand up for ecclesiastical claims as he afterwards did; he may have seemed to be a despiser of the canon law and the clergy; and yet he may (which is what John of Salisbury really says that he did) have withstood acts of oppression whether directed against churchmen or laymen. The beasts of the court had to be withstood on behalf of both—*pro necessitate ecclesiae et provincialium*."

[1] Gervase, *Chron.* A.D. 1159 (col. 1381, Twysden): inauditam census exactionem.

instance of scutage. The Red Book of the Exchequer contains a notice of a scutage levied in 1156, the second year of Henry's reign, which the compiler of that record describes as the first of all the scutages. It was assessed at the rate of 20 shillings on each knight's fee, and was confined to the lands of those prelates who held *in capite* of the Crown. Theobald opposed its exaction, as we infer from a remark in one of John of Salisbury's letters; and it is not certain whether his lands were compelled to pay the tax[1]. This first scutage was a new form of taxation; but the novelty consisted apparently in the new basis of rating, the knight's fee (*scutum*) being taken as the unit of calculation instead of the old hide of land[2]. The more famous scutage of 1159 was something very different. It was more comprehensive, extending as it did to all tenants by knight-service,

---

[1] Stubbs, *Const. Hist.* i. 577. Joh. S. *Ep.* 128 (Giles, vol. i. p. 178), writing to William bishop of Norwich, says that a message has come from the king promising to grant certain requests that had been made by Theobald, but declining to remit the scutage. In omnibus enim consiliis domini archiepiscopi adquiescet et honori et utilitati ecclesiae tota mentis intentione studiosus invigilabit. Verum *scutagium remittere non potest* et a quibusdam exactionibus abstinere, quoniam fratris gratia male sarta nequidquam coiit. This allusion fixes the date of the scutage. It was levied for the war against Geoffrey in 1156. The compiler of the *Liber Ruber Scaccarii* (Alexander Swerford) says it was raised for the Welsh war: pro exercitu Walliae super prelatos tantum qui ad militaria servicia tenentur assisum. But the Welsh campaign was in 1157–1158.

Stubbs (*Const. Hist.* i. 454) thinks that this scutage was perhaps suggested by the chancellor; but the original authorities are silent on this question.

[2] Stubbs, *Const. Hist.* i. 581, 582.

whereas the earlier scutage was only levied on the fees in possession of bishops and abbots[1]. It was assessed at a heavier rate, two marks on each fee. But the real innovation consisted in the fact that it was levied as a commutation for personal military service. Such is the meaning attached to the term *scutagium* from this date onwards. The only persons exempt from the charge were the barons of the Exchequer[2]. The clergy seem to have objected to the exaction on the ground that they were not liable to military service; but this objection was ignored. The lands of the Church were considered as held by the same feudal tenure as those of the secular barons, and no distinction was made between the two classes in levying this scutage.

It was the second exaction that roused the indignation of the Church[3]. The blow was resented by the clergy all the more keenly because it was believed to come from the hand of the chancellor, himself an officer of the Church. Years afterwards the charge was flung in the teeth of Thomas the

---

[1] Notices of the scutage of 1156 occur in plenty in the Pipe Roll of 2 Henry II., e.g. the sheriff of Hampshire accounts for £49. 10s. de scutagio militum episcopi Wintoniensis, and £16. 13s. 4d. de scutagio militum abbatis de Hida (p. 56, Hunter).

[2] *Dial. Scacc.* i. 9: ab hoc (scutagio) quieti sunt ad scaccarium residentes.

[3] Miss Norgate (*England under the Angevin Kings*, i. 433), speaking of the scutage of 1156, remarks that "at the moment no resentment seems to have been provoked by the measure; its ultimate tendency was not foreseen, the sum actually demanded was not great, and the innovation was condoned on the ground of the king's lawful need and in the belief that it was only an isolated demand."

archbishop by the leader of the ecclesiastical opposition, Gilbert Foliot bishop of London. Foliot told him plainly in the famous remonstrance of 1166 that his election to the primacy was the result of sheer coercion. The Church, he said, had yielded for fear of a worse evil; she had submitted to his intrusion in order to avoid a repetition of the cruel exaction under which she had already groaned when he robbed her of so many thousand marks for the war of Toulouse[1]. John of Salisbury is the only one of the chancellor's friends that has dealt with this measure in particular. In a letter written in exile to Bartholomew bishop of Exeter in 1166 he describes the failure of the king's ambitious projects as a retributive judgment on his oppression of the Church, and singles out this scutage as the crowning enormity. He hints that an arbitrary and undue proportion of the tax had fallen upon the Church in comparison with the share paid by the baronage[2]. Then turning to deal with the assertion that it was the work of the chancellor, whose influence was then supreme with the king, he says that the charge was false. The chancellor did not suggest the exaction;

[1] Foliot, *Ep.* 235 (v. 525): stabat regni gladius in manu vestra......ille quidem gladius quem in sanctae matris ecclesiae viscera vestra paulo ante manus immerserat, cum ad trajiciendum in Tolosam exercitum tot ipsam marcarum millibus aporiastis.

[2] Joh. S. *Ep.* 194 (v. 378): omnibus contra antiquum morem et debitam libertatem indixit ecclesiis ut pro arbitrio ejus et satraparum suorum conferrent in censum, nec permisit ut ecclesiae saltem proceribus coaequarentur in hac contributione vel magis exactione...nam ecclesiae in deteriori calculo vertebantur. The churchman's indignation is concentrated in the opprobrious title of *satrap* with which he brands the rapacious sheriff.

he only sanctioned what he could not prevent[1]. Yet even John is compelled to admit that Thomas was at least the instrument of this injustice (*minister iniquitatis*); and he recognises an appropriate Nemesis in the punishment of the archbishop by the hand of the very monarch whom the chancellor had obeyed in preference to God. This is an important admission, coming as it does from one who was perhaps the truest, certainly the most candid, of Thomas' friends and his most impartial biographer. It does not stand alone. The view which John takes of the chancellor's conduct is echoed by one anonymous biographer, who explains at great length the difficulties of the position in which Thomas was placed, apologising in general terms for his acquiescence on the ground that it was not safe to oppose king and court beyond a certain point. It was the chancellor's place not to argue but obey, and tolerate where he could not praise. He adds that Thomas did sometimes feel the zeal of God's house burn within him, and did venture more than once to protest in the name of the Church within the limits allowed by his fear of the king's displeasure[2]. There is no reason

---

[1] Joh. S. *Ep.* 194 (v. 379): non auctoritatem praestitisse libidini sed obsecundationem necessitati.

[2] Auct. Anon. II. iv. 87. After recording the newly elected primate's resolve to defend the threatened liberties of the Church, the writer briefly states the crying grievances of the day: (1) the loss of judicial power,—contra ecclesiae leges in disponendis ecclesiasticis rebus, ut laicis, plus agebat manus regia quam censura canonica, (2) the loss of wealth under the royal exactions,—personis etiam ecclesiasticis indebitarum exactionum et concussionum onere multiplici saepius fatigatis. Sed *et ejus enormitatis ipse*,

to doubt this statement; the chancellor's remonstrance against the marriage of the abbess Mary in 1160 is an obvious instance in which he proved that he had convictions and the courage to give them vent; and more than one unfortunate cleric owed his escape from the king's vengeance to the timely interposition of the chancellor. But the fact remains that not one of the original authorities says a single word about any protest on the part of the chancellor against this scutage of 1159.

Whatever share the chancellor had in the royal exactions, he can scarcely be acquitted of something like personal extortion as archdeacon in the diocese of Canterbury. Our authority for the facts is a letter addressed by Theobald to the chancellor himself. The old archbishop, just recovering from a dangerous illness, writes to say that he intends to spend his last days in reforming certain abuses which had arisen in his time or by his own fault in the administration of his see, especially the custom of "second aids" imposed by his brother the arch-

(b) The archdeacon and his "aids."

quia regis ab eo videbatur pendere consilium, suasor et laudator ab aemulis dictus est. Verius autem ipsa per se regis animositas haec usurpabat. The young king, he adds, was carried away by his thirst for power, and his impetuosity was stimulated still further by the flattery of his courtiers. *His igitur omnibus obviare cancellario soli tutum non fuerat;* sed nec censoris ad corrigendum personam gerebat, *cui manebat necessitas obsequendi, non auctoritas arguendi.* Propterea que cum potestas esset et hora tenebrarum, prudentius in medio navigaverat, *usurpationes magis dissimulans quam suadens, magis sustinens quam laudans.* Zelo tamen domus Dei nonnunquam ingemuerat; interdum etiam talium dissuasor esse praesumpserat, ea tamen quae decuit modestia, ne regis offensam incurreret.

deacon. He has already released the churches from this burden, and forbidden its imposition in future on pain of excommunication,—a resolution which he has confirmed by written instructions of his own[1]. He is quite sure that Thomas would sooner have his

[1] Theobald, *Ep.* 7 (v. 10): ...Deo vovimus inter caetera quod consuetudinem de secundis auxiliis, quam frater noster archidiaconus ecclesiis imposuit, destrueremus, et ab ea relaxantes ecclesias et liberantes, sub anathemate prohibuimus ne ulterius ab aliquo exigantur. Et ne hoc nostrum beneficium aut potius debitum in posterum valeat infirmari, hoc ipsum scripto nostro confirmavimus. The *frater* is Walter, Theobald's own brother, who was archdeacon of Canterbury until his promotion to the see of Rochester in 1147. Lord Lyttelton takes this letter to be addressed to Henry II. and explains *frater noster archidiaconus* as referring to Thomas, and *secunda auxilia* as the second scutage (1159). Father Morris, though right in interpreting the *frater* to be the archbishop's brother Walter, makes the same mistake as Lyttelton in explaining the *auxilia* as a part of the great scutage, in which, he adds, "there can be little doubt St Thomas cooperated with Henry." Strangely enough, in the very next sentence the learned Jesuit remarks by way of clearing his hero-saint,—"But the archbishop attributes these subsidies to his own brother years before, and he is far from saying that the chancellor was responsible for them." The very fact that Theobald lays the original blame at his brother's door proves that the *auxilia* cannot refer to the scutage levied twelve years after his brother's promotion from Canterbury to Rochester.

The "aids" in question are evidently a provision for the benefit of the archdeacon. The letter, though addressed *Thomae cancellario*, is an appeal to Thomas as archdeacon of Canterbury; and the exaction which the old man's conscience condemned in what threatened to be the hour of death is clearly something which it was in his power as archbishop to control or abolish with the cooperation of the archdeacon, whose vested interests were at stake. It was a personal matter between the two: tu quoque si nostras praesens vidisses angustias, nostram malles animam liberari quam de peccatis et damnatione nostra pecuniam et divitias infinitas acquirere.

old master's conscience set at rest than enrich himself at the cost of his master's honour. For the present therefore he cannot listen to Thomas' demand for the exaction of this "aid" without breaking the vow made during his illness and endangering the welfare of his own soul; but he trusts that on his recovery he will be able to provide for Thomas without having recourse to such methods of raising money. The letter ends with a pitiful entreaty for the chancellor's sanction, which shows how strongly the old primate felt the need of this reform. "I pray thee, welcome what I have done, for the whole world would avail me nought, if I had lost my soul."

The archdeacon of the twelfth century was a proverbial character. It was an essentially secular office, usually reserved for a deacon as incompatible with the sacred calling of the priesthood, and notorious for its peculiar temptations, which made the eternal welfare of an archdeacon a stock theme for scholastic disputation,—*an possit archidiaconus salvus esse?*[1] The rights of visitation and the

[1] Joh. S. *Ep.* 166 (Giles, i. 260), written to Nicolaus de Sigillo: erat, ut memini, genus hominum, qui in ecclesia Dei archidiaconorum nomine censentur, quibus vestra discretio omnem salutis viam querebatur esse praeclusam. Nam, ut dicere consuevistis, diligunt munera, sequuntur retributiones, ad injurias proni sunt, calumniis gaudent, peccata populi comedunt et bibunt, quibus vivitur ex rapto, ut non sit hospes ab hospite tutus. Cp. Freeman, *Norm. Conqu.* v. 497. Stubbs, *Med. and Mod. Hist.* pp. 139, 301, 303. At the Council of Westminster, October 1163, the archdeacons as a class were accused of lording it over the flock and harassing the laity with false charges of crime, the clergy with undue extortion (Auct. Anon. II. iv. 96). A flagrant instance of extortion was brought home to an archdeacon and a rural

judicial functions which belonged to the office were utilised to the full as means of extortion, until the bishop's archdeacon became as unpopular in the diocese as the king's sheriff was in the county. Thomas was preserved from the fate of an ordinary archdeacon by his constant attendance upon his royal master; but it is quite evident from this letter of Theobald's that he was not beyond reproach. He drew without compunction—with avidity almost, if we may so infer from the archbishop's doubtful and pathetic plea for a little self-sacrifice—the excessive profits that were wrung from the churches of the diocese for the benefit of its archdeacon.

(2) *Church patronage.* According to Fitzstephen it was part of the chancellor's office to administer the revenues of vacant sees and abbacies, as well as the lay-fiefs, as they reverted to the Crown[1]. It is certain that Thomas had a large amount of church preferment passing through his hands, either ex officio or by special favour of the king. Out of the fifty-two clerks in his household, we are told, many were engaged solely in the administration of vacant sees and abbeys or his own ecclesiastical benefices[2].

dean at York in 1158 in the king's presence, and he remarked, as he insisted on the punishment of the offending clerics, that the archdeacons and deans extorted more money in a year in the shape of fines from the inhabitants of his realm than he himself received as revenue (Fitzst. iii. 44).

[1] Fitzst. iii. 17: ut vacantes archiepiscopatus, episcopatus, abbatias et baronias, cadentes in manu regis, ipse suscipiat et conservet.

[2] Fitzst. iii. 29: quinquaginta duos clericos cancellarius in obsequio suo habebat; quorum plurimi in suo erant comitatu,

Here and there we get an occasional glimpse of the
way in which Thomas discharged the responsibility
which his influence with the king involved. Fitzstephen—the only biographer who has dealt with
the subject of the chancellor's patronage—is emphatic in his praise of Thomas' conscientious disposal
of church preferment. His own demands were
modest, as Fitzstephen remarks with artless sim-
plicity. He could have had all vacant parochial
churches for himself, if he had so pleased. None
would venture to refuse, if he chose to ask. But he
showed the greatness of his heart by leaving them
to poor clergy[1]. *Magnanimus magna potius re-
quirebat.* His ambition soared to higher levels,—
the provostship of Beverley, for instance (which had

plurimi curabant episcopatus, et abbatias vacantes aut ejus proprios honores ecclesiasticos. Some of these clerics superintended
the revenues of vacant sees and abbeys; others discharged the
spiritual duties attached to the many livings and prebends which
the chancellor held.

[1] Fitzst. iii. 20. Fitzstephen relates elsewhere (iii. 25, 26)
a striking conversation that took place at Rouen between Thomas
and Aschetinus prior of Leicester, who found him whiling away
the hours of convalescence in a gay courtier's garb over a game of
chess, and frankly avowed his dissatisfaction at the sight of such
frivolity in a dignitary of the church "already archdeacon of
Canterbury, dean of Hastings, provost of Beverley, canon of more
than one church, entrusted with the care of the vacant archbishopric (*procurator etiam archiepiscopatus*), and marked out by
court gossip as the coming archbishop." Thomas replied that he
knew three poor priests in England whose promotion to the
primacy he would welcome sooner than his own. The date of
this conversation is fixed by the allusion to the vacant see of
Canterbury in Thomas' charge. It must have taken place after
Theobald's death in April 1161.

come with his archdeaconry), and a prebend or two
at Hastings[1] (the gift of the count of Eu), in
addition to the secular preferment bestowed upon
him by the king. But, pluralist as he was, Thomas
did not forget his duty to the Church. It was at the
suggestion of the chancellor that the king found
honest occupants without delay for vacant sees and
abbeys, instead of retaining " the inheritance of the
Crucified" for the benefit of his own royal treasury,
as he did later in his reign[2]; visited, and at his own
cost completed and endowed, the abbey church at
Merton[3]; and infused fresh blood into the Church of
England by recalling from France famous English
monks and scholars and finding them preferment at
home. Robert of Melun was installed as bishop of
Hereford[4], and William, a monk of S. Martin des

---

[1] Fitzst. iii. 20: donationem praebendarum Hastinges a comite
Augensi. The prior of Leicester addresses Thomas as *decanus
Hastingiae* (iii. 26). Freeman suggests that he may have been
dean with the nomination of the prebendaries also entrusted to
him. Robertson (*Becket*, p. 30) remarks that Hastings was a
royal chapel with a college of secular canons attached (Dugdale,
Monasticon, vi. 1470).

[2] Fitzst. iii. 23: ut fisco suo patrimonia crucifixi inferrentur.

[3] Cp. Ch. I. of this essay for Thomas' connexion with Merton,
the scene of his early school-days. The Pipe Rolls of the 2nd and
4th years of Henry II. contain several royal grants or exemptions
conferred upon the *canonici de Meritona*.

[4] Fitzst. iii. 23. Robert may have been invited to England
while Thomas was chancellor, but he was not promoted to the see
of Hereford till 1163, after it was vacated by Foliot's translation
to London. Herbert of Bosham (iii. 260, 305) says that Robert
was both ordained to the priesthood and consecrated by Thomas
the archbishop. Cp. Ch. I. of this essay on Robert's possible
connexion with Thomas during his student days at Paris.

Champs, as abbot of Ramsey[1]. All this Fitzstephen attributes to the judicious influence of the chancellor. It is also a significant fact that in each of the three instances which Fitzstephen gives of the chancellor's interposition to break the force of the king's displeasure, the sufferer reprieved was an ecclesiastic. Nicolas archdeacon of London had incurred the king's anger for some unknown reason. His family were driven from hearth and home, and his house confiscated by royal command. But Thomas pleaded his cause, and the king yielded to his entreaties. A still more notorious instance occurred in Normandy in July 1160. The kings of England and France had met at Neufmarché in conference with the Norman and French clergy, to decide between the claims of the rival popes Octavian and Alexander. Unfortunately first Gilo archdeacon of Rouen, acting on behalf of his uncle Hugh archbishop of Rouen, and after him the bishop of Le Mans, had anticipated the verdict of the conference by giving their allegiance at once to the nuncios of Alexander. Henry, infuriated by their independent action, ordered the immediate destruction of the archdeacon's house; but Thomas persuaded him to countermand the order. The bishop's case was more serious. Henry

The chancellor a friend at court.

---

[1] Fitzst. iii. 23. Robert de Monte gives 1161 as the date of William's promotion to Ramsey. One other instance of the chancellor's patronage is preserved in an insertion in the *Quadrilogus* (perhaps due to its compiler, the monk Elias of Evesham), which states that one of the commissioners who fetched the *pallium* for Thomas after his consecration—Adam abbot of Evesham—owed his abbacy to the chancellor (Robertson's note, *Materials*, iii. 189).

in his rage would not listen to reason, and the chancellor saw that it was useless to attempt to calm his violence at once. The king's marshals had already sacked the prelate's hostelry at Neufmarché, and turned him adrift in disgrace, and other messengers from Henry, armed with a writ that he had brandished in the face of his awe-stricken court, were on their way to Le Mans to raze the bishop's palace to the ground; but the chancellor was equal to the emergency. His only hope was to gain time, and he gave the messengers secret instructions to spend four days on the journey instead of two. The next day he sent the bishops to intercede with the king for their brother prelate; but they pleaded in vain, and the chancellor himself fared no better. Undaunted by his repulse he went again the following day, and at last the king yielded, but not until he thought that time enough had elapsed for his officers to complete their work. The chancellor did not lose a moment. He despatched a messenger of his own with the king's counter-orders, and warned him, as he valued his master's friendship, to rest neither day nor night till he came to Le Mans. The chancellor's plan had succeeded. His messenger reached Le Mans just in time; the king's writ had been handed to the city authorities that morning, but the bishop's palace was intact; and the king was honestly grateful afterwards for the stratagem that had robbed him of his vengeance and saved him in spite of himself from a deed of wild injustice[1].

[1] Fitzst. iii. 26–28. The date of the conference is given by Robert de Monte, A.D. 1160.

One other instance of the chancellor's intercession on behalf of his brother clergy remains to be noticed before returning to the question of his patronage. John of Salisbury had for a time incurred the king's displeasure, and made use of the chancellor's friendship to reinstate himself in Henry's favour. He forwarded to the chancellor letters of recommendation from his master the archbishop of Canterbury and from his friend the Pope, and begged the chancellor to exert his influence, which was the one thing wanted to give them their full weight with the king[1]. John also wrote to Ernulf, the chancellor's secretary, explaining that he was afraid that without a monitor at his side the busy chancellor might not find time to plead a friend's cause, and asking him first to urge the chancellor to lay the case before the king, and then to write as soon as possible and tell him how the king received the letters from the Pope and the archbishop and the plea which he expected the chancellor to put forward on his behalf. We do not know the actual result of the intercession; but these two letters are at least a proof that the chancellor was recognised by his brother clergy as "a friend in deed in time of need[2]," upon whose personal sympathy and support they could rely, in cases of individual distress, what-

---

[1] Joh. S. ad Thomam regis cancellarium, *Ep.* 6 (*Materials*, v. 8, 9).

[2] Joh. S. ad magistrum Ernulfum, *Ep.* 5 (*Materials*, v. 7). This Ernulf remained secretary to Thomas after his consecration, and conveyed the seal to the king, when his master resigned the chancellorship.

ever attitude he took up towards the Church as a whole.

See of Exeter.

To return to questions of ecclesiastical administration, John of Salisbury was not always quite so sure of the chancellor's principles at the time as Fitzstephen was when he wrote his biography years afterwards. The letter which John wrote to Thomas in Theobald's name, asking him to exert his influence in the nomination of a new bishop of Exeter, casts just a shade of suspicion upon the chancellor's integrity in the matter of church revenues. Robert Warelwast bishop of Exeter died in 1160, and the vacant see was not immediately filled. The king had already favoured the suit of Robert Fitzharding, a local baron, on behalf of an illiterate and inefficient candidate for the see, and had written to archbishop Theobald in the man's interest; while some persons had even gone so far as to intrude upon the bedridden primate on the same errand. The canons of Exeter, however, had rejected the nomination; and Theobald now put forward Bartholomew archdeacon of Exeter—without Bartholomew's knowledge, John of Salisbury is careful to state—as a candidate for the king's approval. John was doubtful of the result. There was a rumour afloat, he writes, that the king had granted the revenues of three vacant bishoprics to swell the chancellor's income[1]. Still Theobald relied upon his patronage. If he were

[1] Joh. S. *Ep.* 9 (v. 14): fama est apud nos quod trium vacantium episcopatuum reditus ad liberationem vestram vobis dominus rex concesserit. Ducange gives *liberatio* = salary. The word occurs frequently with that meaning in the Pipe Rolls.

only willing to speak, a word to the king would suffice; his good services to the Church in similar cases at Lincoln, York and elsewhere were signal proofs of his influence. Theobald was hoping for a speedy decision, but almost against hope, it seems; for John concludes with a warning that if the archbishop's petition were to be postponed until the king's arrival in England, he would feel that king and chancellor alike were merely waiting for his death. The aged primate was spared that pang of disappointment, though he did not live to consecrate his friend. We learn from other sources that Bartholomew was consecrated bishop of Exeter, just after Theobald's death in April 1161, by Walter bishop of Rochester in accordance with his brother's dying request[1].

One other incident of the chancellor's ecclesiastical administration is recorded in an extant letter from Foliot to the king. The see of London was thrown upon the chancellor's hands by the helplessness of its bishop, Richard de Belmeis, who broke down under an attack of paralysis some time before his death in May 1162[2]. Thomas tried to provide for the administration of the see by a stroke of economy which would meet the spiritual require-

See of London.

---

[1] R. Diceto, i. 304 (ed. Stubbs). Bartholomew after his election went into Normandy to do homage to the king for the temporalities of his see, and returned only to find Theobald dead.

[2] R. Diceto, i. 304, 306 (ed. Stubbs). Robertson, in a note on p. 15, vol. v., gives 1161 as the date of Richard's death, apparently by a slip of the pen, for in a note on p. 23 he mentions that Richard survived Theobald by a year.

ments of the diocese and at the same time turn its misfortune into a source of profit for the king's treasury. In other words he did his best to serve two masters, and discharge his duty to the king without forgetting his duty to the Church. He asked Gilbert Foliot, then bishop of Hereford,—afterwards, as bishop of London, his bitterest enemy, though now apparently they were on terms of friendship—to take charge of the disabled see and pay the expenses of the bishop's household out of its revenues, reserving the rest for the Crown, to be expended at the royal pleasure[1].

Whether Foliot suspected the chancellor's intentions with regard to the revenues of the see or only dreaded the strain of the responsibilities which its administration would add to the cares of his own diocese of Hereford, is an open question. He wrote to the king and declined the honour in vague terms. It would be a dangerous task, he said, and a grievous burden on his soul, and he implored the king to leave him free to serve God with greater devotion and intercede for him with a heart that would be the purer for its release from such a

---

[1] Foliot to Henry, *Ep.* 10 (v. 15, 16): sollicitat me dominus cancellarius ut curam Londoniensis episcopatus suscipiam et ex parte redituum episcopatus episcopum ipsum et domum ejus exhibeam, reliquum vero domino meo regi, prout sibi spiritus Dei suggesserit, erogandum conservem. It is immaterial whether *sibi* refers grammatically to *cancellarius* or *regi*: practically the result is the same. The chancellor was entrusted with the revenues of vacant sees to be administered on behalf of the king; and the revenues of the see of London would pass through his hands as the king's agent.

weight of care[1]. Eventually Foliot and the bishop of Lincoln with great difficulty induced Hugh dean of London and Nicolas the archdeacon to undertake the responsibility of managing the affairs of their helpless bishop, who was still lingering out his days. Their reluctance was more than justified, for in less than twelve months Foliot had to appeal to the new archbishop of Canterbury on their behalf against the persistence of the late bishop's creditors[2].

[1] Father Morris (*S. Thomas Becket*, pp. 41, 42) speaks of the see as already vacated by the death of its bishop, and takes the chancellor's proposal to be an offer of the see, refused by Foliot "in consequence of the disgraceful condition annexed to the offer of the translation." This view he supports by taking the words *episcopum ipsum et domum ejus exhibeam* to mean "maintain myself and my household as its bishop." He afterwards mentions with approval the explanation that Foliot was only asked to administer the see during its vacancy, regarding this as a less reprehensible proposal, amounting merely to a retention of a part of what the king usually confiscated *in toto*; and suggests that "S. Thomas, who as we know used his influence with the king to prevent long vacancies, may in this instance have been able to gain nothing more liberal to the church than the compromise here offered." But Foliot's "evident indignation at the offer" and his subsequent translation to the see compelled the learned Jesuit to incline reluctantly in favour of the former view. That view however is untenable, for two reasons: (1) the words *episcopum et domum suam fideliter exhibere* are used in a subsequent letter in reference to the trusteeship of Hugh and Nicolas. They cannot therefore mean "to maintain oneself as bishop." (2) Richard was still alive when the bishops of Hereford and Lincoln forced the administration of his affairs upon the dean and the archdeacon. The see was therefore not vacant at the time of the chancellor's offer to Foliot.

[2] Foliot, *Ep.* 15 (v. 23, 24), addressed T. Cantuariensi, i.e. Thomas, for the bishop of London, who is mentioned as dead, survived Theobald by a year.

(3) Ecclesiastical jurisdiction.

The attitude which Thomas the chancellor took up towards the rival claims of royal and ecclesiastical jurisdiction is clearly illustrated by the part which he played in the long litigation between the bishop of Chichester and the abbot of Battle. The trial of 1157 has been already described in outline, and it will be sufficient here to recall Thomas' share in that trial and in the previous stages of the dispute. Early in 1155 the abbot obtained the king's consent to the confirmation of his privileges; but at the instigation of the bishop Theobald remonstrated with the king, and persuaded him to withhold his seal from the abbey charter until the rights of Chichester and Canterbury obtained what he considered due recognition. The abbot lost no time in procuring once more the royal order for the confirmation of the charter; and, in spite of an urgent remonstrance from the bishop, the king instructed the chancellor to affix the royal seal to the charter, and required the bishop, the abbot and the chancellor to meet in conference before the archbishop and revise any clauses that needed revision. If they separated without coming to an agreement, the charter was to be kept by the chancellor in the royal chapel until the king should decide what was to be done. The persons interested met at Lambeth. The charter of William I. was read out as the model of all the subsequent charters, which were practically mere confirmations of the original grant; and the clause declaring the abbot's exemption from episcopal jurisdiction gave rise to a fierce discussion. Some objected to it as contrary to the principles of canon law, others as inconsistent with the rights and dignities of Canterbury. Some loudly asserted that the clause was too sweeping; others as violently enforced the opposite view[1]. The bishop required the excision of the clause, as it was not signed by any of his predecessors in the see of Chichester; and the archbishop supported his demand. The abbot argued calmly on rational grounds, but in vain; his opponents still clamoured for their point. At last the chancellor ended the dispute abruptly by removing the charter into the royal chapel in compliance with the king's previous instructions. The bishop was happy, for he felt sure that the abbot and his church had lost the royal sanction to their charter. But the abbot persevered, and, once more procuring the king's consent to its confirmation, returned this time in triumph to his abbey with the precious document in his possession.

Such briefly is the narrative of the Abbey Chronicle. At the trial of 1157 the bishop of Chichester referred in a tone of complaint to the abbot's conduct at this court of revision in 1155. The clause, he said, which infringed upon the rights of Chichester and Canterbury—the very clause which the conference in accordance with the king's instructions was to revise and modify, if necessary—had after due consideration been pronounced untenable on the ground of its sweeping and arbitrary character; and yet the abbot, ignoring this authoritative

[1] *Chron. Monast. de Bello* (Wilkins, i. 428, 429): nonnullis nimium clamantibus hoc verbum peremptorium esse; multis etiam hoc aliter objurgando interpretantibus.

expression of opinion, had given vent to his indignation and assailed him with marked insolence, not only on that occasion, but subsequently in the chapter-house itself at Chichester[1]. The bishop, it will be noticed, regarded the archbishop's assent to his objection as settling the question in his favour, and practically annulling the provisions of the charter. But the chancellor in his speech on behalf of the abbot took a very different view of the relative weight of a bishop's complaint supported by an archbishop's judgment and an old royal charter with the present king's seal recently affixed in confirmation of its contents. The abbot, he says, was acting in accordance with the king's instructions. He had taken his stand upon a perfectly legitimate ground, namely, the fact that the privileges denounced as arbitrary by the bishop originated from a royal grant, and as a matter of fact his defence, far from being an abusive attack upon the bishop, had been based on principles of sound reason[2].

[1] *Chron. de Bello* (*Materials*, iv. 249): the bishop's speech to the king: praecepit igitur vestra clementia quatenus coram archiepiscopo ego et abbas cum cancellario vestro domino Thoma conveniremus, ibique lecta abbatis charta consilio archiepiscopi ea quae corrigenda erant (ea scilicet quae contra dignitates praedictarum ecclesiarum, Cantuariensis scilicet et Cicestrensis exsistebant) correcta, unusquisque quae sui juris esse videntur, adquisisse gauderet. Convenimus ibi. Lecta igitur coram assistentibus carta abbatis, ea quae contra dignitates Cantuariensis ecclesiae et Cicestrensis erant, justa consideratione *peremptoria esse praecepta sunt.* Abbas ira commotus multis me ibidem et maximis aggressus est injuriis. Nec solum duntaxat tunc, sed anno etiam praesenti Cicestriam veniens capitulum nostrum cum nimia nimis arrogantia intravit, &c.

[2] *Chron. de Bello* (iv. 253): quas (dignitates, i.e. the privileges

The chancellor's attitude at the Lambeth conference of 1155 was marked out for him by his position as the representative of the Crown. His contribution to the debate is not recorded; perhaps he was little more than a keen spectator; but his withdrawal with the abbey charter after the authority of the archbishop had been thrown solidly on the side of the bishop against the abbot is a clear indication that as a minister of the Crown he was prepared to uphold the prerogative of the Crown to grant or confirm ecclesiastical privileges independently of the ecclesiastical powers. This view of his attitude is confirmed by his action throughout the great trial of 1157. When the bishop waxed eloquent on the supremacy of the ecclesiastical jurisdiction, the chancellor lost no time in following up the king's protest with a pointed reminder of his own. "You are disloyal to my lord the king, to whom you have taken the oath of allegiance, as all men know." When the abbot withdrew with his friends to deliberate in private, it was Thomas the chancellor who was entrusted with the delivery of the defence thus prepared. Theobald, significantly enough, was not among this chosen circle of friends and partisans. His sympathy and support as the champion of episcopal rights were of course given to the bishop.

The evidence of the Chronicle of Battle seems

---

of the abbey) etiam praecepto domini regis coram domino nostro archiepiscopo Cantuariensi, non vobis pessima ingerendo, sed ratione vigenti easdem a vobis peremptorias judicatas defendendo, ut regales nobis audientibus retinere cupiebat.

unmistakable[1]. On the one hand was the Crown —for it was a royal charter that was at stake—, on the other hand the representatives of episcopal jurisdiction, with a papal brief at their back; and Thomas sided unhesitatingly with the king against the pretensions of the papal supremacy which he had once done his best in the service of Theobald to enforce as the final authority in the ecclesiastical affairs of England. The only difficulty in the way of accepting the evidence of the Chronicle is the fact that Thomas himself took a very different view of this trial afterwards when he was archbishop. In a letter written to Pope Alexander in 1168 the exiled primate, bent on clearing himself from the charge that he was himself responsible for the evils that troubled his native land and Church, enumerates the instances of royal oppression that had taken place before he came to the archiepiscopal throne, and among them he ranks the verdict of the king and council at Colchester in 1157. He condemns it as an act of coercion which showed how futile the claims of "apostolic" jurisdiction were in conflict with a self-willed monarch and a subservient court[2]. This

---

[1] The impression which the chancellor's action left upon the friends of the abbey comes out clearly in the reference made in the Chronicle to his promotion to the primacy (*Materials*, iv. 256): Thomas...quem superior edidit narratio cum abbate Walterio adversus Cicestrensem episcopum Hilarium viriliter stetisse, seque pro defensione libertatis ecclesiasticae S. Martini de Bello advocatum exhibuisse.

[2] Thomas, *Ep.* i. 54, Giles; *Materials*, iv. 244: sed et Cicestrensis episcopus quid profuit adversus abbatem de Bello? qui privilegiis apostolicis fretus, cum ea nominasset in curia,

letter has been made the basis of an attempt to prove in spite of the Chronicle of Battle that Thomas must have taken the ecclesiastical side in the trial of 1157[1]. But after all the letter only proves that Thomas the archbishop ignored or repudiated the action of Thomas the chancellor[2]. Circumstances had changed, and Thomas had changed with them. Even Thomas' own comment eleven years later can scarcely outweigh the evidence of the Abbey Chronicle. Whatever his attitude was in 1168, he had ranged himself in 1157 on the side of his master the king against his old friend and master the archbishop.

One other aspect of the question has yet to be considered, and that is the archbishop's own view of his archdeacon's conduct as chancellor. The story is soon told. It is a tale of bitter disappointment, a

(4) *The archbishop and his archdeacon.*

et abbatem denuntiasset excommunicatum, eidem incontinenti coram omnibus communicare compulsus est sine absolutione et eum recipere in osculo pacis. Sic enim placuit regi et curiae quae ei in nullo contradicere audebat. *Privilegia apostolica* may cover both the episcopal rights and the papal brief. Probably it refers specially to the latter. *Apostolicus* in mediaeval literature usually means *papal*, cp. mandatum apostolicum, auctoritas apostolica, aures apostolicae (=the Pope's ears), all of which expressions occur in this same *Chronicon de Bello*.

[1] R. H. Froude, *Remains*, iv. 577. It was Froude's aim to reestablish the reputation of Thomas by disproving the prevalent idea of an absolute contrast between the chancellor and the archbishop in life and conduct.

[2] Robertson, *Becket*, Appendix vii. p. 326: Thomas "seems to have fancied that in exchanging the chancellorship for the primacy he had not only been released from all obligations as to money, but had got rid of his former self." Freeman practically endorses this view (*Contemp. Review*, vol. 32, p. 486, note).

tale of promises unfulfilled and affection unrequited. It was to Theobald mainly that Thomas owed his training and experience, ecclesiastical, legal and political, and his first footing on the ladder of promotion in Church and state. Theobald naturally looked for some return. He relied on Thomas the archdeacon, his adopted son and, as he fondly hoped, his successor on the throne of Canterbury, to lift from his shoulders something of the care of all the churches which came upon him daily. He relied on Thomas the chancellor to maintain the traditional rights and privileges of the Church amid the dangers with which he was himself too old and weak to grapple. Both expectations were doomed to disappointment. The duties of the archdeacon were neglected for the duties of the chancellor. The interests of the archbishop were postponed to the interests of the king. Already Theobald and Thomas had come twice into collision. The chancellor had at least consented to the exaction of a scutage which the primate condemned; and in the Battle Abbey case they had met as the representatives of the opposing claims of Church and king. The correspondence which passed a year or two later between the archbishop and his faithful secretary on the one side and the king and his chancellor on the other shows how deeply the iron had entered into the old man's soul. He writes in sorrow to his archdeacon, then absent with the king in Normandy: "You have now been recalled again and again to your post, you who ought to have returned at the first summons of your old and ailing father. Indeed it is to be feared that the Lord may punish your delay, if you still turn a deaf ear to my appeal, forgetful of all my kindness and regardless of the father whom you ought to have borne upon your shoulders in his sickness. There would have been no excuse for you, you would have well nigh merited my curse, if it were not that my lord the king excused your absence on the pretext of his own necessity. But as I put the public interests of the king's business before all private interests, I have allowed his will, which I have always preferred before my own where it was possible and right, to overrule my command to you on this condition only, that as soon as you can obtain his consent you no longer delay your return to my side. I make this concession for the present out of regard for your welfare as much as his wish, because I am afraid of the risk you may run if you should offend him by returning home. For if you incur the loss of his favour for my sake, I fear you could not regain it by any efforts of mine[1]." At the same time, conscious of his approaching end, Theobald wrote more than once to the king, and pleaded piteously for a glimpse of his face, "the face of the Lord's anointed," once more in England, or at least for a visit from the archdeacon, "his first and only counsellor," as soon as the king could spare him[2]. Still Thomas did not

[1] Theobald 'ad archidiaconum suum,' *Ep.* 8 (*Materials*, v. 11). The earlier editions have the initial R. before *archidiaconum*, but the contents of the letter are only applicable to Thomas, and it must have been attributed to his predecessor Roger (archdeacon of Canterbury, 1147–1154) by mistake (Robertson, v. 11 n.).

[2] Joh. S. *Ep.* 90 (Giles, i. 93): qui (Thomas) nobis unicus est et consilii nostri primus.

come. At last John of Salisbury, the trusty clerk who tended the helpless primate to the last and bore the burdens of the see in his master's stead[1], wrote a letter to Thomas which proves how seriously the archbishop's affection for his archdeacon was strained by his apparently wilful absence. John began by explaining that he had already in compliance with the chancellor's suggestion written letters in the primate's name to the king and to Thomas, recalling the chancellor to his archdeaconry on pain of excommunication and forfeiture of his ecclesiastical income[2]; but the king's plea that he could not spare

---

[1] Joh. S. *Metalogicus* (dedicated to Thomas), iv. 42 (ed. Giles): siquidem pater meus et dominus, immo et tuus, venerabilis Theobaldus Cantuariensis archiepiscopus in aegritudinem incidit, ut incertum sit quid sperare, quid timere oporteat. Negotiis more solito superesse non potest: injunxitque mihi provinciam duram et importabile onus imposuit, omnium ecclesiarum sollicitudinem.

[2] Joh. S. ad Thomam Angliae cancellarium, *Ep.* 9 (v. 13, 14): *Juxta mandatum dilectionis vestrae*, litteras domini mei ad dominum regem et vos sub ea austeritate conceperam ut vobis redeundi festinata necessitas indiceretur nisi crimen inobedientiae malletis incurrere et cum poena anathematis dispendium bonorum quae a Cantuariensi ecclesia habetis, sustinere. Lord Campbell (*Lives of the Chancellors*, i. 68) takes this threat in earnest and places it at the time of the scutage of 1159. "Upon this the heads of the church uttered the most violent invectives against him. Foliot, bishop of London, publicly accused him of plunging a sword into the bosom of his mother, the church; and archbishop Theobald his former patron threatened to excommunicate him." This is a double inaccuracy. Foliot's remonstrance first appears in his pamphlet of 1166, seven years after the great scutage; and Theobald's threat was a suggestion of the chancellor's own in 1160. Possibly however Lord Campbell was thinking of the excommunication on pain of which Theobald had forbidden the exaction of *auxilia* in his diocese (v. supr. p. 162; see his letter

his chancellor till peace was firmly established in France had induced Theobald to countermand the letters. Still Theobald was perplexed to reconcile the contradiction between the statements and requests of king and chancellor with all that he heard of their unanimity from other sources of foreign news; for this very threat of deprivation had been suggested by Thomas himself as a way of inducing the king to release him. Theobald was half-inclined to suspect that the king and the chancellor were in collusion; but John fancied that he could understand the difficulties of his friend's position, and thought better of his sincerity. Still even John confessed that he was growing more and more anxious as Theobald's strength sank, and after pleading for the speedy appointment of Bartholomew to the see of Exeter for the sake of the dying archbishop, he ended his letter with an earnest appeal to the truant archdeacon to come home at all costs before his master's death. Still Thomas did not come[1]. He

to Thomas, *Materials*, v. 9, 10, *Ep.* 7). Father Morris, while right in correcting Lord Campbell's mistake (note C, p. 529), is surely wrong himself in calling this excommunication "a sportive threat." The dying primate was in no mood to jest. The threat was perhaps not meant eventually to be carried out, but it was prepared sternly enough as the last chance of moving the king, who had turned a deaf ear to every gentler call.

Strange to say, in the text of his book, Father Morris (like Dean Hook, *Archbishops, Life of Theobald*) takes the threat seriously: "They had even thought of forcing S. Thomas to return by threat of censures. But they had been induced to be patient by the report............of the perfect unanimity between the king and the chancellor" (Morris, p. 59).

[1] Miss Norgate (*England under the Angevin Kings*, i. 506)

had been set to serve two masters; and when the inevitable crisis came he held to the one and despised the other. His affection for his old patron was not strong enough to outweigh the attractions of foreign diplomacy and the danger of the royal displeasure. Thomas procured the appointment of Bartholomew to Exeter; but he stayed with the king, and Theobald died without seeing his archdeacon.

NOTE A.

THE MEANING OF THE WORD 'PEREMPTORIUS'
(Battle Abbey Chronicle).

The traditional rendering of the word *peremptorius* in modern versions of the Battle Abbey case is '*frivolous.*' This translation occurs first in a note on p. 101 of the Latin text of the *Chronicon de Bello* (published by the Anglia Christiana Society in 1846) where the meaning there given is said to be derived from late Latin writers. It was embodied in Mr Lower's translation of the Chronicle in 1851 (pp. 83, 111), and thence found its way into the works of Dean Hook (*Archbishops of Canterbury*, ii. 372) and Father Morris (*Life of S. Thomas*, Note D, pp. 536, 545), who remarks that in giving this singular meaning to the word Mr Lower is borne out by a passage given by Ducange from the

gives him the benefit of just the faintest doubt: "If he did go, it can only have been for a flying visit; and there is no sign that he went at all."

statutes of Liège of the year 1287 : 'cum judex viderit aliquam partium per exceptiones frivolas, dilatorias et *peremptorias* litem protrahere.' But this meaning of the word is by no means certain. I have in fact felt compelled to abandon the traditional interpretation, and substitute some such word as '*sweeping*' or '*arbitrary*'; and I take this opportunity of giving my reasons. The word *peremptorius* occurs in four passages in the *Chronicon de Bello* :

(i) in the narrative of the conference at Lambeth in 1155 (p. 74, Angl. Christ. Soc.): 'nonnullis nimium clamantibus hoc verbum *peremptorium* esse.'

(ii) in the bishop's reference to this incident at the conference in his speech before the Curia in 1157 (*ib.* p. 96; *Materials*, iv. 249), where he remarks as evidence in his favour that the disputed clauses 'justa consideratione *peremptoria* esse praecepta sunt.' (Mr Lower, p. 106, says " were *perceived*," as though he read *percepta.*)

(iii) in the king's indignant interruption of the bishop: "a strange thing this I hear, that the charters of the kings my predecessors, confirmed by the full authority of the Crown of England, and by the testimony of our great men, should have been pronounced peremptory by you, my lord bishop" (p. 96, Angl. Christ. Soc., 'a vobis *peremptorias* esse judicatas'). There is no need to account for the king's interruption, as Father Morris does, by supposing that the chancellor had reported this expression to the king after the conference in 1155. He probably did report the proceedings to his master on that occasion; but the bishop had just repeated the expression himself in the king's hearing.

(iv) in the chancellor's subsequent reference to the same conference, where he asserts in reply to the bishop that the abbot in 1155 had confined himself to sound logic in defending as a royal grant the privileges condemned by the bishop: 'ratione vigenti easdem a vobis peremptorias judicatas defendendo' (*ib.* 101; *Materials*, iv. 253).

There are several points to be noticed in the passages quoted above:

(1) the word *peremptorius* must have the same meaning in all four cases.

(2) it refers not to the judicial verdict of a court but to an expression of party-feeling.

(3) the king's remark makes it clear that it was the bishop and his partisans who applied the term *peremptorius* to the clause securing the independence of the abbey.

It is evident therefore that the usual technical signification of the term, derived from Latin jurists (='final, precluding further debate') will not stand. It is inconsistent with (iii) and (iv). But the rendering 'frivolous' will not meet the case; it is too vague an indictment.

Ducange (vol. v. p. 201) gives it no support. The passage quoted by Father Morris (p. 545) proves on inspection to be given by Ducange under the heading of the t. t. *exceptio peremptoria*. Ducange in fact suggests the reading *non peremptorias*, to avoid the contradiction between the two technical terms *dilatorias* and *peremptorias*, and refers to the jurists in illustration of the technical meaning of the latter (Dig. 44. 1. 3; Gaius 4. 117). Besides, if *peremptorias*, usually so strictly technical, is to be turned, as Father Morris turns it, into a synonym for *frivolas*, why should not the other technical term *dilatorias* be similarly treated? I am inclined myself to translate the passage, 'unmeaning, frivolous pleas, whether intended to postpone or to preclude discussion of the question.'

It remains to suggest some other meaning for these expressions in the *Chronicon de Bello*. The clause condemned as 'peremptory' was a clause giving the abbot absolute exemption from the jurisdiction of the bishop of the diocese. The bishop and his supporters were indignant that this question should be regarded as settled once for all by an old royal charter which invested the abbot permanently with a freedom that was not qualified by any safeguard or restriction in the interests of the bishop or the archbishop. It was this absence of any saving clause that roused their indignation. I should therefore translate *peremptorius* by some such word as '*sweeping*,' '*arbitrary*,' a transitional meaning between the legal t. t. 'final,' 'decisive' and the looser modern use of the word 'peremptory' in the sense of 'autocratic.'

NOTE B.

THE CHANCELLOR AND THE BATTLE ABBEY CASE
(Father Morris, *S. Thomas*, pp. 47, 48; Note D, pp. 533–557).

In the text of his life of S. Thomas of Canterbury (pp. 47, 48), Father Morris just alludes incidentally to the Battle Abbey case as an oft-quoted example of the chancellor's readiness to side with the king against the principles of ecclesiasticism, but rejects the evidence of the Chronicle as biassed and fragmentary, and refuses to allow it to modify the judgment which he formed of the chancellor's character from the other acts of his chancellorship. For this summary dismissal of the question he makes full atonement in a long appendix (Note D, pp. 533-557), in which he traces the history of the dispute from beginning to end as it is related in the Abbey Chronicle, and explains in detail his reasons for declining to join in the almost universal vote of censure against the chancellor's action in this famous suit.

The learned Jesuit's case for S. Thomas may be analysed briefly as follows.

J. The trustworthiness of the Abbey Chronicle as historical evidence is discredited

(a) by the fragmentary shape in which the chancellor's speech has come down to us. The MSS. show unmistakable signs of erasure and correction. The chancellor's remonstrance with the bishop at the trial of 1157 apparently ran thus in the original MS. ......tis in dominum nostrum regem, cui fidem sacramentum...... As it now stands the second lacuna is filled thus: cui fidei sacramentum vos fecisse nulli dubium est. The addition is evidently written over an erasure. The word ...*tis* has been completed into *peccatis* by the editor of the *Chronicon de Bello* (Anglia Christiana Society, 1846), but this is after all only a conjecture.

(b) by the *ex parte* character of the Chronicle, written as it was by a monk of Battle Abbey, who would naturally take pains to represent the great chancellor as siding with the abbot against the bishop.

(c) by the letter to Pope Alexander in 1163 in which Thomas the archbishop enumerates the discomfiture of the bishop among the acts of oppression to which the Church had been compelled to submit before his own promotion to the see of Canterbury. "This does not read like the statement of the man who had taken the part ascribed to him by the chronicler of the Abbey."

II. Assuming however for the sake of argument that the chronicler's report of the trial is mainly correct, Father Morris puts forward one or two valuable suggestions by way of explaining the chancellor's real attitude towards the question at issue.

(*a*) Pope Adrian in his letter of remonstrance to the abbot on his disloyalty to the bishop had referred to the profession of obedience which the abbot had made to the bishop. Apparently therefore the Pope was under the impression that the Abbey was not exempt, in which case alone could the abbot's refusal of obedience be made a ground of censure. As a matter of fact the original exemption had been sanctioned by archbishop Lanfranc and Stigand bishop of Chichester.

(*b*) Battle Abbey was a *dominica capella*, and therefore had all the privileges of a royal chapel.

(*c*) A founder was at liberty to impose any condition of his own authority at the time of foundation. "It was for the Church to choose whether she would accept the foundation so hampered; and in this case the Church was a party to the conditions imposed in the Conqueror's charter."

Father Morris is inclined therefore to regard the opposition of the bishop of Chichester and the evident sympathy which Theobald gave him as arising "not so much from zeal for ecclesiastical liberty as from jealousy of monastic exemption." He then proceeds to point out that

(1) the chancellor in his concluding speech in no way claimed the right to decide the matter by secular authority.

(2) the point of grievance emphasized by Thomas

in his letter to Pope Alexander eleven years afterwards was not that the king had encroached upon a papal privilege by exempting an abbey from episcopal jurisdiction, but that he had compelled the bishop to give the kiss of peace to an abbot whom he had excommunicated. As a matter of fact, the conclusion arrived at in this case in 1157, far from being repudiated by the Church, was sanctioned by archbishop Theobald, who confirmed the exemption of the Abbey, and afterwards by Pope Honorius and Pope Gregory, who recited with approval the recognition of the rights of the Abbey by bishop Hilary at Colchester in 1157.

Father Morris has done good service in clearing up the precise point at issue and proving that the chancellor was acting in accordance with the technical rights of the case in upholding the royal charter. But still the fact remains if we may trust the Chronicle, that Thomas was quick to follow the king's lead in interrupting the bishop in the midst of his injudicious assertion of the supremacy of the spiritual power, even though the exact terms of the interruption cannot be with certainty restored, owing to the fragmentary condition of the manuscripts; and it is difficult to avoid the suspicion that the chancellor's deliberate persistence in bringing home to the bishop's door the responsibility of having called in the papal intervention against a royal charter was prompted by the conviction that this was the surest way to bring down the king's anger upon the bishop and secure a verdict in favour of the abbot.

CHAPTER VIII.

THE PRIMACY.

THEOBALD died in April 1161, and for a whole year the see was left vacant. In May 1162 Thomas of London, archdeacon of Canterbury and chancellor of England, was elected archbishop on the king's nomination. His conduct at this crisis has been a veritable *crux historicorum*. The motive is the first thing to be examined in estimating the moral value of a man's actions, and it is usually the last thing to be determined with certainty, especially where different motives are at work in combination or in conflict, as is frequently the case. It is just this complexity of motive which makes the attitude of Thomas on this occasion so hard to understand; and the problem is still further complicated by the discrepancy of the data at our disposal for its solution. The statements of Thomas and his friends are not easily reconciled with the statements of his opponents. In some case they have to be left in almost absolute contradiction.

One thing is certain at the outset, and that is Henry's intention in placing Thomas on the archi- *Henry's intentions.*

episcopal throne. The biographers are all agreed on this point, and their testimony is in accordance with all that we know from other sources of the general character of his early policy. It was his intention to rule the Church through the archbishop as he had ruled the baronage and the people through the chancellor[1]. The divided jurisdiction of Church and Crown which dated from the Conqueror was now seriously threatening the royal supremacy and the unity of the kingdom. A large section of the king's subjects was withdrawn from his control by the separate jurisdiction of the bishops and the primate over all who had received the orders of the Church, readers and acolytes as well as priests and deacons.

[1] Joh. S. ii. 305: quo totam facilius ecclesiam regeret. Fitzst. iii. 25: confidens quod sibi ad placitum et nutum, ut cancellarius fecerat, archiepiscopus obsequeretur. Auct. Anon. I. iv. 14: credens itaque rex propositum suum adversus ecclesiam per eum potissimum impleri. Henry had also a secondary purpose in view which should not be overlooked. Theobald's services in promoting his accession and in governing the country during the interregnum of 1154 had apparently impressed him with the capacities of the primacy as a bulwark of the Crown; at any rate more than one biographer credits Henry with the design of securing in Thomas a faithful guardian for his heirs in the event of his own death occurring early. Joh. S. ii. 305: si vero dies suos mors immatura praecideret, haeredibus suis tutorem fidelissimum providebat. Cp. Gervase (*Act. Pontif. Cant.* s. v. Thomas), and Will. C. i. 6, where the two motives of dynastic and ecclesiastical policy both come out clearly. *Thomas Saga* (Rolls Series, i. 70): "he trusted Thomas best of all men to aid his heirs to the throne, in case he himself should be no more." The *Saga* avowedly attaches less importance to the other reason for the king's insistence, "in that he thought Thomas would be yielding to his will in the keeping of the laws and the kingly customs in the realm."

The danger was twofold. The only penalties at the disposal of this spiritual jurisdiction—fines, penance, imprisonment, and degradation—were impotent to check crime within the Church. In fact the comparative licence which they gave was rapidly converting the lower orders of the Church into a criminal class. The ecclesiastical jurisdiction was weak where it should be strong, in the coercive element of justice. But at the same time it was aggressive in its pretensions. As a spiritual power it claimed absolute independence and superiority in the face of the secular power, and it encroached upon the province of the king's jurisdiction by extending its power over the laity. The boundaries of canon law and common law were not yet sharply defined; and questions of marriage and inheritance, the validity of oaths and contracts and the like, were appropriated by the Church courts. The commutation of penance into fines made their procedure popular with the rich, and the merciful character of their punishments in comparison with those of the lay courts won the goodwill of the lower classes of the people. This state of things was intolerable to Henry. He had met with a striking case in the diocese of York in 1158, in which the extortions of clerical justice and the pretensions of clerical immunity both stand out in vivid relief. The king was at York, and a citizen of Scarborough came before him with a grave complaint. A certain rural dean had extorted from him twenty-two shillings by bringing an unsupported charge of adultery against his wife, though a royal edict had ordered that no accusation should be entertained on the evidence of a single witness only. The king summoned the dean before him, and the case was investigated. The archbishop of York was present, and also the bishops of Lincoln and Durham, and John treasurer of York. The dean had been provided with a defence. The woman, he said, had been accused by two persons, a deacon and a layman. She denied the charge, and was permitted to choose her ordeal; but her husband came forward and paid the archdeacon twenty shillings as a bribe and the dean himself two shillings. The dean was unable to prove this statement, and the king insisted on his trial, remarking that the archdeacons and deans extorted more money from the people of the realm in this way than the king received as revenue. The king's barons went with the clergy to try the case. At last John the treasurer suggested that the money should be restored to the citizen, and the question of the dean's degradation submitted to his archbishop. This roused Richard de Luci. "What share then in the decision will you allot to my lord the king, whose authority the man has disobeyed?" "Nothing," replied John; "the man is a clerk." Richard refused to lend his sanction to such a proposal, and went back with the barons to the king. The clergy came in shortly with the proposal which John had made; but the king angrily refused to recognise the validity of their sentence, and gave notice of an appeal to Theobald archbishop of Canterbury. The appeal however was not prosecuted. The death of Geoffrey intervened in July

1158, and Henry dropped the case and went off to Normandy[1].

None the less Henry was determined to remedy the evil; and the death of Theobald gave him his opportunity. He was bent on being king in fact as well as in name over the whole nation,—bent on asserting his supremacy in all causes and over all persons, ecclesiastical and civil alike. The refractory barons had been compelled to submit to his authority; the administration of royal justice in the provinces had been set on a firm basis; and the Church was now from the king's point of view the only insubordinate element in his kingdom. His early reforms had been carried out with the help, if not at the suggestion, of his trusty chancellor. Thomas' attitude—real or assumed—towards ecclesiastical claims had been distinctly unsympathetic[2]; and the king, convinced of his ability and devotion, thought that Thomas would prove as archbishop an invaluable instrument in securing ecclesiastical reform. "Where the problem was to reconcile the rights of the clergy with the law of the land, it would be convenient, even essential, that the chancellorship and the primacy should be combined in the same person[3]."

[1] Fitzst. iii. 44, 45.

[2] Auct. Anon. I. iv. 14, hints that the king was misled by Thomas' deliberate assumption of severity against the Church. Cp. Ch. VII. of this Essay (p. 155).

[3] Prof. Froude, *Short Studies*, iv. 33. In the original article in the *Nineteenth Century* for 1877 the passage quoted above was followed by the remark that Frederic Barbarossa "was finding the value of such a combination in Germany, where with the

The king's intention is certain beyond a doubt. We have now to notice how his nomination was received first by Thomas himself, and afterwards by the chapter of Canterbury and the clergy of England.

archbishop of Cologne for a chancellor of the empire he was carrying out an ecclesiastical revolution." The revolution was Mr. Froude's own addition; the rest of his comment is a mutilation of the remark which Diceto makes in explanation of Henry's surprise and disappointment at Thomas' resignation of the seal (R. Diceto, i. 308, ed. Stubbs): audierat namque quod Maguntinus archiepiscopus in Teutonica sub rege, quod Coloniensis archiepiscopus in Italia sub imperatore nomen sibi vendicent archicancellarii. There were two chancellor-archbishops. Cp. Miss Norgate, *England under the Angevin Kings*, ii. 6.

Freeman (*Contemp. Review*, vol. 32, pp. 494–496) admits that Henry probably had these "imperial models" in view, but points out that this fact does not make his design with regard to Thomas much less remarkable. There was as yet no precedent in England (1) for the promotion of a chancellor straight to the *primacy*. Ordinary bishoprics were frequently given to royal chancellors as the reward of secular services, but never the see of Canterbury, which was almost invariably filled out of the ranks of monasticism. (2) for the *retention* of the chancellorship by a bishop or archbishop. Up to this date it was considered below the dignity of a bishop to remain chancellor. The greatest of Thomas' predecessors in the chancellorship, Roger bishop of Salisbury, had resigned the lower position of chancellor to his son on his own promotion to the higher offices of bishop and justiciar. It was not until after the chancellorship had gained prestige and dignity in the hands of Thomas that it came to be retained by a bishop or an archbishop. This fact has an important bearing on Thomas' speedy resignation of the seal after his consecration. The king was certainly surprised and indignant; he was so intent on having a chancellor-archbishop of his own like the emperor that he had procured a papal dispensation to sanction the combination of the two offices (Garnier, ed. Hippeau, p. 29). But Thomas in resigning the chancellorship was only acting in accordance with precedent.

(1) The circumstances of the king's offer are described in detail by Herbert of Bosham, who says that he often heard the story from the lips of the exiled archbishop[1]. The death of Theobald after a primacy of more than twenty-two years aroused the keenest expectation and curiosity at court. Some hinted, others openly pointed at the chancellor as the coming archbishop[2]. The people were loud in their prophecies. But the king kept his own counsel, and took no steps beyond entrusting the vacant see, as usual, to the care of the chancellor. Thomas guessed the king's design, but held his peace. They were then in Normandy. Henry had resolved to send Thomas to England to deal with the incursions of the Welsh, and transact other affairs of state[3]. It was on this occasion that Thomas received the first intimation of the king's purpose. He had gone to take leave of the king at Falaise. Henry took

Thomas and the king's offer of the primacy.

---

[1] Herb. iii. 180-182.

[2] Cp. the language attributed to the prior of Leicester in his interview with Thomas at Rouen: vos estis...procurator etiam archiepiscopatus, et, sicut rumor in curia frequens est, archiepiscopus eritis. Fitzst. iii. 26.

[3] Grim, ii. 366, says that Thomas was sent to England on more errands than one, but especially to secure the homage of the nobility for Henry the king's son, who was soon to be crowned as the future king. Auct. Anon. I. iv. 13 mentions with admiration his success in this matter, which, he says, was considered a difficult task even for a king himself to accomplish in person. R. de Diceto (A.D. 1162) records that in that year the bishops and abbots swore fealty to the young Henry by command of the king (mandato regis); "but Thomas the chancellor did homage to him before any one else, saving only his allegiance to the king as long as he should live and wish to remain at the head of the realm."

him aside, and revealed the secret of his mission to England. He was to be made archbishop of Canterbury. Thomas by way of reply drew the king's attention with a jest to his gay costume, and contrasted his own worldly appearance with the bearing of the grave monks of Canterbury over whom the king proposed to place him in authority. Then changing his tone he warned the king seriously that a rupture would be inevitable[1]. As archbishop he could not sanction the encroachments upon ecclesiastical privilege which Henry, he knew, was meditating and had in fact begun[2]. His enemies besides would seize the first opportunity to alienate him from the king.

Henry was not deterred, continues Herbert, by this affectionate warning. He next announced his intention publicly in the presence of Thomas and the rest of the commissioners bound for England;

[1] Robertson (*Becket*, p. 38) suggests that the warning was given with a smile which robbed it of its force by casting a doubt upon its sincerity. But there is no indication of this in the text of Herbert's narrative.

[2] Herb. iii. 181: novi quippe te nonnulla exacturum et etiam in ecclesiasticis te jam multa praesumere quae ego aequo animo sustinere non possem. According to the Icelandic life (*Thomas Saga*, i. 65), the chancellor advised the selection of some fitter person than himself: "And withal you have in your realm such laudable persons as that my fleshly looseness fareth low before their feet...I therefore pray, in all humbleness, that you go somewhere else." The writer adds, after recording Henry's charge to Richard de Luci, that "at the same time the king settled privily with the cardinal (Henry of Pisa) that he should give such aid to the affair that his own furtherance thereof should not be needed" (ib. pp. 67, 69). But there is no hint of this secret understanding in any of the other biographers.

and turning to one of them, Richard de Luci, commanded him to forward Thomas' advancement as loyally as he would exert himself in placing young Henry on the throne, if his father lay dead on his bier.

Herbert is the only biographer who has given the actual circumstances in full. But the other biographers are equally emphatic on the subject of Thomas' hesitation and reluctance. They all lay stress on the fact that he foresaw the certainty of a conflict with the king. Some of them suggest other reasons besides,—the heavy responsibilities of the care of all the churches[1], the danger from jealous enemies at court[2], the necessity of adopting a stricter manner of life as archbishop[3]. Only one writer speaks of him, and that incidentally, as casting an eager glance at the vacant primacy. William of Canterbury says that he was in a strait 'twixt two[4]. He was anxious for the greater opportunities of meditation which the new life would bring, and yet he dreaded the very appearance of a grasping ambition. Whatever the meaning of Thomas' resistance was, it only made the king more determined; and eventually the chancellor's "faint and lingering scruples[5]" were overcome by the arguments of a fellow ecclesiastic, Henry of Pisa, a Cistercian monk, cardinal and papal legate,

---

[1] Joh. S. ii. 305. Will. C. i. 7.
[2] Joh. S. ib. Will. C. ib.
[3] Auct. Anon. II. iv. 85.
[4] Will. C. i. 7.
[5] Milman, *Latin Christianity*, iii. 453.

who had remained in Normandy after lending his
sanction on behalf of the Pope to the marriage of
the royal children Henry and Margaret in 1160.
He urged Thomas in the interests of the Church as
well as for his own spiritual benefit to accept the
great opportunity now at his disposal[1], and at last
Thomas yielded to the legate's entreaties and the
advice of his friends, and withdrew his opposition to
the king's design.

That is the story as told by the contemporary
biographers. Two facts stand out clearly in their
narrative. One is the fact that Thomas was sincerely
reluctant; the other is the fact that Thomas gave
the king clear proof of his reluctance. Against the
first of these statements we have to set the inevitable contradiction of his rivals and opponents. One
of the anonymous biographers admits that Thomas'
election was opposed by some on the ground that he
had forced his own way into the sacred eminence of
the primacy[2]; but he says that the accusation was

---

[1] Will. C. i. 8, Joh. S. ii. 306, Auct. Anon. i. iv. 18, just state
the bare fact of the cardinal's intervention. Auct. Anon. ii. iv. 86
gives the substance of his appeal to Thomas: ut munus tam
instanter oblatum pro Christi ecclesia non respueret, nec occasionem tam honestam sperneret, qua liber ab humano, Dei deinceps
vacare posset obsequio. Froude's unwarranted addition in the
Nineteenth Century for 1877 (p. 562)—to the effect that the
cardinal also told Thomas that "he need not communicate
convictions which would interfere with his appointment"—is
omitted in the reprint of the essay in his *Short Studies* (vol. iv.
p. 34), possibly in consequence of its scathing exposure by Freeman (*Contemp. Review*, vol. 32, p. 493).

[2] Auct. Anon. ii. iv. 85: tam sanctum dignitatis fastigium non
horrens renuisse, sed ultroneus ascendisse.

prompted by jealousy, and he only quotes it to give it a flat denial. Gilbert Foliot in his famous letter of remonstrance four years afterwards openly charged Thomas with having bought the chancellorship deliberately, according to the usual interpretation of the passage, as a stepping-stone to the primacy[1]. He certainly accused him in the same letter of indecent haste in securing the prize when the death of Theobald brought it within his reach. "You were waiting," wrote Foliot, "with a watchful eye for this event, and you lost no time in hurrying back from Normandy to England." This haste may be explained on other grounds; we know that Thomas had urgent business of state to transact on this visit to England. But it is doubtful whether it was such a hasty proceeding. The chancellor was still at Rouen, convalescent after his illness, when the prior of Leicester addressed him as 'procurator archiepiscopatus'; and had he been as busy in his own behalf as Foliot hints, it is scarcely likely

[1] Foliot to Thomas, *Ep.* 225 (*Materials*, v. 523, 524): vos certa licitatione proposita cancellariam illam dignitatem multis marcarum millibus obtinuisse, et aurae hujus impulsu in portum ecclesiae Cantuariensis illapsum ad ejus tandem sic regimen accessisse. The deliberate design upon the primacy from the outset is an inference which perhaps the language will scarcely justify. The words 'illapsum...accessisse' seem rather to imply that the course of events had brought Thomas within reach of the primacy; and perhaps Foliot is merely hinting that Thomas had made an unjustifiable use of the influence with the king afforded by a chancellorship which had itself been obtained by a transaction that suited ill with his eventual promotion to a spiritual office, however permissible it might be regarded as a means of obtaining a secular office.

that twelve months would have been allowed to elapse before his election[1].

The testimony of the biographers on this point is confirmed by a review of his previous conduct. The whole tenor of his life as chancellor had been the opposite of what might have been expected of an intending candidate for the sacred office to which Lanfranc and Anselm had bequeathed such a heritage of saintly tradition. Ordinary bishoprics might fall to worldly ecclesiastics as the reward of secular services to the state, but not the archbishopric of Canterbury; and though more than one primate had proved himself a statesman, it was not on the score of his statesmanship that he had been selected to occupy the primacy. Men still looked to the abbey or the monastery for a scholar or a saint to tread in the footsteps of the great Norman archbishops. But Thomas had taken no pains to conciliate the churchmen who would have a voice in his election. Worldly and secular in his outward bearing, his love of sport, his grandeur, his extravagance, and anti-ecclesiastical in his policy, he had done everything to alienate the men whose good-

---

[1] Dean Hook (*Archbps.* ii. 387) attributes the delay to the opposition of the English clergy; Froude (*Nineteenth Century*, 1877) thinks it was caused by the reluctance of Thomas. It is quite possible that Milman is right (*Latin Christianity*, iii. 453) in supposing that Henry did not offer the primacy to Thomas until the end of the year. The chancellor was in charge of the temporalities of the see, and its revenues would go into the royal treasury, so that Henry would have an obvious motive in delaying the appointment of a new archbishop.

will he should have striven to win if he had set his heart on filling the throne of Canterbury.

His disinclination to accept the primacy, after all, was only natural. He was quite at home in the chancellorship. His military ardour, his diplomatic talent, his administrative powers, all had full scope in that office, and room was left for the display of the luxury and magnificence which he loved so dearly. But the change of position would necessitate a change of life. The pastimes of the court, the excitements of war, permissible in a deacon, not always foregone even by the bishops and papal legates of that age, were inconsistent with the ideal of the priesthood, still more of the primacy, which Thomas would feel bound to copy to the best of his ability from the life of his great prototype Anselm. It might involve, it was certain to involve a change in his relations with the king. The archbishop would consider himself called upon to oppose the royal will which it was the chancellor's duty and pleasure to obey; and friendship might have to give place to enmity. Thomas may well have shrunk from the prospect. His biographers emphatically say that he did shrink from it; and there is no valid reason for rejecting their testimony.

There is no reason either why we should not believe the further statement that Thomas did give Henry full notice of his reluctance to accept the primacy, and full warning of the conflict that must ensue if he did accept it. Unless Herbert of Bosham is to be ruled out of court as a partial witness on a point of fact which he states on the direct authority of Thomas himself, we must admit that the warning was given. It has been pronounced "incredible that the king would have persevered in the appointment, if he had been made distinctly to understand what Becket meant to do," and that incredibility has been regarded as a sufficient ground for doubting Herbert's veracity[1]. But it is far more probable that the warning was given and disregarded. Perhaps Henry mistook it for "the decent resistance of an ambitious prelate[2]"; perhaps, blinded by his attachment to Thomas and his implicit faith in Thomas' devotion to himself, he was content to risk all contingencies. Whatever the reason, he persisted in defiance of the warning; and it was not repeated. The conscience of the nineteenth century might require a second warning where the first had fallen on an unheeding or mistaken ear, but the code of honour by which Thomas regulated his conduct like his contemporaries, laymen and clerics, in the twelfth century would be content with one plain intimation[3]. Thomas would have satisfied his conscience; and Henry alone would now be responsible for the consequences of his ill-

---

[1] Froude, *Short Studies*, iv. 34. "Herbert of Bosham introduces a speech which Becket is *supposed* to have addressed to Henry, intimating that the king would find him a most determined antagonist." The italics are my own. In a foot-note to this passage Mr Froude has another fling at the devoted biographer. "Herbert considers his master's frankness on this occasion a miracle of magnanimity." So he does (Herb. iii. 181); but this comment need not damage the credit of the fact to which it is appended.

[2] Milman, *Lat. Christ.* iii. 453.

[3] Freeman, *Contemp. Review*, vol. 32, p. 493.

advised persistence. It is quite possible that Thomas having done all that his duty seemed to require began to "listen to the promptings of ambition[1]." He may have reflected that perseverance in his refusal would probably drive the king to find a more compliant ecclesiastic elsewhere[2]; and Thomas could ill brook to see the primacy of all England pass into other hands when it had once been placed within reach of his own. He may have dreaded the weight of the king's displeasure[3], which might visit his obstinacy with loss of wealth or influence. We cannot tell what thoughts did or did not pass through his mind. We only know the result. Thomas let things take their course, and waited for the sequel "with the consistency and dignity of a man who knows not exactly what to wish; of one who has been forced into an election in which he would not have volunteered to be a candidate[4],"—in the words of the faithful Herbert,

"non honorem ambientis nec respuentis tamen."

(2) The king's nomination had now to be confirmed by the voice of the Church[5]. The decision lay primarily with the chapter of Canterbury, and their choice was ratified by the clergy of the

The election at Canterbury

---

[1] Hook, *Archbps.* ii. 386.   [2] Froude, *Short Studies*, iv. 35.
[3] Auct. Anon. II. iv. 86: cui (regi) procul dubio necesse fuit obsequi, vel ipsum (Thomam) indubitato proscriptionis et odii subjacere discrimini.
[4] Hook, *ib.*
[5] Grim, ii. 366: aliquamdiu differtur negotium donec a conventu consensum extorqueat, qui liberam ab antiquo solet habere vocem in electione pontificis; nam illo reclamante nulli regum licuit intrudere quemquam propria auctoritate.

province. The *congé d'élire* was conveyed to the monks of Christ Church by a deputation from the king, consisting of three bishops, Bartholomew of Exeter, Hilary of Chichester, and Walter of Rochester, the justiciar Richard de Luci, and his brother Walter abbot of Battle[1]. The procedure is described at great length by one of the anonymous biographers[2]. The bishops began by greeting the chapter, and after enlarging upon the king's favour called on Richard to explain the king's intentions. The justiciar announced that the king was graciously pleased to allow full freedom of election, but he recommended them to fix their choice upon a person acceptable to the king, and hinted ominously at the dangers and difficulties that must otherwise beset the Church[3]. The prior retired, by permission of the bishops, with a few of the older and wiser monks; but they found the responsibility of the choice too great, and came back to request the advice of the bishops and the justiciar, who were acquainted with the royal pleasure on which the election was felt to depend. The joint consultation ended in their choice falling upon the chancellor. The monks

---

[1] Garnier, pp. 16, 17 (ed. Hippeau). Auct. Anon. I. iv. 14–16, only mentions Exeter and Chichester. Grim, ii. 366 says there were three bishops; and the name of the third, Rochester, is supplied by Gervase, i. 169 (ed. Stubbs), who also mentions Chichester's old opponent, the abbot Walter.

[2] Auct. Anon. I. iv. 14–16, whose account is closely followed in the text of this Essay.

[3] Cp. Grim, ii. 366: si talis eligatur qui regi non placeat, in schismate eritis et discordia, sub tali pastore dispersionem, non refugium habituri.

indeed hesitated for a time, unwilling to elect an archbishop from the ranks of the secular clergy. Canterbury had been a monastic church from its foundation by S. Augustine, and all its archbishops but two had been regulars. But this technical objection was compensated by the personal merits of the chancellor, and eventually every voice was given in his favour[1].

The election was confirmed in Westminster Abbey. The king's commissioners summoned to London by royal mandate all the bishops, abbots and priors of the province of Canterbury[2], as well as the barons and royal officials, to hear the result of the election in the presence of the young Henry, who had received his father's instructions to act as his representative. The prior of Christ Church announced the choice of the chapter, the king's

Its confirmation at Westminster.

---

[1] Auct. Anon. I. iv. 14–16. Herbert of Bosham (iii. 183), as will be seen shortly, speaks of a variety of objections raised by the monks of Christ Church; but their opposition is nowhere so vividly depicted as in the *Thomas Saga* (i. 73), which represents the king's commissioners as withdrawing without the formal consent of the prior and his monks to the election.

[2] R. Diceto, A.D. 1162: clero totius *provinciae Cantuariorum* generaliter Londoniae convocato, praesente Henrico filio regis et regni justiciariis Thomas...nemine reclamante sollenniter electus in archiepiscopum (i. 306). Cp. Herb. iii. 184. Fitzst. iii. 36. Matthew Paris says, 'congregato clero et populo totius *provinciae Cantuariensis.*' Garnier (p. 19, ed. Hippeau), Will. C. i. 9, Auct. Anon. I. iv. 16 speak of the council as representing the clergy and people of the whole realm; and this no doubt misled Baronius, who styles it 'generale concilium, omnibus convenientibus episcopis' (Wilkins, *Concilia*, i. 434). The Icelandic life gives a full account of these proceedings at London; see Note at the close of this chapter.

commissioners expressed their approval, and the assembly of clergy and nobles acquiesced in the election. Little Henry, only eight years of age, gave his consent in his father's name at the request of the body of bishops headed by Henry of Winchester, and his example was followed by the ministers of state, to whom the king had already communicated his intentions. One other formality had yet to take place before the archbishop-elect could be consecrated. That was the release from all secular obligations which has already been discussed. It was made the subject of an earnest appeal by Henry bishop of Winchester, and it was readily granted by the royal ministers on behalf of the king[1].

Opposition of the clergy. The royal purpose was now attained. But the course of events had not run quite as smoothly as some of Thomas' friends assert. Edward Grim and the anonymous biographer who relates the proceedings of the chapter of Christ Church in such detail both describe the election at Canterbury as unanimous. We are also told that the only voice raised in opposition at Westminster was that of Gilbert Foliot, bishop of Hereford[2], a man of strict monastic life and eminent learning, a vegetarian and a total abstainer[3], known to be in high favour with the king, and widely mentioned as a probable

---

[1] Auct. Anon. I. iv. 16–18. Grim, ii. 367.

[2] Fitzst. iii. 36: solus quod potuit dissuasit. Will. C. i. 9, Grim, ii. 367, Anon. Auct. I. call him "bishop of London," but it was not until 1163 that Gilbert was translated from Hereford to London.

[3] Fitzst. iii. 36: habitu monachus, vinum vel carnem non gustans.

successor to Theobald[1]. He stood alone, it is said, and withdrew his opposition when he saw that he was unsupported[2], though he afterwards remarked that the king had wrought a miracle in turning a soldier and a worldling into an archbishop[3]. But two of the biographers, Herbert of Bosham and the second anonymous writer, frankly and unsuspectingly supply us with the materials for reconstructing the other side of the case. The former distinctly states that there was a great difference of opinion, and that this difference was especially marked in the chapter, which had the most vital interests at stake. The chancellor's friends, he says, were convinced that the Church would enjoy a firm and lasting peace

---

[1] Auct. Anon. II. iv. 98.

[2] Auct. Anon. I. iv. 17. Diceto, i. 306, says the election was confirmed 'nemine reclamante': this can only be true of the formal acceptance of the archbishop elect after Foliot had withdrawn his protest.

[3] Fitzst. iii. 36. Cp. the language attributed to Foliot by Garnier (p. 19):

"Kar de seinte Eglise ad persécuturs esté,"

and again,

"Destruite ad seinte Eglise: si l'at mise en despit;

Et a dispersunée: à tort l'i unt eslit"

(i.e. they have done wrong in electing him).

Bishop Henry's only reply to this charge was an appeal to Thomas, which indicates that he too felt the need of a miracle to change the wolf into a shepherd, the persecutor Saul into a second apostle Paul (Garnier, p. 18):

"Tu fus lus a veillis: or seies pastre et prestre;

De Saul persécutur, Pols serras et deiz estre."

Cp. the story of the election in *Thomas Saga*, i. 81, 82, where bishop Henry appeals to Thomas to accept the primacy in similar words. See Note C at the end of this chapter.

"with such a welcome mediator between the king and the priesthood." But others, he adds, looked askance at the royal gift to the Church. There was the risk of material loss. With a primate hailing fresh from court, the royal officials and barons would grasp still more boldly at the possessions of the Church. There was also the risk of moral and spiritual decline. It was a patent absurdity, a flagrant wrong, to set over such a holy band of monks a man who wore a soldier's belt with a better grace than the garb of a clerk,—to place as pastor in charge of the fold a man who preferred to follow the hounds and feed a hawk, who would bring with him the appetite of a wolf sharpened by his courtier's life, and sacrifice all spiritual interests to pomp and popularity[1]. It was sheer presumption, said others, that one scarce fit to hold an oar should take the helm of the Church into his own hands[2]. The personal character of Thomas was not the only objection raised. The circumstances of his election were equally unsatisfactory. Some looked upon his apparent reluctance as grasping ambition in disguise[3]. Others condemned his election as un-

---

[1] Herb. iii. 183. Cp. Foliot's language in his letter to Thomas in 1166, *Ep.* 225 (*Materials*, v. 535): id dixeritis inauditum, officialem curiae repentino transitu ad illam sic ecclesiam umquam hactenus ascendisse ut quis curiam, cras dispensaret ecclesiam, ab avibus et canibus ceterisque curiae jocundis usibus cito quis adstaret altaribus et episcopis totius regni spiritualia ministraret et sacerdotibus.

[2] Auct. Anon. ii. iv. 85.

[3] Auct. Anon. ii. iv. 85: non horrens renuisse (creditur) sed ultroneus ascendisse.

THE PRIMACY. 211

canonical on the ground that the royal pressure at his back had carried the day in spite of the wishes of the clergy and the people[1]. Foliot may have been the only man who spoke out his mind when the time came; but he was evidently not the only man who objected in his heart to the elevation of Thomas to the primacy. Foliot's opposition may have been what the biographers say it was, the outcry of a disappointed rival[2]; but there was evidently a large body of feeling against Thomas which cannot be explained away by the supposition of personal jealousy. It was apparently suppressed at Westminster. It had no influence on the result[3]. It was perhaps driven inwards, to come out again—such is the irony of fate—on the side of the king against the recalcitrant archbishop. But its existence is proved beyond a doubt by the admissions of Thomas' own friends and biographers.

A still stronger light is thrown upon the election of 1162 by the correspondence which passed between

---

[1] Auct. Anon. II. iv. 85: magis operata est regis instantia quam cleri vel populi vota. Fitzst. iii. 36 admits this one flaw in the election: praecedente notaque omni clero Angliae regis voluntate, quod solum electionis illius meritis derogavit.

[2] Fitzst. iii. 36: ut putabatur, non bene zelans electionem sed male electum; aspirare enim et pro se laborare credebatur. Auct. Anon. I. iv. 17: ut ferebat opinio, ad archiepiscopatum ex diu aspiraverat.

[3] Auct. Anon. II. iv. 87: licet (sicut evenire solet in talibus) aemuli quidam non parum suspiraverint, nihil tamen palam propositum est quod rem vel praepediret vel differret. This seems conclusive against Dean Hook's supposition that it was the opposition of the English clergy that was responsible for the long delay in the appointment.

Thomas and the English clergy in consequence of his fulminations at Vezelay in 1166. The first letter of the four—a remonstrance from the bishops and priests of the province of Canterbury, accompanied by a copy of their appeal to the Pope—charged Thomas in strong language with ingratitude to the king who had befriended him at the outset of his career and had left no means untried to exalt him to the sacred dignity of the primacy, "in spite of the warnings of his mother, the loud protest of the whole realm, the sighing and groaning of the Church of God, as far as she dare give voice to her complaint[1]." Thomas replied to the body of the clergy with a flat contradiction. He defied them to point to a single flaw in his election. All due formalities had been observed; the choice of the Church had been unanimous; the king's son and the king's commissioners had given their assent; and lastly the English clergy had joined the king in the despatch of an urgent message requesting the Pope to forward the pallium to the archbishop who had been thus duly elected and consecrated[2]. In his letter to Foliot, the prime mover of the appeal, Thomas quoted the accusation verbatim as Foliot's handiwork, only to give it a full denial. He had heard the voice of the realm; but it had been loud in acclamation, not in protest. The warning of Matilda, the king's mother, if given at all, had never

---

[1] *Ep.* 205 (v. 410): dissuadente matre sua, regno reclamante, ecclesia Dei, quoad licuit, suspirante et ingemiscente, vos...omnibus modis studuit sublimare.

[2] *Ep.* 223 (v. 498).

found public expression. But it was quite possible that a few ambitious ecclesiastics, when they saw their hopes dashed to the ground, had given vent to a sigh of disappointment,—the very men perhaps who had revenged themselves afterwards by fomenting the ill-feeling between himself and the king[1].

Foliot returned to the charge with a trenchant reply to this apology. He complained of the archbishop's injustice in singling him out from the whole body of clergy for personal attack. He disavowed the very idea of having aspired to the primacy. Thomas, he said, knew better, if he would only acknowledge what he knew. The favour of Thomas was the one thing essential for all seekers after preferment. But had he ever taken pains to ingratiate himself with the chancellor? He had not, and Thomas knew that he had not[2]. It was

[1] *Ep.* 224 (v. 516): regni reclamationem non audivimus, sed potius acclamationem. Dissuasio vero genitricis domini nostri, si fuit, usque ad publicum non prodiit...Potuit autem fieri aliquas ecclesiasticas personas ad eandem promotionem, ut solet, aspirantes suspirasse, cum se sentirent ab ea quam conceperant spe decidere: qui et hodie fortassis, in ultionem sui casus, praesentis dissensionis auctores sunt et consiliarii.

[2] Foliot to Thomas, *Ep.* 225 (v. 522, 523). Robertson, in a foot-note on p. 43 of his "*Becket, a Biography*" (in the midst of a long digression on Foliot's life and character, pp. 41–45) points out that this argument of Foliot's was "not worth much in a case where the chancellor himself was the rival marked out by public rumour." The charge of aspiring to the primacy was brought against Foliot once more after the see was vacated by the murder of Thomas, and was then again denied by him (Foliot, *Ep.* 269, ed. Giles). Foliot's merits have been briefly discussed by Milman (*Latin Christianity*, iii. 454, 455) and more thoroughly

not his own defeat, or the defeat of his friends, that had set him mourning over the promotion of Thomas. It was the degradation of the primacy, now fallen into the hands of a mercenary intruder of notorious unsanctity, who had bought his way into the king's service, and forced his way thence into the archbishopric for which he had been waiting. The death of Theobald had brought him back in hot haste to England, while Richard de Luci did not follow until some time afterwards with the royal mandate to the chapter. This mandate was practically, says Foliot, a command to elect the royal favourite on pain of the royal displeasure[1]. Threats of proscription were held out as the penalty of free choice, if it ran counter to the royal will[2]. The king's messengers were urgent; the chancellor's design was obvious; his friends plied threats and

by Miss Norgate (*England under the Angevin Kings*, i. 492–497, ii. 47–49).

[1] Foliot, *Ep.* 225 (v. 524): regis hic ad omnes habebat imperium ut Cantuarienses monachi, ut ecclesiae ipsius episcopi suffraganei vos expeterent, vos eligerent, vos in patrem et pastorem, negotium nulla deliberationum mora protrahentes, assumerent: alioquin iram regiam non utique declinarent, verum se regis hostes et suorum proculdubio ipsis rerum argumentis agnoscerent.

[2] Foliot, *Ep.* 225 (v. 524): quid loquimur experti novimus: attendentes enim ecclesiam Dei suffocari graviter, *ob quod in ejus libertatem quodammodo proclamavimus, verbum proscriptionis audivimus, et exsilio crudeliter addicti sumus*, nec solum persona nostra sed et domus patris mei et conjuncta nobis affinitas et cognatio tota. *Hoc quidem calice et aliis propinatum est.* Apparently Foliot's outspoken protest at Westminster was silenced by a naked threat of confiscation and exile; and he was not the only man thus coerced into acquiescence.

promises, intimidation and flattery, thick and fast; opposition was hopeless. The chancellor's vengeance was too terrible to risk. The sword of the civil power was in his hand. He had plunged it once already into the heart of his mother Church and drunk deep of her blood, when he drained her revenues for the war of Toulouse. A second blow was inevitable, if his designs upon the primacy were thwarted; and the Church yielded in self-defence. Her fears proved stronger than her reluctance[1]. "It was thus that you entered into the sheepfold," wrote Foliot in conclusion, "not by the door, but by climbing up another way."

We may perhaps hesitate to accept Foliot's disavowal of all ambitious aspiration to the primacy; but after making due allowance for the bitterness of personal jealousy and the recklessness of a "party pamphlet," there must remain a certain residuum of fact in his assertions. These two letters written to Thomas the archbishop four years afterwards—one Foliot's own, the other perhaps dictated by him—go far to explain the discrepancy between the accounts that come from the friends of Thomas,—between the admission on the one hand that there was a striking divergence of opinion as to the merits of the royal candidate, and the statement on the other hand that the election at Canterbury was unanimous, and the consent of the clergy at Westminster equally unanimous after the withdrawal of the one dissentient

---

[1] Foliot, *Ep.* 225 (v. 525): qui (gladius) ne limatus denuo per vos aptaretur ad vulnera, jussis obtemperavit ecclesia, et *declinando quae metuit, simulavit se velle quod noluit.*

voice. It was a forced unanimity. There were probably many, like Henry of Winchester, reduced to hoping against hope for a change in the character of their archbishop-elect. Objections were entertained, perhaps expressed; but the objectors were over-awed and silenced, when the time came to enforce their opinion at Canterbury and at Westminster, by the pressure of the royal authority, and, under tacit or open compulsion, they gave their consent to the promotion of a man whose fitness for the primacy they questioned, some perhaps prompted by the baser motive of personal jealousy and biassed by prejudice, others (we cannot doubt the fact) influenced by a sincere desire for what they considered the welfare of the Church, and led to their conclusion by an honest review of the chancellor's personal conduct and ecclesiastical policy.

The archbishop elect.

The election was confirmed in the monks' refectory at Westminster on the Wednesday before Whitsunday, 1162[1]. No time was lost by the archbishop-elect and his friends in proceeding to Canterbury. Herbert of Bosham tells the story of this journey from personal reminiscence[2]. Thomas

---

[1] R. Diceto, i. 307, A.D. 1162: electionem factam sine aliqua contradictione recitavit Henricus Wintoniensis episcopus apud Westmustier in refectoris monachorum iiii[a] feria ante Pentecosten.

[2] Herb. iii. 185, 186. *Thomas Saga* represents the archbishop-elect as riding away from London with a large following of clerks and laymen to Merton, where he joined the monastic order, and changed "his costly weeds and silk attire" for the garb of a canon regular. This done, he rode off towards Canterbury, and on the way confided to Herbert the vision of the ten pounds, and asked

was lost in anxious reflection, absorbed in the thought of what his life had been in the past, and what it must be in the future. Like a man awaking out of deep slumber, he saw before him the prospect of a life in which his real self, hitherto buried and almost forgotten as a dream of the past, could and must come to the front. On the way down from London to Canterbury he called Herbert to his side, and related to him a dream of the previous night, in which a man of venerable appearance had placed ten talents in his hands. Herbert could not interpret its meaning at the time, but after-events made the interpretation plain. It must have been a prophecy of the reward prepared for the future saint—the faithful servant who had received five talents, and was in the end to gain other five. But a more signal proof of Thomas' confidence and esteem was in store for the faithful Herbert. Thomas requested him there and then to act in future as his private monitor, to call his attention to any impression that his conduct might make upon the world outside, and quietly remind him of faults that might escape his own notice. "Four eyes," said Thomas, "see further and clearer than two." The value of Herbert's testimony to what was passing in the mind of his master may be doubted; but this request for friendly criticism is at least an illustration of what seems to have been the ruling principle of

him to report all rumours current about his conduct and point out his failings (*Thomas Saga*, pp. 85, 87). But it is scarcely likely that the faithful Herbert should have omitted the ordination at Merton if it took place on this journey.

218   THE PRIMACY.

Thomas' life,—the determination to act up to his ideal of the position, whatever it was, in which he found himself. As archbishop he must take heed to his ways, and aim at a new and saintlier type of life, even if the attempt involved an artificial and unreal attitude, as in this case it seems to have done; and we can easily understand his looking for a friend to act as his mirror and reveal the defects that might escape his own notice, however earnest he might be in self-examination.

His consecration. At Canterbury, where bishops, abbots, monks and barons were thronging in crowds, a solemn reception awaited Thomas and his friends at the hands of clergy and citizens alike[1]. The archbishop-elect was still a deacon, and he had first to receive priest's orders. This was done on the Saturday after Whitsunday[2]. He was ordained priest in the cathedral by Walter bishop of Rochester, who usually acted as the vicegerent of Canterbury. A question had been raised as to the right of consecrating the archbishop[3]. It was the privilege of the bishop of London as provincial dean, but that see was now vacant[4]. The right was claimed by the bishop of Winchester as the vicegerent of the bishop

---

[1] Herb. iii. 188. Auct. Anon. I. iv. 18, 19. *Thomas Saga,* i. 89.

[2] Diceto, i. 307: electus autem sabbato Pentecostes ordinatus est in presbyterum in ecclesia Cantuariensi a Waltero Rofensi episcopo, in ordinationibus et in dedicationibus faciendis ecclesiae Cantuariensis vicario.

[3] Herb. iii. 188.

[4] Richard bishop of London died on the 4th of May, 1162. R. Diceto, i. 306.

THE PRIMACY. 219

of London; and a counter-claim was made by the bishop of Rochester, as the special chaplain of the archbishop in virtue of the privileges of his see[1]. There was a third claimant of importance, the rival archbishop of York, who, after holding aloof up to this point, now came forward to assert the dignity of the northern see; but the primate-elect and the bishops of the southern province were unwilling to let him perform the rite until he had made due profession of allegiance to Canterbury; and with this condition Roger of York refused to comply[2]. At last the bishop of Rochester consented to waive his claim in deference to the veteran Henry of Winchester[3], who, as a prelate of royal blood and "the father of the whole English episcopate," was acknowledged to be the most fitting person to consecrate the new primate. The ceremony took place in the cathedral on Sunday, the octave of Whitsunday, June 3, 1162[4]. The order of the service

[1] Herb. iii. 188.
[2] Gervase (*Act. Pontif. Cant.* s. v. Thomas). In his chronicle (i. 170, ed. Stubbs) he says that one Welsh bishop claimed the right as senior member of the episcopate; but it is not clear who this can have been. Winchester was consecrated in 1129. His claim was supported by a letter from the London clergy (Robertson, *Becket*, p. 47).
[3] Herb. iii. 188: salvo in hac parte jure Rofensis ecclesiae, de Rofensis consensu Henrico Wintoniensi episcopo archipraesulis consecratio delata est. Diceto, i. 307: sequenti die Dominica consecratus est a Henrico Wintoniensi episcopo vice Londoniensis ecclesiae tunc vacantis: quod ad jus suum spectare dicebat Rofensis episcopus, sed non obtinuit.
[4] Gervase, *Chron.* i. 170, gives the date (iii. *Non. Jun.*) and the names of the bishops present:

Henry of Winchester,   Bartholomew of Exeter,

is described in full detail in an extant fragment of an unknown biography. At an early hour on that Sunday morning, in full view of an eager congregation of barons, knights and commoners, who thronged the nave, with the little king and the ministers of state in the forefront, while the choir was occupied by the fourteen bishops and their attendant clergy and the crowd of monks and canons, Thomas came out from the vestry robed in the black cassock and white surplice of a simple priest. It was an impressive sight, as he moved slowly up the choir to the great altar, and bent over its steps for a time in prayer. Thence he rose and was conducted back to the entrance of the choir, where the release of the primate-elect from all secular obligations was formally requested by his consecrator in the name of the church of Canterbury[1], and formally granted in the

Nigel of Ely,	Robert of Lincoln,
Robert of Bath,	Walter of Rochester,
Jocelin of Salisbury,	Nicolas of Llandaff,
William of Norwich,	David of Menai,
Hilary of Chichester,	Godfrey of Llanelly,
Richard of Chester,	Gilbert of Hereford.

Herb. iii. 189 merely mentions that there were fourteen, including the consecrator.

[1] Lansdowne MS. (*Materials*, iv. 154, 155). Most of the biographers place this release from secular claims at London, immediately after the election: Auct. Anon. I. iv. pp. 17, 18; Will. C. i. 9; Grim, ii. 367; Herb. iii. 185; Garnier, p. 19; and *Thomas Saga*, i. 81. Fitzstephen's language (iii. 36), though not quite clear, seems to fall in with the statement of the Lansdowne MS., and Miss Norgate is inclined to regard the Auct. Anon. I., Will. C., and Grim, as borrowing their statement from Garnier. This would reduce the weight of authority in favour of the release

king's name by little Henry[1], the justiciar Robert of Leicester, and the rest of the ministers of state[2]. This done, the bishop of Winchester proceeded with the solemn rite; and Thomas of London, archdeacon of Canterbury and chancellor of England, now in the forty-fourth year of his age, was consecrated archbishop of Canterbury and primate of all Britain[3].

at London; but Herbert, who travelled with Thomas from London to Canterbury, has still to be reckoned with.

It may be possible to combine the two statements. Perhaps the release was actually secured at London immediately after the election, and was formally repeated and confirmed on the day of consecration.

[1] The young king is described in the Lansdowne MS. (p. 155) as ten years old or more (tunc major decenni): but he was born in March, 1155 (Gervase, i. 161, ed. Stubbs), and was therefore little more than seven years of age at the time of the consecration.

[2] The Lansdowne MS. describes Robert of Leicester as 'principalis justitiarius Angliae.' Elsewhere, e.g. in Herbert's account of the consecration, it is Richard de Luci who is present at the consecration and is designated by the above title.

[3] The Sunday on which Thomas was consecrated was soon afterwards elected by him to be the festival of the Holy Trinity (Gervase, i. 171, ed. Stubbs), which has always been kept on that day in England since his time. Fitzstephen in his account of the consecration describes the day thus: Octava Pentecostes, Ecclesiae Cantuariensis festa die Sanctae Trinitatis (iii. 36). Father Morris remarks that "the Convent of the Blessed Trinity" occurs even in papal letters as an alternative title for Christ Church, Canterbury, and probably the festival of the Holy Trinity was already observed at Canterbury as a titular feast of the cathedral, if not a feast of the Church. He takes Gervase therefore to refer to the extension of the festival to the whole province of Canterbury (S. Thomas, p. 70). The festival thus instituted in the Church of England was adopted in the Roman Church by Pope John XXII. early in the 14th century.

NOTE C.

THE ELECTION AT LONDON. (*Thomas Saga*, i. 73—83.)

The Icelandic version of this event in the life of Thomas is much fuller than that of any of the other biographers, and it is reproduced here in summary, partly because it deserves a place to itself as a connected whole, and partly because I was unable to consult it in time to embody it in the text of the essay. The *Saga* paints a vivid picture of the difference of opinion in the chapter of Canterbury as to the fitness of the royal candidate. At last, runs the *Saga*, the king's messengers, "finding that they had to deal with contentions instead of an election and with tardiness instead of goodwill," summoned the representatives of the chapter to London, there to meet certain bishops and magnates of the realm. The election is described in detail. Thomas was waiting outside within easy reach; but "the lord cardinal Henry" of Pisa, whose assistance the king had secured by a private understanding in Normandy (*Thomas Saga* p. 67), was present from the outset by the side of the king's little son, who had seen the letter which gave him full powers to act on behalf of his father. The bishops began by offering a prayer for guidance in their choice to "God, who seeth the hearts of all men." The royal messengers then opened and read the king's letter recommending Thomas for election; but the same divergence of opinion which prevented the chapter from coming to a decision at Canterbury now threatened to baffle the king's design at London, "some urging fulfilment of the king's words, others withstanding them stubbornly, saying that Thomas is in no wise a person fitted for such a station, a man of mark though he be among lay powers." Gilbert Foliot proposed that the matter should await the king's decision; but Hilary bishop of Chichester pertinently replied that they had just received plain proof of the intentions of the king, who was represented by his son. A certain abbot ventured to plead for the appointment of a regular to the chair of the monk Augustine; but Hilary silenced this protest in a fashion quite consistent with the anti-monastic prejudice that had marked his conflict with the abbot of Battle in years gone by. "Deem ye, sir abbot," replied the bishop, "that none may be acceptable to God unless he be of your manner of living? far from it!" Henry of Winchester now put in a good word for Thomas; but the feeling of the assembly swayed from side to side, as one speaker after another gave vent to the promptings of reason or self-interest, and the issue seemed more uncertain than ever. At last the cardinal came to the front and silenced the malcontents by an unmistakable hint at the consequences of their obstruction; "and now through his guidance they all say now yea to Thomas being elected, although," the *Saga* significantly adds, "the hearts of some of them went right another way." The cardinal now requested his namesake the bishop of Winchester to lay the case before the chancellor. Thomas was admitted into the hall, and informed of his election "for the glory of the Holy Trinity, for the governance of the Church and for the good of the people." The bishop concluded by requesting the chancellor's assent to the choice of the assembly; but Thomas prayed to be spared the responsibilities of such an exalted office, weighed down as he was already by the cares of state and unredeemed from his own burden," the chancellorship. Richard de Luci then came to the rescue and explained that it was part of the commission entrusted to himself and his fellow-messengers and part of the instructions contained in the king's letter to his son that the chancellor was to be absolved from all claims of state; and the absolution was formally given there and then in the presence of witnesses. Still Thomas shrank from accepting the offer of the primacy with its new responsibilities and its prospect of conflict with the king; and he only yielded at last to an earnest appeal from the bishop of Winchester, crediting him with sorrow for his old offences, and urging him to let the future atone for the past. "Call to mind how he did, Paul, who aforetime withstood the Church of God, but was sithence the greatest prop of her in word and example, and glorified her at last in his blood at his death." The chancellor resisted no longer, but gave a reluctant assent. The whole assembly rose to its feet, and the hymn Te Deum was sung amid the ringing of bells; and thus the meeting ended. "So he rideth away from London, having first resigned into the hands of the young Henry all the feofs and properties which he had held of the Crown anigh and afar[1]."

[1] Mr Magnússon (*Thomas Saga*, i. 82, note 10) interprets this as referring to the resignation of the chancellorship, which he is inclined to place "immediately following the election." Such is his inference from Wendover's description of the step as "resignatio tam subita" (*Chron.* ed. Coxe, ii. 292, 293). But not one of the other authorities mentions the resignation until after the consecration,—though they do not say how long or short the interval was. Cp. Will. C. i. 12. R. de Diceto (i. 307) merely places it in 1162.

CHAPTER IX.

CHARACTER OF THOMAS OF LONDON.

THE character of Thomas of London has suffered equally at the hands of friends and enemies. It has been depicted chiefly from the facts of his life as archbishop; and as those facts are frequently susceptible of a twofold interpretation, the chancellor's portrait has been painted in very different colours. The historian who, blinded by anti-ecclesiastical prejudice, sees nothing but arrogance and insincerity in the archbishop, condemns the chancellor off-hand as "a tyrannical and unscrupulous minister." The churchman who reveres the primate as a saint and martyr strives to make out a plausible case for the incipient sanctity of the chancellor. Both views are wide of the mark. The *a priori* element is obvious in either estimate. Characteristic facts are selected or ignored to suit the presupposition with which the writer comes to his work; and the result is sheer contradiction between the two.

It is only with Thomas the clerk and Thomas the chancellor that we are now concerned. The character of Thomas the archbishop falls outside the limits of this essay, which leaves him on the threshold of the third and last stage of his career. His early training at home, at school, at college and at the desk, his rise to eminence in Church and state, have all been traced in detail. It now remains to sum up what information may be gathered from the contemporary biographers as to the character of the man up to this point. The task is rendered all the easier by the fact that each stage in his development is clearly marked in their narratives. They note each change of manner as it came with the change of position; and on the whole their evidence has the air of truth. They record the failings of their hero without hesitation, though they naturally dwell with greater satisfaction on his merits. One biographer —the anonymous writer identified until recently with Roger of Pontigny—modestly claims for himself at the outset the credit of impartiality[1], and the claim is well supported by the calm judicial tone of the character-sketch which follows. It is a vivid picture of the man as his friends knew him. Quick of sight and hearing[2], endowed with a memory that rarely failed him and a ready perception that gave him the start of men more deeply learned than himself, yet too keenly appreciative of the pleasures of city-life to derive the full benefit of his studies

[1] Auct. Anon. i. iv. 5: qualiter primaevae aetatis tempora transegerit percurramus, nihil more laudantis vel aliquem commendare satagentis apponentes, sed simplicem veritatem simplici et fideli sermone breviter annotantes.

[2] The *Saga* represents him as suffering from an impediment in his speech; but it can only have been slight, for it is not mentioned elsewhere.

at school and at the university; vain and proud of his personal appearance, yet open-hearted and open-handed to a fault; given at times to the frivolities of love, yet never crossing the bounds of decency and purity; a winning handsome youth who found his way to the hearts of young and old, and did not forfeit the affections even of the men from whose coarseness he shrank with undisguised aversion,—such was Thomas of London in the days of his early manhood[1].

With his entrance into the household of Theobald —whether that step was taken of his own deliberate choice or at the call of circumstances—there came a marked change[2]. He was thrown among new faces and new surroundings, and associated with a new set of men, some of them his seniors in age and his superiors in learning and experience, others his eager rivals in the race for promotion; and his character took a more serious turn. The influence of older and graver men and the stimulus of competition did their work. Thomas had now found a profession to follow, a position to improve, and he threw himself into his new calling with a vigour that soon told upon his prospects. Before long he had won not only the approval but the affection of

---

[1] Auct. Anon. i. iv. 5, 6, 8. Cp. Joh. S. ii. 303. Will. C. i. 3, 4. There is no sign as yet of deep religious feeling. Herbert hints in fact that his growth in grace would not bear comparison with his progress in popular estimation (iii. 163): crevit et industria et gratia apud homines sed apud Dominum non adeo.

[2] Grim, ii. 361: ludis et levitate postposita, seniorum sapientumque sermonibus ad meliora semper animum informabat.

the archbishop, and had become his dearest friend and trustiest servant[1].

So far the character of Thomas presents no difficulty. There is plenty of variety but no contradiction in the statements of his biographers; and the general effect is natural and intelligible. It is the life and conduct of Thomas the chancellor that has left such different impressions upon his biographers and given rise to such a wide divergence of opinion among modern writers. The simplest plan will be to let the original authorities tell their own tale. They agree on the whole in speaking of a distinct change of life, a relapse, as some of them practically describe it, from the high aims and serious occupations of the clerk to the lower level of the man of the world. They depict the chancellor as a courtier of courtiers, fond of luxury and display in dress and living, bent on popularity above everything, equally at home in the chase and on the field of battle, condescending even to the coarse humour of the barons at court, while he forgot, if he did not despise, his clerical brethren[2]. Grim dwells with regretful emphasis upon one new feature which showed itself in his character at this stage—the ruthless cruelty with which he visited the enemies

---

[1] Grim, ii. 361. Auct. Anon. i. iv. 9. Joh. S. ii. 303. Will. C. i. 3, 4. *Thomas Saga* (i. 37) says on the authority of "Prior Robert" that Theobald found in Thomas' gentle tact a timely corrective to his own quick temper, and in Thomas' eloquence a supplement to his own poverty of language. There is however no parallel to this in the original authorities.

[2] Will. C. i. 5. Auct. Anon. ii. iv. 85. Herb. iii. 176, 183. Cp. Joh. S. Ep. to Baldwin of Exeter in 1166 (vi. 101).

of his lord the king; and he paints a vivid contrast between the peaceful temper of Thomas the clerk and the relentless ferocity of Thomas the soldier-chancellor in his assertion of the king's power[1]. It was a startling revelation to his friends. These pictures may perhaps have been coloured to enhance by contrast his later sanctity, but they are probably in the main true. As Herbert quaintly says, on entering the king's service he put off the deacon and put on the chancellor[2]. This however is only one phase of the man's character. Side by side with these painful admissions there are indications of positive merits to be placed to his credit. Far from being entirely destitute of virtues, he had retained or developed qualities of rare excellence. He was truthful, and hated slander as he would a lie. He was faithful to his earthly lord[3]. Above all, he was scrupulously chaste. His biographers are justly emphatic upon this point[4]; for it was apparently

---

[1] Grim, ii. 365.

[2] Herb. iii. 173: levitam pro tempore exuit et cancellarium induit. Herbert cannot resist the temptation to jest upon the word (iii. 172): nec enim levita factus mox supposuit humeros *levitarum oneribus* sed *levitatis* potius et saeculi hujus *operibus* ex tunc magis operam dabat.

[3] Herb. iii. 166: labia mendacia et linguam semper detestabat detrahentem. iii. 167: castitatis amator, ut diximus, veritatis aemulus, fidem etiam quae terrenis debetur dominis summa semper colens devotione.

[4] Grim, ii. 365. Joh. S. ii. 303. Will. C. i. 5, 6, tells how he refused the advances of an old mistress of the king's at Stafford, and how his host, who thought he had gone to the lady's house, found him sleeping on the floor of his own room, wearied out with his devotions. The same story is told in *Thomas Saga* (i. 53, 54)

an unusual virtue in kings' palaces. It was the one exception to the community of taste and occupation between the king and his chancellor. Thomas kept his personal purity intact in spite of the atmosphere of the court and the direct temptations placed in his way by the king himself[1]. More than that, Thomas did what he could to maintain a good tone in his own household, and prevent its luxury and magnificence from degenerating into vice. He expelled from his service and imprisoned in the Tower of London one of his clerks, Richard d'Ambli, who had invaded the sanctity of the home of an absent friend[2]. Truthfulness and chastity were not his only virtues[3]. He was liberal in almsgiving[4]. The merit of this

and by Garnier (p. 12), who gives the names. The lady was Avice of Stafford, the host 'Vivien le clerc.'

[1] Fitzst. iii. 21, says that he had the fact from Thomas' confessor, Robert of Merton: ex quo cancellarius factus est, nulla eum polluit luxuria. This need not imply that his life had been unchaste before his appointment; it simply means that Robert's personal knowledge of Thomas' chastity dated from the very outset of his chancellorship. Auct. Anon. I. iv. 14, quotes similar testimony to Thomas' purity from those who were in attendance upon him for twenty years or more: this period, if it included his later life as archbishop, would still carry us back at least four years beyond the date of his appointment to the chancellorship.

[2] Fitzst. iii. 21.

[3] Mr Froude, in the *Nineteenth Century* for 1877, wrote: "The only virtue which Edward Grim allows him to have preserved unsullied was his chastity." Freeman was justly severe upon this unwarranted assertion (*Contemp. Review*, vol. 32, pp. 478–480); and it has been omitted in the *Short Studies*, vol. iv.

[4] Grim, ii. 303: pauperibus absque aestimatione necessaria ministrabat. Cp. Auct. Anon. I. iv. 13. Fitzst. iii. 21.

may perhaps be discounted by regarding it as part of his general magnificence. Grim says that it was so regarded, even when he was archbishop. But there is another fact which cannot be explained away. Fitzstephen tells us that in the midst of all his worldly grandeur the chancellor bared his back in secret to the lash. When he was in the neighbourhood of London, Ralph the prior of Holy Trinity acted as his father flagellant; in the neighbourhood of Canterbury, Thomas priest of St Martin's[1]. False and unnatural as this idea of spiritual discipline may seem to us now, it was dear to the mediaeval seekers after sanctity, and Thomas deserves at least credit for sincerity in his asceticism. Robert of Cricklade is responsible for an anecdote which speaks as forcibly for the chancellor's devotions. A kinsman of Robert's who went early one morning to lay a petition before the chancellor saw in the dim twilight a figure prostrate in prayer at the door of a certain church. On his admission a little later to the chancellor's presence, he recognised at once the very dress that he had noted in the grey light of the dawn, and found to his great astonishment that the king's chancellor and the unknown worshipper at the church-door were one and the same[2]. If this story be true, then it proves that the chancellor had not discarded the habit of prayer with which he was credited while yet a clerk in the service of the archbishop[3]. His severest critic denies

[1] Fitzst. iii. 22.
[2] *Thomas Saga*, i. 51, 53.
[3] *Thomas Saga*, i. 39.

that he showed as chancellor any of the "features of the Becket of Catholic tradition[1]." But this is an estimate which can only be accepted by a wholesale rejection of the evidence of his biographers. They distinctly attribute to the chancellor three of "the main features of a personally devout life, strictness of moral conduct, abundance of almsdeeds, and severe religious mortifications[2]." They assign to him a private character that would be more than creditable in a layman of that age and might put many a clerk to shame. Secularity is the only fault with which he can be charged. Ecclesiastical duties were neglected for the employments of the court and the camp, and the archdeacon lived the life of a layman and a courtier; but, in the words of one who has analysed his character with masterly insight, it was "the life of a layman and a courtier who, while he left certain official duties to others, never forgot his personal moral and religious duties......Had he only been a layman instead of a deacon, we should have in him a model minister of his age. The misfortune was that except by the path of the ecclesiastical calling he could never have found his way to a position for which he was exactly suited, but with which the ecclesiastical calling was altogether inconsistent[3]."

It is precisely this inconsistency which is the

[1] Froude, *Short Studies*, iv. 29: "except in the arbitrariness of his conduct," he adds significantly. Such a touch as this reveals the bias of the writer unmistakably.

[2] Freeman, *Contemp. Review*, vol. 32, p. 484.

[3] Freeman, *Contemp. Review*, vol. 32, p. 474.

real difficulty in the life of Thomas. His private character will bear the closest inspection, but Thomas was not a private individual. He was a public character, and private virtues are not incompatible with public vices. Such a vice in general estimation is inconsistency. Rightly or wrongly, consistency is the one quality which the world requires most rigidly of its great statesmen; and it is no easy task to justify the conduct of a public man who turns his back upon the past, joins issue with his old comrades in Church or state, and attacks the cause he once defended. It can only be done by proving that the apparent inconsistency was after all consistent,— that the same principle was at work all along, necessitating or justifying a change of action to meet a change of circumstances. Now the inconsistency of which Thomas stands convicted by the evidence of his biographers proves after all to be consistency of a kind. The very change of attitude towards the great questions of his day, which has brought the accusation upon his head, is seen to be the natural result of the change in his position. A brief review of his public career will make the crucial point clear. We are not concerned here with the policy of the archbishop, except to notice that the change from chancellorship to primacy, bringing Thomas as it did back to the old ground on a higher level, brought back the old views intensified. The archbishop resumed and extended the ideas that he had begun to work out in the service of Theobald. Our attention is concentrated by the limits of this essay on the inconsistency between the first two great phases of Thomas' career,—between the aim and bearing of his actions as the servant of Theobald, and the aim and bearing of his actions as chancellor. The contrast between the ecclesiastical calling and the secular conduct of the chancellor has been already dealt with. The point now at issue is the change that came over his ecclesiastical views and his attitude with reference to the rights and wrongs of the Church.

Two facts stand out distinctly in connexion with the services which "Thomas the clerk of London" rendered to Theobald. Both in his efforts to procure the legatine commission for the primate and in the steps which he recommended or took to prevent the coronation of Eustace, Thomas on behalf of Theobald accepted and by his acceptance strengthened the papal claim to jurisdiction in England. And in his study of civil and canon law abroad with the consent, if not at the suggestion of Theobald, we have indications of a design of extending and solidifying the episcopal jurisdiction in the Church courts at home, with a systematic code of Church law that would hold its own, if it did not gain ground, in the face of the common law of the state. Thomas in short bade fair to prove a staunch ecclesiastic on the points at issue between the Church and the Crown. His attitude at this stage is clearly defined. It is not so simple a matter to pronounce upon the ecclesiastical policy of the chancellor; but, to sum up the results already obtained, the case stands briefly thus. In the tenure of preferment the chancellor was a pluralist in an age of pluralities, rather above than below the standard of his day, for he did observe limits in the accumulation of benefices for himself. In the disposal of patronage he was judicious in his selection of men, and exercised a salutary influence over the king; nor should his frequent intercession for clergy in distress be forgotten in this connexion. So far the chancellor's conduct leaves little room for dissatisfaction; but there is unfortunately more to be said. His ecclesiastical duties as archdeacon of Canterbury were neglected, at the cost of Theobald's loving confidence. His ecclesiastical views fell into the background. They were either abandoned or kept in suspense. He seems, it is true, on his entrance to the king's service, to have encountered opposition through his efforts on behalf of the rights of suffering clergy as well as laymen,—*pro necessitate ecclesiae et provincialium*, as John of Salisbury says; he seems to have protested strenuously against one breach at least of the ecclesiastical laws of marriage; but we have no trace of the views of ecclesiastical policy upon which he had acted as the servant of Theobald, and which he afterwards upheld so obstinately as archbishop. On the contrary we find him twice in conflict with Theobald on the question of the powers and privileges of the Church. By enforcing the scutage of 1156 and 1159 upon the clergy, he practically denied their right to immunity from taxation; and in the Battle Abbey case of 1157 he threw the whole force of his eloquence and influence on the side of the Crown against the papal claim to intervene in ecclesiastical causes in England.

It is an unmistakable change of front, whatever explanation lay behind. The staunch ecclesiastic of the archbishop's court proves as staunchly anti-ecclesiastic in the service of the king. It is a clear case of inconsistency, as that word is generally understood. It is not a case of conversion. The supposition that Thomas changed his views of ecclesiastical policy in the light of fuller experience and maturer judgment only postpones the difficulty. A second conversion will be requisite to explain the archbishop's return to his former standpoint, and by that time our belief in his powers of judgment will be reduced to a minimum. But there is no need for such a supposition. On closer inspection we find that there is a consistency in the actions of Thomas, —a link connecting the two phases of his career which at first sight seem to have little or nothing in common. It is not the consistency of the great mind which shapes its own ideal at the outset, takes that ideal as its guiding principle, and keeps it always in view, adapting circumstances to its purpose where they can be so adapted, and avoiding them where they cannot. It is not the consistency of the man who follows his principles where they bid him take a new departure even at the cost of a painful wrench from old associations. It is the consistency—less lofty, but not less real on its lower level—of the man who is faithful to the ideal of the office in which he is placed, but allows himself to be placed in office without any definite choice of his own; who holds to his principles, but takes them from his position, instead of carrying them into it;

who does whatever he finds to do with all his might, but leaves circumstances to find it for him. It is, if the expression is permissible, a fragmentary or sectional consistency. The life of Thomas of London is not a consistent whole. It falls into distinct sections, each of them inconsistent with the previous section, but each of them having a consistency of its own. Removed from the secular atmosphere of a city office to the service of the Church, Thomas throws himself heart and soul into the aims and pursuits of the ecclesiastical calling. Removed from the service of the archbishop to the service of the king, Thomas sets himself loyally to carry out his ideal of the chancellor's office, and looks at everything in Church and state with the eyes of a chancellor, whose first duty is to execute his royal master's will. Removed once more from the chancellorship to the primacy, Thomas resolutely begins to act up to his ideal of a great archbishop, involving as it did to him the pursuit of personal sanctity and the maintenance of ecclesiastical privilege. "Twice in his life he was placed in altogether new positions in the hope that he would carry the spirit of the old position into the new. Both times he disappointed the hopes of those who put him in the new place[1]." The spirit of the new position was more powerful than the associations of the old, more powerful even than the recollections of his former patron's intentions in procuring his elevation.

This is not a lofty type of character. Thomas

[1] Freeman, *Contemp. Review*, vol. 32, p. 475.

cannot in fact be ranked among statesmen or prelates of the highest order. A man of high moral and intellectual capacity, it has been forcibly said, "would not have changed from one object to another in this way. Such an one would do his official duty in any office in which he was placed; but he would have settled objects of pursuit to be followed through life. He would either keep himself clear of offices which were inconsistent with those objects, or he would adapt his offices to his purposes and not adapt his purposes to his offices. This last is what Thomas did[1]." His strength lay not in creative genius, but in his faculty of self-adaptation. He had not the originality of the reformer, but he was invaluable as a minister to a king who was himself a reformer. He belonged to the class of men who make the best servants and the worst masters. But he was not merely an efficient instrument in the fulfilment of the king's purposes. Within certain limits he had a real power of his own. As chancellor he allowed his office to shape his views, but in return he remade the office. There were two potent factors in his character. One was personal ambition; the other was that "strong sense of immediate duty" which from another point of view we may call official pride; and the two together led him to magnify his office, and carry its powers and claims to their fullest extent. At the beginning of the reign of Henry II. the chancellor was merely the king's secretary, an ordinary official of the royal

---

[1] Freeman, *Contemp. Review*, vol. 32, p. 475.

household. From his time onwards the chancellor was a great minister of state. So marked had been the growth of the chancellorship under Thomas that when he resigned the office there was no man for a time to fill his place.

The merits of Thomas the archbishop, martyr, and saint, have been long before the world. The merits of Thomas the chancellor have yet to be recognised. For seven centuries his title to greatness was based upon his primacy, but it may perhaps prove after all to lie in the chancellorship which he held for eight eventful years as "the great minister of a great king." It is certain, to quote Dr. Freeman once more, that "a fame which was partly factitious has robbed him of a fame which was truer and better deserved"; and the labour of this essay will be well repaid if it is found to contribute anything towards the fuller appreciation of "the man who was the most striking embodiment of the fusion of Normans and English on English ground, who in his own day brought back peace and order to a troubled realm, and who has left the personal impress of his own administrative power on several of the most important institutions of our country[1]."

[1] Freeman, *Contemp. Review*, vol. 32, p. 132.

NOTE D.

"*The Real Thomas Becket.*"

The *Nineteenth Century* for February 1893 contained under the above title a passionate vindication of the merits of Thomas of London which excited considerable interest at the time. It came from the pen of Miss Agnes Lambert, and took the form of a tribute of praise to the late Poet Laureate, the first writer, in Miss Lambert's opinion, who has done adequate justice to the "historical" Becket. The article falls roughly into two parts, (1) a history of the traditional prejudice against Thomas which dates from the day when the coarse vulgarity of Henry VIII. held him up to public scorn by a mock trial and condemnation as a traitor to king and country, (2) an attempt to dispel the cloud of slander and odium by a revelation of "the real Thomas Becket" of history.

The earlier half of the article consists mainly of a summary verdict of censure on nearly every historian who has dealt with Miss Lambert's hero, from Lord Lyttelton downwards. Not only Lord Campbell, Southey, Canon Robertson and the present Mr J. A. Froude, but Dean Milman, the late Professor Freeman, and Bishop Stubbs are condemned as slaves in a greater or less degree to the influence of this inherited bias from which the learned Jesuit, Father Morris, and the elder Froude alone among prose-writers and among poets Aubrey Vere and Tennyson have broken away,—a bias which sooner or later proves too powerful for the loyalty to original authority and the desire to be just which Miss Lambert is willing to recognise as underlying the work of the great Oxford historians of the age. This is not the place to deal in detail with the specific charges brought against each name in the long roll of writers thus condemned. That is a task which would involve the repetition of much that has been already stated in the foregoing pages. But it is not too much to say that the general reader will hesitate a long time before he abjures his faith in the judgment of the master-historians of this century at the bidding of even the most fervid advocate of the historical drama. It is too large a demand upon our credulity, unless it is supported by something like adequate historical evidence; but it is precisely on this ground that Miss Lambert's case breaks down.

In the second part of her article the writer begins by insisting upon "the perfect continuity of the mind and character of Thomas Becket. His circumstances, duties and surroundings changed suddenly and greatly, but he never changed. The man was the same throughout. Let us read him as those read him who lived with him" (p. 282). The sketch of his life which occupies the rest of the article is necessarily inadequate. The space is limited, and its avowed aim is to rehabilitate Thomas by an appeal to his contemporaries. It was natural therefore, perhaps inevitable, that some of the facts which tell against Thomas should be omitted; and it was natural too, considering the primary purpose of the whole article, that a good deal of space should be devoted to quotations from the late Laureate's "Becket" and the writer's own comments thereon. We are only concerned here with her judgment of the chancellor. To her vindication of many of his moral qualities—his purity, his truthfulness, his devotional habits—the heartiest assent must be given. It is however a work of supererogation; it has been done already and better done. The late Professor Freeman insisted sixteen years ago, in his controversy with the present occupant of the Oxford chair of history, that if contemporary authority is worth anything at all, we are bound to acknowledge the sterling merits of Thomas' private character. But Miss Lambert is satisfied with nothing less than the recognition of his absolute consistency even in matters of churchmanship. "As regards his ecclesiastical policy, even this underwent no real intrinsic change when Becket became archbishop." All the proof alleged is the fact that once, if not twice, during his chancellorship Thomas protested against a dynastic marriage that was contrary to the laws of the Church; and without a word of evidence beyond this the case is summed up as follows : " In fact, allowing for the difference of circumstances, position and responsibility, no change of principle can be discovered between the ecclesiastical policy of the chancellor and that of the archbishop." There were "many things that as long as he was chancellor he might use persuasion, counsel, diplomacy to prevent, or might even let be, but that once archbishop he would have to forbid" (p. 283). This undefined concession may be meant to cover the Battle Abbey dispute of 1155–1157 and the great Scutage of 1159; but not a word is said of either. Yet in both cases—especially in the latter—the conduct of Thomas calls for explanation. There is no sign of "persuasion, counsel or diplomacy" used with a view to prevent; and contemporary opinion—which is a factor that cannot be neglected in any historical problem—attributed to Thomas more than a passive attitude of *laisser faire*.

CHARACTER OF THOMAS OF LONDON. 243

Even Miss Lambert's "seer" felt the stubbornness of one historical fact, the great Scutage, and met the difficulty by assigning a conscientious motive for his hero's action:

Becket. "O Herbert, Herbert, in my chancellorship
I more than once have gone against the Church."
Herbert. "To please the king?"
Becket. "Ay, and the King of kings,
Or justice,—for it seemed to me but just
The Church should pay her scutage like the lords."

This is a credible view of the case. It may have been loyalty to the principles of abstract right that led Thomas to initiate or second what seemed to the world outside an act of injustice prompted by the exigencies of finance. But the point at issue is not so much the moral aspect of the case—its rights and wrongs judged by modern standards of policy and justice. It is rather the simple question, which side was Thomas as a consistent churchman intended and expected to take by his ecclesiastical friends and patrons? The answer to that question involves the charge of inconsistency which was examined in the preceding chapter. Thomas lived in an age and was brought up in a school that regarded the exemption of the Church from secular jurisdiction and secular exaction as the two bulwarks of ecclesiastical independence; and the churchmen of his day undoubtedly regarded him as directly or indirectly responsible to a certain extent for the breach that was made in those defences while he was chancellor.

APPENDIX.

THE BIOGRAPHERS OF THOMAS.

It may perhaps enhance the value of this essay to add some account of the biographers who came forward to pay their tribute to the memory of Thomas,—all but one of them within a decade of his murder. Canon Robertson has collected all that is valuable of their personal history in his introductions to the first four volumes of the *Materials*; and the chronological order of their writings has been thoroughly investigated by Mr. Magnusson in his introduction to the second volume of *Thomas Saga*. There is little to be done therefore beyond summarizing their conclusions for the convenience of the reader, except perhaps to note more particularly the nature of each biographer's connexion, if any, with his subject, and his acquaintance with the facts of Thomas' life before 1162, so far as it affects the value of his testimony. The order adopted is that worked out on chronological grounds by Mr. Magnusson, except that the writer known as Auctor Anonymus II., omitted by him as not yet identified, is here inserted in the list.

1. BENEDICT OF PETERBOROUGH was apparently the earliest writer of the group. After holding the office

of chancellor or secretary to Richard archbishop of Canterbury, he became prior of Christ Church, Canterbury, in 1175, and in 1177 was promoted to the abbacy of Peterborough, where he died about 1193. From the *Quadrilogus* we learn that he was with Thomas on the day of his death; but there is no trace of any earlier connexion between the two. Benedict was responsible for the first collection of *Miracles*, which Mr. Magnusson dates 1171-1172 (*Thomas Saga*, ii. pp. lxxii-lxxv), and a *Passio* of which some fragments are preserved in the *Quadrilogus*. The Icelandic *Thomas Saga* (ii. 44) credits him besides with a *Life of Thomas*; but this is a doubtful point. The writer identified with Roger of Pontigny, Edward Grim, and Elias of Evesham all assign to him only the collection of *Miracula* and the *Passio*; and Benedict's work was not used in the compilation of the *Quadrilogus* until the events immediately preceding the murder. The language however of *Thomas Saga* is specific enough, and Mr. Magnusson is inclined to accept its statement, and assign to Benedict a good deal of the narrative in *Thomas Saga* which is there ascribed to prior "Robert of Cretel." Some of these passages—e.g. the relations between Thomas and Theobald (i. 36), Theobald's motive in procuring the chancellorship for Thomas (i. 44, 46), the first dissension between Thomas and the king (i. 138)—seem from their tone of positive certainty to imply a personal acquaintance with the actors and an insight into the secrets of the primate's household, which in Mr. Magnusson's opinion points to an inmate of Canterbury rather than an Oxford prior, as the authority for these statements.

2. WILLIAM FITZSTEPHEN, whose *Life of Thomas* is placed by Mr. Magnusson about 1171-1172, bases his own claim to credibility on his intimate connexion with

his hero. He states in his prologue that he was a fellow-citizen of Thomas, and a clerical member of his household, that he was admitted into his confidential service by special invitation, and acted as *dictator* (i.e. remembrancer) in his *cancellaria*, as subdeacon at mass in the chapel when his master was celebrating, and as clerk of the court and occasionally as advocate when his master sat to hear cases of law. These are ample credentials for the biographer of the archbishop; but it is doubtful whether the first item on the list can be taken as a proof that Fitzstephen was ever in the service of the chancellor, at any rate before his consecration. The *cancellaria* may have been the office where the primate's business was transacted (cp. p. 116). On the other hand, the fact that he has given us the only full and detailed record of Thomas' chancellorship is strongly in support of the view that he was officially connected with the chancellor. He was in close attendance on his master at the Council of Northampton in 1164, visited him once in his exile, and remained by his side at Canterbury on the 29th December, 1170, to the bitter end. The greater part of his narrative of the archbishop's, if not the chancellor's, career is therefore, as he says himself, the work of an eye-witness; the rest (probably including the earlier portions of Thomas' life) he learned from responsible sources. Strange to say, however, though his biography seems to have been written among the very first, there is no notice of him in the contemporary writers either as an associate or as a biographer of Thomas. His name occurs nowhere, not even in Herbert's *Catalogus Eruditorum*; and his work was not laid under contribution by the compilers of the *Quadrilogus*. Various explanations of this fact have been offered.

(1) Canon Robertson (*Materials*, ii. pp. xv, xvi)

suggests that perhaps Fitzstephen had alienated the archbishop's extreme partisans by his indifference to the cause of the Church. He saved himself from exile by presenting to the king a conciliatory poem in Latin from his own pen, and apparently was employed by the king as an envoy to the Pope. Foss (*Judges of England*, i. 373) identifies him with the Fitzstephen who was appointed sheriff of Gloucestershire in 1171 and afterwards became an itinerant justice; and Canon Robertson is inclined to explain the absolute silence of his contemporaries with regard to his name and work as due to "their anger against him as a deserter from the hierarchical party to the service of the Crown."

(2) Mr. Magnusson (vol. ii. p. lxxix) rejects this explanation on the ground that the eulogistic strain of Fitzstephen's biography would have atoned for his own half-hearted allegiance to the cause of the Church. He prefers to suppose that Fitzstephen withheld the biography from publication for fear that its appearance at a time when party feeling ran high might damage his own chance of promotion. If the biography was not given to the world until perhaps after the death of Henry II. in 1189, the absence of any reference to it is easily explained; but this supposition, as Father Morris points out (p. xvii), still leaves unexplained the absolute silence about Fitzstephen himself and his association with the archbishop.

3. JOHN OF SALISBURY'S place in the "Becket cycle" of biographers does not correspond either to his merits as a writer or to his authority as a witness. His intimacy with Thomas began at an earlier date than that of any other biographer. They were contemporaries, if not acquaintances, at the university of Paris. They were certainly thrown together in that

little school of the prophets which found a home under Theobald's roof, and which had already known Thomas the clerk for some six years when John came to be the archbishop's secretary. The acquaintance which sprang up there or ripened into friendship there retained its vigour to the end. It was kept up by correspondence when Thomas followed the king to France and the faithful John remained with the old primate at Canterbury, and afterwards again during their occasional separation when Thomas the archbishop was himself an exile and a wanderer among the monasteries of the Continent. John's letters breathe throughout the spirit of true friendship, in fearless remonstrance as well as in helpful sympathy, and set the reader vainly longing for a biography of Thomas from the same pen that dealt out wise advice and frank rebuke with such unerring insight and such impartial justice. But John's contribution to our positive knowledge of Thomas, beyond the incidental allusions in their correspondence, is but slight. His *Polycraticus*—a treatise on "*The Triflings of Courtiers and the Footprints of Philosophers*," dedicated to Thomas during the war of Toulouse in 1159—gives a vivid glimpse of the life of England as it was and as it might be,—the sad reality of injustice and corruption in Church and state contrasted with the bright ideal of his own fancy—which would have made a fitting background for a life of the chancellor and archbishop. But instead of a full portrait from the master-hand we have but a sketch, "a succinct and brief account," as John calls it in his preface. It was all that he thought necessary. Detail was superfluous when the knowledge of the facts had been carried through many a channel over "almost all the Latin world[1]." Fuller information

[1] Joh. S. ii. 316, "ex relatione plurimorum," i.e. by *oral*

on particular points of Thomas' career must be sought in the "great volumes written *by him* and about him[1]." Something however of the same regret with which modern writers and readers accept this outline was already felt in John's own day. We learn that his contemporaries were sadly disappointed. They had expected more from one "who wrote in a style that knew no rival and who had the fullest acquaintance with the facts, as he had been linked to Thomas by a bond of friendship from his youth upwards and had remained his constant companion in persecution" (Auct. Anon. I. iv. 2).

4. EDWARD GRIM was but a stranger brought into contact with the archbishop just before his murder. He was not a member of the archiepiscopal household or even a monk of Christ Church, but a secular clerk from Cambridge, who visited Canterbury in December, 1170, for the purpose of seeing the primate (Fitzst. iii. 132, Herb. iii. 498, 529, 530). The date of his biography of Thomas, which yields to none in loyal devotion to its hero, is uncertain. Mr. Magnusson places its *terminus a quo* in 1174, the year of Henry's penance, to which

circulation. Auct. Anon. I. iv. 2 mentions only two written works, John's *succinctum eloquium* and the *Miracula* of Benedict prior of Canterbury. Benedict was made prior in 1175; John became bishop of Chartres in 1176, but is described by Auct. Anon. I. merely as "vir illustris." Mr. Magnusson therefore dates John's sketch 1175–1176.

[1] Joh. S. ii. 302, "a magnis quae *ab illo* et de illo scripta sunt voluminibus." Canon Robertson takes this to refer to a collection of Thomas' letters. Mr. Magnusson (*Thomas Saga*, ii. p. xc) explains it as an allusion to minutes (taken by Thomas or by order of Thomas) of speeches and proceedings in important matters. The former view seems to me to be confirmed by the parallel expression a few lines further on in John's preface: "*epistolae ejus* et scripta aliorum."

Grim alludes (ii. 447), and its *terminus ad quem* in 1177, the year in which Benedict, to whom Grim refers as prior of Canterbury (ii. 448, 9), became abbot of Peterborough. Nothing further is known of Grim except that he was dead when Herbert compiled his *Catalogus Eruditorum* (iii. 530). Grim's personal acquaintance with the archbishop began too late for him to rank among the inner circle of authentic witnesses. His testimony is mainly given at second hand. His biography bears a marked resemblance in places to those of Garnier and Auctor Anonymus I., a resemblance more easily explained by the assumption that he consulted the one or the other than by the supposition that all drew independently from a common tradition; and it is significant that in his own description of his editorial *modus scribendi*, Grim gives the first place to the information derived from Thomas' intimate acquaintances, and the second to his own immediate knowledge of the facts (ii. 355).

5. AUCTOR ANONYMUS I. Such is the title which Canon Robertson prefixes to the more important of the two anonymous lives now extant, a work attributed by Dr. Giles to ROGER OF PONTIGNY. The evidence for this identification is only slight. The writer mentions in his preface that he ministered to the archbishop in his exile, and was ordained by him to the priesthood; and in Thomas Froimont's composite life of Thomas (Giles, ii. 52) it is stated that a monk named Roger was attached to Thomas during his exile at Pontigny. Canon Robertson (vol. ii. pp. xii, xiii) gives various reasons for doubting this identity; and Mr. Magnusson, while pointing out that the biographer was evidently a foreigner, to judge from his peculiar handling of English terms and names (*Thomas Saga*, ii.

p. lxxxiv), adopts the name Roger of Pontigny "more for the sake of convenience than from conviction." The biography is assigned by Mr. Magnusson to the year 1175–76, on the ground that he mentions Benedict in his preface as prior of Canterbury, and refers to John of Salisbury merely as "vir illustris," not as bishop of Chartres, to which see he was promoted in 1176. But Father Morris (p. xviii) is inclined to place it a little later, as its writer evidently borrows from Garnier, whose work was not finished till 1176.

The preface in which this anonymous biographer explains his motives for writing is almost as valuable as the life itself. He begins by remarking that it was a matter of regret to many that no full account of the life and conduct of Thomas had yet appeared. It was a serious want, for ignorance of the facts had given rise to different and even contradictory views of the man's real merits. John of Salisbury had given the world a sketch that was too brief to satisfy, and Benedict had only dealt with the "Passion" and the miracles that followed. This deficiency it was the writer's aim to supply by a biography in detail in which "nothing should find a place beyond what he himself had seen and heard or ascertained from trustworthy evidence of those who had been present on different occasions" (Auct. Anon. I. iv. 2).

6. WILLIAM OF CANTERBURY, whose personality has only recently emerged from its confusion with that of William Fitzstephen, was a monk of Christ Church, Canterbury, one of many admitted to the monastery during the archbishop's exile, but the only one approved by the archbishop. The rest were remanded for further inquiry; William alone was admitted to the diaconate in December 1170 (i. 119). His acquaintance with the

primate was brief. He was in attendance upon him on the fatal day, but his new-born devotion was too weak to share his master's death. "Conscious of his sins and feeling unfit for martyrdom," to quote his own confession (i. 133, 134), he saved his life by flight. Apparently he was attached to the martyr's tomb in some official capacity, for he seems to have been entrusted with the task of receiving pilgrims and listening to their stories; but the tradition which made him sub-prior of Christ Church is practically disproved by Canon Robertson (vol. i. p. xxix). William's tribute to his dead master consisted of two important works, (1) a collection of *Miracles* begun in 1172, and (2) a brief but judicious *Life of Thomas*. The preface to this life was written after the *Miracles* were undertaken, but the date of its completion is a matter of conjecture.

7. GARNIER, a clerk of Pont S. Maxence, was the author of a French life which seems to have been consulted both by Grim and Auctor Anonymus I. From his own pen we learn that he first wrote a summary of Thomas' life, which was circulated by a dishonest scribe before the tone of its expression here and there had received the necessary modifications at the hand of its author. He then undertook a more ambitious work, for which he went to Canterbury in 1172 to collect fuller information. There he consulted the friends of Thomas, among them his sister Mary (afterwards abbess of Barking, 1173) and the prior and monks of Christ Church, and others who had been associated with him from his younger days. The *Sermun*, as Garnier calls it, was written in 1167 five-line stanzas, and was completed in the year 1176 (Garnier, p. 206, ed. Hippeau).

8. ALAN OF TEWKESBURY is here included in the list as the first editor of the correspondence relating to Thomas. Originally a monk of Christ Church, Canterbury, and afterwards canon of Benevento, he returned to England in 1174, became prior of Canterbury in 1179 and in 1186 abbot of Tewkesbury, where he died about 1202. His *Life of Thomas* from January 1164 to January 1169 was written (1) as a supplement to John of Salisbury's biography, (2) as a preface to his own edition of 529 letters, which he had already collected and arranged. This collection is mentioned by Herbert (iii. 396) as the work of the prior of Canterbury, and should probably therefore be dated between 1179 and 1186.

9. AUCTOR ANONYMUS II., called ANONYMUS LAMBETHIENSIS by Dr. Giles from the fact that the MS. is preserved in the archiepiscopal library at Lambeth. Wharton, who was librarian to Archbishop Sancroft, attributed this anonymous life to a monk of Canterbury, an eye-witness of the murder, and placed its date within two years of that event (*Anglia Sacra*, ii. 523). It is true that the murder is described in full detail, with several touches that occur in no other life, but Canon Robertson points out (vol. iv. p. xiv) that (1) there is no such claim made in the rest of the narrative, (2) the same prologue occurs at the head of a fragment of a different biography in a MS. in the Bodleian Library, (3) the life is more general and less circumstantial than its contemporaries, and seems the work of a writer not personally connected with the events which he is describing. He draws here and there from John of Salisbury; but there is no indication of his date, and Canon Robertson inclines to place him later than Wharton, about 1172–74.

10. HERBERT OF BOSHAM'S biography, painfully tedious as it is, and prolonged to an unconscionable extent by ponderous reflections on almost every other incident, is nevertheless valuable as the work of a man who had opportunities for knowing his subject scarcely inferior to those enjoyed by John of Salisbury and Fitzstephen. He may or may not be identical with the Herbert on the chancellor's staff who conveyed a letter and an oral message from Henry II. to the Emperor (p. 76, note); but it seems certain that he was in the service of the chancellor. Immediately after his election as primate at London in May 1162, Thomas chose Herbert for his confidential friend and mentor, and this choice can only be explained by the supposition of a previous intimacy of the closest kind. From this day forward Herbert was rarely away from his master's side. He was present at the Councils of Tours, Clarendon, and Northampton, and during the time of his exile was either in attendance upon him or absent on missions undertaken on his behalf. His absence from Canterbury on the fatal 29th was due to the forethought of his archbishop, who had despatched him on an errand to the Continent.

Herbert's contribution to the memory of his master includes (1) a *Vita Thomae* in six long books, with a seventh book or appendix entitled *Catalogus Eruditorum Thomae*, a list of the scholars and clerks, a score or so in number, who formed the inner circle of the primate's acquaintance; (2) a *Liber Melorum* of practically no historical value,—mainly a comparison between Thomas the "martyr miles" and his Lord "Christus Imperator." The date of Herbert's biography is fairly certain. He states himself (iii. 192) that he began the work in the fourteenth year after his master's death, i.e. 1184. It was finished before 1187; for Pope Urban III., who was in his earlier days one of the *Eruditi* and is mentioned in the *Catalogus* as "hodie totius ecclesiae rector," died in October 1187. Of its composition we know practically nothing beyond the fact that he spent some time " in the British world" while engaged in writing the work— probably for the purpose of collecting materials[1].

It was apparently the last of the contemporary lives, and it breathes here and there a spirit of regretful disappointment. Most of his fellow-witnesses to Thomas' conduct and character had already departed this life, and he was left to mourn his own isolation. The primate's memory and even the relics of his person were already treasured and revered, but the faithful servant who had survived his master by half a generation was still in exile, neglected and ignored by the bishops and clergy of his native land (iii. 553). Canon Robertson is half inclined to see in this lament an explanation of Herbert's ostentatious attempts to do justice here and there to the motives and measures of the king.

11. ROBERT OF CRICKLADE, who became prior of S. Frideswide's, Oxford, in 1154, and chancellor of Oxford in 1159, is nowhere mentioned by the Latin biographers; but he seems entitled to a place in their company. A letter of his to Benedict, describing the miraculous healing of his own leg (Benedict, *Miracles*, ii. 97–101), is given in *Thomas Saga* (ii. 92) as the work of the same prior Robert who elsewhere in the *Saga* is called Robert of Cretel, and who is credited with a Latin life of Thomas (*T. Saga*, i. 32). The date of this

[1] Herb. *Lib. Mel.* iii. 553, periclitor enim et peregrinor adhuc, sublato mihi domino meo...adeo solus derelictus, ut orbis Britannicus, in quo, dum hanc martyris historiam scriberem, aliquandiu sum moratus, mihi communicare vix velit.

life by Robert of Cretel (Cricklade) is unknown, but it is acknowledged by the compiler of the *Saga* as the source from which he drew several striking passages, e.g. (1) Thomas' escape from drowning (i. 32), (2) the personal relations of Thomas and Theobald (i. 36), (3) Thomas' devotion, almsgiving, and missions in the service of Theobald (i. 38), and (4) the stories told in illustration of the chancellor's devotion and chastity (i. 50 foll.).

12. "*Thomas Saga Erkibyskups*" is the title prefixed by Mr. Magnusson to his edition of the Icelandic *Saga*, the story of Thomas the archbishop as it has come down to us in a manuscript nearly five centuries old. The history of the *Thomas Saga* in general has been worked out at length by Mr. Magnusson in a most interesting preface to the second volume of his edition (pp. vi–xxxv), which I take the liberty of summarizing here as follows. From the earliest times Iceland had been in touch with England, and from the close of the eleventh century onwards the two countries were drawn closer and closer in peaceful intercourse. The practical monopoly enjoyed by English trade is marked by the introduction of the English yard measure about the year 1200. But this activity was not confined to commerce. English missionaries had visited Iceland before the Norman Conquest, and Rudolph, the Norwegian priest who founded the first Icelandic monastery, ended his days as abbot of Abingdon. Anglo-Saxon literature found its way to Iceland; the Anglo-Saxon language was recognised by the Icelanders as practically identical with their own; the Anglo-Saxon alphabet was used to supplement the Roman and the Runic characters when the Icelanders revised their alphabet early in the twelfth century; and fragments of Anglo-

Saxon history were embodied in Sagas evidently derived from English sources. First one and then another Icelander of note visited the southern island. Thorlak, bishop of Skalholt 1178–1193, divided his theological studies between Paris and Lincoln, and returned to Iceland about 1161, when Thomas the chancellor was at the height of his fame. Thorlak's nephew Paul Jonsson, born in 1155, who succeeded his uncle as bishop of Skalholt, studied in England about 1178, when the memory of Thomas was still fresh and some of his biographies already current. Rafn Sveinbjarnarson, a contemporary of Thorlak and Paul, wended his way as a pilgrim to Canterbury in fulfilment of a vow made in 1195 or thereabouts to "the holy bishop Thomas." Mr. Magnusson is of opinion that Rafn, if not Paul, must have brought home to Iceland materials, written or unwritten, for the compilation of the *Saga*. There are indications of the existence of a *Thomas Saga* early in the 13th century. At the southern see of Skalholt, bishop Thorlak's peculiar observance of fast-days and Paul's reluctance to accept the bishopric look like a reminiscence of incidents recorded in the contemporary lives of Thomas. The northern see of Holar was occupied from 1201 to 1237 by a bishop—Gudmund by name—who seems to have taken Thomas for his prototype. His masterful ways had already driven the poet Kolbein, who died in 1208, to compare him to Thomas; and his later insistence upon clerical immunities—a policy new to the Icelandic episcopate—made the comparison a commonplace in Icelandic tradition and literature before another generation had passed away. The story of Thomas' life was evidently familiar to the Icelanders in the earlier part of the 13th century. The first actual mention however of a *Thomas*

Saga occurs in the year 1258, when the recital of the last days of Thomas cheered the soul of an Icelandic martyr on the eve of his own death. From that time onward proofs of the reverence with which the memory of Thomas was regarded come thick and fast. Vows were already made to him before the year 1200; but in the 13th and 14th centuries churches were dedicated to his name in all parts of Iceland.

The extant MS. of *Thomas Saga*, edited by Mr. Magnusson and styled "T." in his preface, has been assigned partly to the 14th century and partly to the 15th; but Mr. Magnusson places the whole of it in the 14th century. The authorship of the *Saga* itself is generally ascribed to Arngrim, abbot of Thingeyrar in the north of Iceland, who died in 1362. The sources from which it was probably compiled have been noted under the names of Benedict and Robert of Cricklade; and the chief statements for which we are indebted to it alone are pointed out as they occur in the notes to this essay.

13. One other name is added to the list of biographers by Father Morris in his preface,—the name of GERVASE of Canterbury. He wrote no biography of Thomas, but in his *Chronicon* he gives Thomas a more prominent place than he occupies in any other chronicle, and apologises for the digression on the ground of his personal connexion with the archbishop. He tells us in his Chronicle that he was admitted to Christ Church, Canterbury, and ordained by Thomas during the early days of his primacy. We are indebted to him also for a list of the Becket literature already in existence when he wrote his Chronicle,—the writings of Herbert of Bosham, John of Salisbury, Benedict of Peterborough, William of Canterbury, and Alan's collection of letters.

14. No sketch of the biographical authorities for the life of Thomas is complete without some notice of the *Quadrilogus*, the composite life drawn from the writings of John of Salisbury, Alan of Tewkesbury, William of Canterbury, and Herbert of Bosham, with the addition of Benedict of Peterborough's "Passion" where John of Salisbury's narrative ceases. The *Quadrilogus* exists in two separate forms.

(1) The *first Quadrilogus* was compiled at the suggestion of Henry, abbot of Croyland, by a monk of Evesham, apparently named Elias. Henry lent a helping hand, and the work was finished about 1198–1199. It was not printed until the close of the 17th century, when it was edited by Christian Wolf (Lupus) and published in 1682, the year after his death. This *Quadrilogus prior* was recast by Roger of Croyland at the request of abbot Henry, and finished about 1212–1213. It was never printed in its revised form, but the MS. is preserved in the Bodleian Library.

(2) The *second Quadrilogus*, a work of later authorship, was printed at Paris in 1495. The prologues of the two *Quadrilogi* are entirely different, but the subject-matter is on the whole identical, except that the second *Quadrilogus* contains the legend of Thomas' eastern origin and passages from two biographers not used in the earlier compilation—Edward Grim and William Fitzstephen.

INDEX.

Acre, knights of, connexion with S. Thomas, 10 n.
Adam, abbot of Evesham, 167 n.
Adelais of Blois, 93
Adrian IV., *see* Popes
Alan of Tewkesbury, 253; his life and letters of Thomas, 253, 258
Alexander, bishop of Lincoln, 59
Alexander III., *see* Popes
Anjou, 77, 78
Anselm, archbishop, 202, 203
apostolicus, 179 n.
Aquitaine, 77, 78
Archdeacons, judicial work of, 35, 36; legal training at Bologna, 37; their worldly and mercenary character, 36, 163, 164, 194
Archdeaconry of Canterbury, 52–54
Argentan, conference at, 146
Arnulf, advocate of Stephen and claim at Rome, 46; bishop of Lisieux, 58; relations with Henry II. and Thomas, 16
Aschetinus, prior of Leicester, 165 n., 201
assisa, communis, 128
Assize, meaning of the term, 113 n; assize of Clarendon, 112
Auctor Anonymus I., his identification with Roger of Pontigny, 250, 251
Auctor Anonymus II., Lambethiensis, 253
Augustinian (Austin) canons, 13; *see* Merton
auxilia = "aids," in diocese of Canterbury, 161–163

Baille-hache, nickname of Thomas, 30
Baldwin of Boulogne, recommends Thomas to Theobald, 28
Baldwin, archdeacon of Exeter, 144
Bartholomew, archdeacon, 170; bishop of Exeter, 171, 184, 206, 220
Battle Abbey, dispute about its charter and privileges, 105–111, 174–179, 184–190, 235, 242
Becket, the surname, 2, 3; *see* Gilbert, Thomas
Benedict of Peterborough, his career, 245; his writings, 245, 255, 259
Berkhampstead, "honour" of, 139, 141, 142
Bermondsey, council at, 67
Bernard, Saint, 32 n., 42 n.

bestiae curiae, 154, 156

Beverley, provostship, 54, 56, 165

Bishops of the English Church, their political and military power, 28, 59; opposition to Thomas' election as primate, 4, 207, 211, 223; present at his consecration, 219, 220; letter of remonstrance to archbishop Thomas, 7, 55, 212; *see* Church

Bologna, Thomas' legal studies, 34; home of civil and canon law, 36; training-school for archidiaconate, 37

Boso, cardinal, 43, 48

Brittany, its relations with Henry II., 79, 80, 87

Cahors, 90

cancellaria, meaning of word, 116, 246

cancellarius regis, 68; *reginae*, 68

Canon law, in Italy, 36; its introduction into England, 36, 37, 54, 234; its extension, 193; *see* Law

Canterbury, traditions of the archbishopric, 202; Christ Church, 221, 251; monastic, 207; election of Thomas by the chapter, 205, 206; archbishops, Augustine, 207; Lanfranc, 189, 202; Anselm, 202, 203; William of Corbeuil, 40 n.; Theobald, *see* Theobald; Thomas, *see* Thomas; Richard, 32

Catalogus Eruditorum Thomae, 250, 254, 255

Celestine II., *see* Popes

Chancellorship, character and duties of the office, 68–70; its rank, 67; its relation to bishoprics and archbishoprics, 196 n.; saleable under Angevin kings, 62–64, 70; causes of its growth, 70; elevated by Thomas, 71, 72, 196 n., 238; official allowance of chancellor, 164; question of his equitable jurisdiction, 119, 120; chancellor and his clerks at the Exchequer, 123–126; the chancellorship in Germany and Italy, 195 n.

Chancery, Court of, 115, 120, 121

Charters, municipal, London, 9; provincial towns, 101; monastic, Battle Abbey, 105, 106, 174, 175, 187

Chichester, *see* Hilary

Chinon, 78

Chronicon de Bello, 188

Church of England, its political influence during the anarchy, 26, 27, 28, 59, 60; its independent jurisdiction, 35, 36, 192–195, 234, 239; its relations with Rome, 39–52, 60, 234; its prospects on Henry II.'s accession, 60, 61, 74, 75, 154

Clarendon, Assize, 112; Constitutions, 122

Clergy of the English Church, low standard of morality, 193, 216; side by side with character and learning, 32, 166, 227; clergy of Canterbury, their opposition to Thomas, 207, 211, 223; their remonstrance with archbishop Thomas, 7, 55, 212

clericus cancellarii, 124, 125

Conan of Brittany, 87

Conrad, bishop of Wurzburg, 20 n.

Constance, sister of Louis VII., 88

Council, the national, 71, 101
Councils; Bermondsey, 67
　Colchester, 106, 178
　London, 41-42
　Neufmarché, 167
　Northampton, 141-143, 150
　Reims, 42-44, 48
　Westminster, 163 n.
　Winchester (synod), 26
Curia, the great, 71, 101
Curia Regis, 71, 72; its justiciars and its work, 101-105, 120; trial of Battle Abbey case, 110; the chancellor at the Curia, 110, 111; Council of Northampton, 143

David, bishop of Menai, 220 n.
Dialogus de Scaccario, 102 n.
Durham, bishop of, 194

Eleanor of Aquitaine, divorced from Louis VII., 77; married to Henry II., 77; her claim to Toulouse, 88
Elias of Evesham, 259
England, anarchy under Stephen, 59, 60; restoration of law and order, 97, 98; fusion of Norman and English races, 6, 118, 239
Ernulf, secretary to Thomas, 169
Eugenius III., *see* Popes
Eustace, Master, recommends Thomas to Theobald, 28
Eustace, son of Stephen; his coronation forbidden by the Pope, 45-48; Thomas' share in the matter, 45, 48-52
Everlin of Liège, fellow student of Thomas, 19, 20
Exchequer, Court of, 101; its barons, 102; the chancellor and its Rolls, 123-126; its work, 103, 126-131; Black Book of Exchequer, 138
Exeter, see of, 140, 170, 171
Eye, "honour" of, 139, 141

Falaise, 197
Fitzstephen, William, his official connexion with Thomas, 115, 246; at Northampton, 141, 246; eyewitness of Thomas' death, 14, 246; his relations to the Church and the court party, 247; his life of Thomas, 246, 247
Flemish mercenaries, expelled from England, 92 n., 97
Foliot, *see* Gilbert
France, kingdom of, its relations with England, 77; with Normandy, 79, 80, 91, 93; with Toulouse, 88
Frederic Barbarossa, Emperor, in communication with Henry II., 76; his chancellor-archbishop, 195 n.

Garnier of Pont S. Maxence, his French life of Thomas, 252
Gascony, scene of Thomas' campaign, 90, 91
Geoffrey of Anjou, at war with Henry II., 78, 157 n.; earl of Nantes, 79; his death, 79
Gervase of Canterbury, ordained by Thomas, 258; his *Chronicon*, 258
Gilbert Becket, father of Thomas, 2; Norman by birth, 5, 6, 29; a merchant, 7, 8; legend of his Eastern travels, 9-11; his hospitality, 9, 16; story of his visit to Merton, 15; loss of wealth, 23;

recommends Thomas to Theobald, 29

Gilbert Foliot, bishop of Hereford, 208, 220, 223; declines charge of see of London, 172, 173; bishop of London, 208 n.; leader of English clergy in opposition to Thomas the archbishop, 7, 212, 213; his assertion that Thomas bought the chancellorship, 62-65, 201; his view of the scutage, 159; of Thomas' procedure at Northampton, 145-147

Gilds, in English towns, 100, 101 n.

Gilo, archdeacon of Rouen, 167

Gisors, 84, 86, 91

Godfrey, bishop of Llanelly, 220

Gratian of Bologna, 36; his codification of canon law, 37

Grim, Edward, his connexion with Thomas, 249; his life of Thomas, 250

Gudmund, bishop of Holar, Iceland, 257

Guido, cardinal, 47

Hastings, deanery, 139, 164

Henry of Blois, bishop of Winchester, papal legate, 26, 28, 60; conflict with Theobald, 40; his ecclesiastical projects, 40; loses the *legatio*, 39-41; his castles, 59; his share in Thomas' promotion to the chancellorship, 57, 58; to the primacy, 208, 209, 216, 223, 224; requests release of Thomas from secular obligations, 140, 144, 208; consecrates Thomas, 219-221; supports him at Northampton, 143, 151

Henry II., count of Anjou, king of England; his accession secured by Theobald and Thomas, 28, 50, 51, 54; recognises services of Thomas, 57; his policy in Church and state suspected by Theobald, 60, 61; plans of reform, 67; personal relations with Thomas the chancellor, 72-74; his generosity to the Merton canons, 14; his position on the Continent, 77; campaign against Geoffrey, 78; policy in France, 78-80; marriage alliance with Louis VII., 84-87; campaign of Toulouse, 87-89; of Normandy, 91; treaty of peace, 93; suppression of anarchy in England, 96-99; revival of judicature, 104; Battle Abbey case, 105-111, 174-179, 184-187, 190; legal reforms, 121, 122; reasons for offering Thomas the primacy, 192, 195; impatient of ecclesiastical insubordination, 193, 195; his influence on the election, 206, 211; prosecution of Thomas at Northampton, 141-143

Henry, son of Henry II., betrothed to Margaret of France, 80, 84, 85, 93, 201; educated in chancellor's household, 134; homage of nobles secured by Thomas, 197 n.; present at Thomas' election, 141, 208, 222; at his consecration, 220, 221

Henry, earl of Essex, constable, 90, 106, 109; itinerant justice, 113

Henry, abbot of Croyland, 259

Henry Murdac, abbot of Fountains, archbishop of York, 43, 44, 46, 49

Henry of Pisa, cardinal, papal

264 INDEX.

legate, 93; his share in Thomas' promotion to the primacy, 198 n., 199, 220, 222
Herbert of Bosham, in the service of the chancellor, 76 n., 254; chosen to be Thomas the archbishop's mentor, 217, 254; his close attendance on the archbishop, 141, 254; his story of the king's offer of the primacy, 197–199; and of Thomas' reluctance, 204; his life of Thomas, 254, 255
Hilary, bishop of Chichester, his conflict with the abbot of Battle, 105–109, 174–176; his share in the promotion of Thomas to the primacy, 206, 220, 223
Historia Pontificalis, 45, 48, 50
homines, meaning of the term, 114 n.
honores, vacant fiefs, 139 n.
Honorius III., *see* Popes
Hugh, archbishop of Rouen, 167, 168
Hugh, dean of London, 173
Huit-deniers, *see* Osbern

Iceland, its early intercourse with England, 256; Icelandic visitors in England, 257; story of Thomas soon familiar in Iceland, 257, *see Thomas Saga*
Innocent II., *see* Popes

Jocelin, bishop of Salisbury, 220 n.
John of Canterbury, member of Theobald's household, 32; treasurer of York, 195
John of Salisbury, student at Paris, 20, 21; contemporary of Thomas,

21, 247; introduction to service of Theobald, 32, 248; his *Polycraticus*, 88, 248; his Latin poems, 116, 117, 119; close correspondence with the chancellor, 248; requests the chancellor's intercession, 169; Theobald's right hand, 182; sometimes uncertain of Thomas, 140, 170, 183; staunch defender of Thomas' reputation, 116, 117, 144, 152, 159; his life of Thomas, 248, 249, 259
Jury, presentment by, 122
Justices, itinerant, under Henry I., 111; under Henry II., 112–114
Justiciar, chief, 67, 69; *see* Richard de Luci, Robert of Leicester
Justiciars of the Curia Regis, 103

L'Aigle, *see* Richer
Lambeth, conference at, 174, 175, 177
Lanfranc, archbishop, 189, 202
Law, canon and civil, 36; in Italy and England, 36–38; fusion of Norman and English law, 118; competition between canon and common law, 193, 234
legatio, *see* Papacy
liberatio, 170 n.
Lincoln, gilds, 101; bishop of Lincoln, 59, 173, 194, 220; his jurisdiction, 113 n.; Thomas' preferment there, 53; his influence, 171
London, its sheriffs, 9; its churches and schools, 15, 16; commerce, 5; recreations, 16; rank of its citizens, 17; their influence in national affairs, 25, 26; fires in

city, 1, 23; Thomas' London preferment, 53; administration of see of London, 171; its privileges, 218; *see* Gilbert Becket, Richard de Belmeis

Loudon, 78

Louis VII. of France, relations with Henry II., 77, 79, 80; with Toulouse, 88-90; war with Henry II., 91; treaty, 93; *see* France, Henry

Luci, *see* Richard

Lucius II., *see* Popes

Ludolf, archbishop of Magdeburg, contemporary of Thomas at Paris, 20

Maine, 77, 78

Malcolm, king of Scotland, 88

Mans, Le, bishop of, 167

Margaret of France, daughter of Louis VII., betrothed to young Henry, 80, 84, 85; married, 93, 200; *see* Henry

Mary of Boulogne, abbess of Romsey, her marriage opposed by Thomas, 94, 161, 235, 242; *see* Matthew

Mary, sister of Thomas, abbess of Barking, 252

Matthew of Flanders, his marriage with Mary of Boulogne, 94, 95; *see* Mary

Matilda, Empress, mother of Henry II., her opposition to Thomas' election to the primacy, 212

Matilda (Mahalt, Machilde), mother of Thomas, 5; his pious training, 12; her death, 22; *see* Gilbert, Roesa, Thomas

Merton, house of Austin canons, 13; Thomas at school there, 13-15; enriched by the king at the chancellor's suggestion, 14, 166; Thomas' admission to the monastic order, 216 n.

Mirabeau, 78

Mont S. Michel, 87

Nantes, 79, 80, 87

Neufchâtel, 86

Neufle, 86

Neufmarché, 167

Nicolas de Sigillo, 106, 163 n.

Nicolas, bishop of Llandaff, 220 n.

Nicolas, archdeacon of London, 167, 173

Nigel, bishop of Ely, treasurer, 65 n., 99, 102, 220

Normandy, 77, 79, 84, 85, 91, 93

Normans, fusion with English, 6, 118 n., 239

Norway, relations with England, 76; with Iceland, 256; reception of Norwegian embassy by Thomas, 135

Nottingham, its gild and charter, 101

Osbern Huit-deniers, 23; Thomas in his service, 23-25

Otford, living of, 44, 53

Oxford, its gild, 101; the university, 22 n., 255; Vacarius and the civil law, 36

Palestinian origin of Thomas, a later fiction, 9-11

Papacy, its claims in England, 39, 52, 178, 234; appeals made to Rome, 40, 42, 60; papal legation, 39-42; *see* Henry of Blois, Thomas, Theobald, Popes

266 INDEX.

Paris, Thomas' student-days, 18–22; the chancellor's visit as ambassador, 80–82; Henry's visit, 84, 87
Patronage, Church, the chancellor's influence, 164–166, 235
patronus, 115, 116
Paul, bishop of Skalholt, Iceland, 257
perdona, 128; the chancellor's share in the granting of perdona at the Exchequer, 128–131
peremptorius, 175, 176, 184–187
persolta (*prosolta*), 127 n., *see solta*
Pevensey, 18, 22
Philip, bishop of Bayeux, 58
Philip, count of Flanders, 94
Pipe Rolls, 102 n., 111, 112; importance of accuracy, 123; method of compilation, 124–126
Pluralism, in feudal and ecclesiastical benefices, 56 n.; Thomas and his pluralities, 55, 165, 234; *see* Patronage
Polycraticus, 248; *see* John of Salisbury
Pontigny, 250
Pont l'Evêque, 33 n.; *see* Roger
Popes: Adrian IV., 106, 189
 Alexander III., 43, 167, 178
 Celestine II., 40, 41, 47, 48
 Eugenius III., 42–44, 47, 48, 50, 51
 Gregory IX., 190
 Honorius III., 190
 Innocent II., 40, 41, 46–48, 50
 John XXII., 221 n.
 Lucius II., 41, 47, 48
 Octavian, 167
 Urban III., 255

Quadrilogus, 11, 258; the first, 259; the second, 259

Rafn Sveinbjarnarson, 257
Ralph the physician, 106
Ralph of London, 30
Ralph de Diceto, 141, 147
Ranulf de Glanville, 122 n.
Raymond V., Count of Toulouse, 88
Reims, *see* Councils
Richard de Belmeis, bishop of London, 107, 171
Richard Fitz Nigel, bishop of London, author of *Dialogus de Scaccario*, 102 n.
Richard, chaplain to Theobald, 32; archbishop of Canterbury, 32
Richard, bishop of Chester, 220 n.
Richard de Luci, justiciar, 65, 99, 113, 139, 194; his share in Thomas' promotion to the primacy, 140, 206, 214, 221
Richer de l'Aigle, guest of Gilbert Becket, 16; intimacy with Thomas, 17, 18
Robert, bishop of Bath, 220 n.
Robert of Cretel (Cricklade), author of Latin life of Thomas, 245, 255, 256
Robert, bishop of Exeter, 170
Robert Fitzharding, 170
Robert, earl of Leicester, justiciar, 99, 107, 221; itinerant justice, 113, 114, 126
Robert, bishop of Lincoln, 173, 194, 220
Robert of Melun, lecturer at Paris, 21; bishop of Hereford, 21, 166
Robert, prior of Merton, 13, 15; confessor to Thomas, 13, 230 n.;

INDEX. 267

attached to Thomas the archbishop, 13, 14; *see* Merton
Robert of Neubourg, 85
Roesa (Matilda), mother of Thomas, 5
Roesa, sister of Thomas, 5 n.
Roger, bishop of Chester, 46, 48 n.
Roger, bishop of Ely, 59
Roger de Pont l'Evêque, member of Theobald's household, 32; jealous of Thomas, 33; archdeacon of Canterbury, 34 n., 42 n., 181 n.; Stephen's envoy to Rome, 50; archbishop of York, 54, 194, 219
Roger of Pontigny, 250; his identification with Auctor Anonymus I., 250, 251
Roger, bishop of Salisbury, 59, 102 n.
Rolls, of Chancery, 121; of Exchequer, *see* Pipe Rolls
Rome, Thomas' missions, 38, 41 n., 44, 49, 50; trial of Stephen's title to the Crown, 46–48
rotulus de cancellaria, 123, 124
rotulus de thesauro, 124
Rudolf of Norway, abbot of Abingdon, 256

Saga, 256; *see* Iceland, *Thomas Saga*
St Edmund's, Bury, 106, 110
scaccarium, 123; *see* Exchequer
scriptor cancellariae, 124, 125
Scutage, the first, 78, 156; the great scutage, 91 n.; anti-feudal, 99; exacted from the Church, 158, 159; attributed to the chancellor, 100, 158–161, 242

Seneschal of France, 87
solta, 127 n.
Stigand, bishop of Chichester, 189
Stephen of Blois, king of England, 26; anarchy of his reign, 27, 28; his conflict with Theobald and the Pope, 42, 44, 51; unable to secure coronation of his son Eustace, 45; discussion of his title at Rome, 46, 47, 50

Theobald, archbishop of Canterbury, his early Norman associations, 6, 29; his political influence in Stephen's reign, 28; admits Thomas to his service, 28–31; *curia Theobaldi*, the home of learning, 32; his reliance on Thomas in ecclesiastical affairs, 34, 228 n.; patron of canon law in England, 36, 37; papal legate, 39–41; at the Council of Reims, 42–44; refusal to crown Eustace, 45; loyalty to Rome, 49; persecuted by Stephen, 51; appoints Thomas archdeacon of Canterbury, 53, 54; acts as regent during interregnum, 34, 54, 192 n.; introduces Thomas to king Henry, 57, 58; his motives in procuring Thomas the chancellorship, 58–62, 152, 153; persuades Thomas to retain it, 75; his share in the Battle Abbey case, 107, 109, 174, 175, 177, 235; disappointed in Thomas, 179–183, 235, 237; prohibits *auxilia* in his diocese, 161, 162; his death, 184, 191
Thomas of London, date and place

of his birth, 1, 2; the surname Becket, 2–4; the prefix à, 4 n.; nationality of his parents, 4–6; their social position, 7, 8; the Saracen legend, 9–11; miraculous element in his biographers, 11; his education, at home, 12; at Merton, 13-15; at the London schools, 15, 16; his intimacy with Richer de l'Aigle, 16, 17; escape from drowning, 17; fondness for country life, 18; student days at Paris, 18–22; enters service of Osbern and the sheriffs of London, 23–26; connexion between municipal and national politics, 26–28; his character at this period, 226, 227; introduction to Theobald, 28–30; his own motives for the step, 30, 31; competition and promotion at the primate's court, 32, 227; rivalry of Roger, 33; services rendered to Theobald, 34, 152, 228 n.; study of canon and civil law at Bologna and Auxerre, 34–38; relations with Rome, 38–52; transference of papal legation to Theobald, 39–42; attendance at Council of Reims, 42–44; papal veto on Eustace's coronation, 45–52; Thomas' ordination, 52; his preferments, 53–56, 139; archdeacon of Canterbury, 53, 54; introduction to king Henry II., 57, 58; accused of purchasing the chancellorship, 62-64; date of his appointment as chancellor, 65–67; his extension of the chancellorship, 71, 72, 196 n., 238; his relations with the king, 72-74, 154, 155, 159 n., 160; with the court, 74, 75, 155 n.; his connexion with foreign affairs, 76, 77; campaign against Geoffrey, 78; embassy to Louis VII. at Paris, 80-87, 134, 135; campaign of Toulouse, 87–90, 135, 136; in Normandy, 91, 92; negotiation of treaty, 93; his opposition to the Flemish marriage, 94, 95; his share in the suppression of anarchy at home, 95–99; municipal charters, 100, 101; his judicial work, in the Battle Abbey case, 105–111; as an itinerant justice, 111–115, 121; no separate equitable jurisdiction of Chancery as yet, 115–121; John of Salisbury's eulogy on his justice, 116–119; his share in Henry's legal reforms uncertain, 121, 122; his place at the Exchequer, 123–126; examples of transactions there, 126, 127; the granting of *perdona*, 128–131; his stewardship over royal revenues, 132; his expenditure, 133–138; his hospitality, 133, 136–138; his fleet, 134; his income, 138–140; the release from secular obligations, 140, 220 n.; challenged at Northampton, 141–144; its meaning and validity, 144–149; his financial integrity, 138, 150-152; ecclesiastical purpose of his promotion to the chancellorship, 61, 62, 153, 154; testimony of his biographers as to its fulfilment,

154, 155; financial oppression of the Church, the chancellor and the scutage, 156-161, 243; the archdeacon and the "second aids," 161-164; his disposal of Church patronage, 164-166; a friend to clergy in distress, 167-169; affairs of see of Exeter, 170; London, 171-173; his ecclesiastical views, 234, 235, 241-243; Battle Abbey case, 174-178, 186-190, 235; personal relations with archbishop Theobald, 179-184, 235; offer of the primacy, 197, 198; his reluctance to accept, 199-205; delay in the appointment, 202 n.; his election at Canterbury, 206; confirmed at Westminster, 207; the *Saga* version of the election, 222-224; opposition of the clergy, 208-216; journey of the archbishop-elect to Canterbury, 216-218; ordained priest, 218; his consecration, 218-221; resignation of the chancellorship, 196 n., 224 n.; character of the chancellor, 226-239; his chastity, 229; his secret asceticism, 231; his devotions, 231, 232; the question of his inconsistency, 233-238, 241-243

Thomas Froimont, 250

Thomas Saga, Icelandic life of Thomas, its history, 257, 258; its sources, 245, 255; its date, 258

Thorlak, bishop of Skalholt, Iceland, 257

Toulouse, campaign of, 87-90, 159

Tower of London, 139; repaired by Thomas, 142

Towns, English, their gilds and charters, 100, 101; *see* London

Trinity Sunday, festival, instituted by Thomas, 221 n.

Ulger, bishop of Anger, champion of Empress Matilda, 46, 47

Vacarius, lectures on Roman civil law at Oxford, 36

Vexin, its fortresses, 79, 80, 86, 93, 94

Vezelay, 212

Wales, campaigns of Henry II., 78, 157 n.; Welsh bishops, 220 n.; Welsh incursions, 197

Walter, abbot of Battle, 105-109, 174-176, 206

Walter, brother of Theobald, archdeacon of Canterbury, 33; bishop of Rochester, 162, 171, 206, 218, 219

Warren, Fitzgerald, 106

Westminster, election of Thomas, 207, 211, 214 n., 215, 216; Council, 163 n.

Wido de la Val, 83

William, brother of Henry II., 95 n., 106

William, Fitzstephen, *see* Fitzstephen

William, abbot of Ramsey, 166

William, archbishop of Canterbury, 40 n.

William, archbishop of York, 42, 43

William of Pavia, cardinal legate, 93

William, bishop of Norwich, 220

William of Canterbury, his connexion with Thomas, 251, 252; his *Miracles* and *Life of Thomas*, 252, 259

William of Ypres, 97

Writs, royal, 69, 120, 125; original and official, 128; writs of *perdona*, 128–131

York, 171; criminous clergy in the diocese, 193; refusal of allegiance to Canterbury, 219

www.ingramcontent.com/pod-product-compliance
Lightning Source LLC
Chambersburg PA
CBHW032113230426
43672CB00009B/1716